# Giving Sorrow Words

*Women's Stories of Grief After Abortion*

Melinda Tankard Reist

Acorn Books
*Springfield, IL*

*Giving Sorrow Words: Women's Stories of Grief After Abortion*

Published by Acorn Books, PO Box 7348, Springfield, IL 62791-7348
Printed in Canada

Cover Design by Alex Snellgrove

**Cataloging-in-Publication Data**
Melinda Tankard Reist
    *Giving Sorrow Words: Women's Stories of Grief After Abortion*
    p.    cm.
    Bibliography: (p.    )
    Includes bibliographical references.
    ISBN 0-9648957-4-9 (paper)
    1. Abortion—Psychological aspects.
    2. Abortion—Moral and ethical aspects.
    3. Abortion—Political aspects.
    4. Abortion—Law and Legislation—Australia.
    I. Title.
    HQ767.4    2006     363.4'6    LCCN: 00-90074
                                CIP

*To the women who created this book,*
*and the memory of their babies*

# CONTENTS

# A NOTE FROM THE PUBLISHER

In preparing this book for publication in North America, the publishers realized that readers might not be familiar with the meaning of some Australian idioms. Therefore, throughout the book readers will find potentially unfamiliar Australian phrases marked with an asterisk (*), with a "translation" appearing at the bottom of the page. (If a word or phrase appears more than once in a chapter, it is only marked the first time.) Additional explanations of some cultural references (for example, in regard to the forced removal of Indigineous children from their families under "assimilation" policies, mentioned in the Introduction) have also been added to the endnotes at the back of the book.

Some additional updates to the author's original endnotes, providing more current information, have also been added.

# Foreword
David C. Reardon, Ph.D.

In 2000, Melinda Tankard Reist, a journalist and women's rights advocate in Australia, published a groundbreaking book entitled *Giving Sorrow Words*. It represented the first major effort to document the experiences of Australian women who have had abortions. Such books are not new in America, but it was an important first for Australia. There, as here, abortion is a contentious issue and women who have abortions are expected to be happy that they had the "right to choose." *Giving Sorrow Words* offered Australian women the opportunity to transcend the political and religious arguments over abortion and simply share their stories.

The book you are reading now is the North American edition of *Giving Sorrow Words*. You may be wondering why a collection of abortion stories from Australia should be relevant to readers in North America. One answer is that abortion has a universal impact; it affects women regardless of their backgrounds or where they live. The emotional, psychological, and spiritual impact of abortion has been felt by women in New York and New Mexico and New-foundland in much the same way as it has been felt by women in New South Wales. At the same time, however, each woman's unique personal and cultural experiences add a new layer of understanding to this deeply complex, personal, and divisive issue.

Second, abortion is a profoundly isolating experience. Often, the woman has no one she can turn to for real support, either when she is pregnant or afterwards. In some cases, her family and friends may not even know that she had an abortion. Even those who do know about it may feel that the best thing is for the woman to "put it behind her" and move on as soon as possible. The result is that she is often left feeling that she is "the only one" who has ever gone through this. Reading the stories of other women who have walked this same path helps break the silence and free women to grieve the past and find resolution and healing. Reading the stories of women halfway around the world who have had the same experience further affirms that one is not alone.

Third, the availability of abortion not only makes a difference in the lives of individual women and those closest to them, but it also influences (and is influenced by) social attitudes and policies toward women, pregnancy, children, work, families, and a host of other issues. Much has been written and said about women's "need" for abortion, but few have actually questioned whether or not abortion really improves women's lives. Melinda Tankard Reist has dared to ask this question and to take an honest look at the state of women's lives in the wake of abortion on demand.

Finally, this collection of stories is simply so moving and poignant that they deserve a wider audience. The reflections of the women included in this book are just too important to dismiss because we are separated by an ocean. You will quickly recognize the universal nature of the themes they present. And if you have read other books on abortion experiences, you will also notice that this book is different from most in that the majority of women who share their experiences here have not yet found healing, of either a secular or spiritual kind. Unlike many American books, very few of the stories end with hopeful remarks that run along the lines of, "Through prayer and fellowship I have found peace at last." In that sense, this selection of stories may be more representative of the vast majority of women who are still struggling with unresolved feelings and thoughts regarding their past abortions. Indeed, when one compares these stories to the stories in *Aborted Women, Silent No More,* in which the women were all members of a post-abortion healing and support group, the striking difference in tone regarding "where I am today" presents a strong argument for the value of post-abortion support groups.

In short, this is a powerful book. The women who share their stories here are not activists. They are simply normal women, with stories that deserve to be heard precisely because they reflect normal truths that affect millions of women like them. They responded to the author's offer to share their stories simply because they wanted you, and I, and your neighbor next door, to understand more about the way abortion has touched and changed their lives.

* * *

It is important to note that the women who shared their stories for this book come from various personal, religious, and ethnic backgrounds. They are rich and poor, Christian and atheist, students and professionals, married and single, teens and older women, immigrants and native-born. Some were pro-choice at the time of their abortions, others felt abortion was wrong but were led to believe it was their only choice—or were not given a choice at all. Some of these women are pro-life today; others, while regretting their abortions, still believe that women need the option to terminate an unplanned pregnancy.

*Giving Sorrow Words* is not a book about the morality of abortion, the sanctity of human life, or healing after abortion. Instead, the author draws on women's personal stories and the insights of researchers, women's rights advocates, counselors, and other experts to portray what women go through before, during, and after abortion. Regardless of one's beliefs about the morality of abortion, no reader can remain oblivious to the injustices experienced by so many women or the sorrow so eloquently expressed in these pages.

Some readers may be uncomfortable with some of the political ideas touched on this book. Melinda Tankard Reist cannot be pigeonholed into the typical categories in American politics occupied by the "left" and the "right." For many American conservatives, the suggestion that government benefits are needed to raise women out of poverty and enable them to afford to care for their children may be rejected as too socialist. Many liberals, on the other hand, may oppose the idea that abortion has not been a "liberating force" in the lives of women.

Still other readers may be disturbed that little space is devoted to emphasizing the importance of the family or to issues such as sexual morality or adoption. However, this book is not so much about finding solutions as it is about recognizing the enormous burdens faced by women experiencing an unplanned pregnancy. These are issues that cannot be bypassed in favor of simply telling women to "do the right thing" and carry the pregnancy to term. Recognizing the conflicts women face is an important first step in finding solutions that will help them overcome these challenges.

To that end, the stories in this book echo several themes that also resonate in the stories of North American women.

First, many—if not most—women who undergo abortions lack emotional and practical support, knowledge of available options, and other criteria necessary to truly "choose" abortion. Many (64 percent of American women in one study[1]) report feeling pressured into abortion by the threats, pressure, manipulation, and even violence of others.[2] Many (83 percent of American women in one survey[3]) say they would have carried to term if they had been given better options or more support from the people in their lives.

Second, abortions are often based on false or misleading information provided by knowledgeable and trusted authorities such as doctors or counselors. Women report being pressured, manipulated, deceived, and ignored by staff at abortion clinics. Usually this misinformation (or complete lack of information) centers on two things: fetal development, and how the abortion will impact the woman. For example, in one study, 84 percent of American women who had abortions reported that they were not adequately counseled before abortion, with 67 percent reporting they received no counseling beforehand, 80 percent saying they were given no information on alternatives, and 52 percent saying they did not have enough time to make the decision.[4]

Many women describe feeling deeply betrayed and horrified when, after being told that they are aborting "just a blob of tissue," they have seen images of developing unborn children in photographs or an ultrasound in a subsequent pregnancy and realized that what was aborted was not just a "mass of cells." They also describe being told that abortion "is no big deal" or that negative feelings will disappear quickly, only to find themselves emotionally shattered by the experience and still unable to find resolution weeks, months, and even years later.

Third, many women report that they feel unable to speak about their experiences and forced to grieve in secret. In the midst of the stormy public debate over abortion, they are often overlooked. Those who believe they speak for women have often never consulted them about their needs and concerns. Further, women who wish to speak of their grief and pain over a past abortion are often shamed, ignored, or dismissed. Some fear being condemned by those who describe aborting women as selfish, callous, or worse. Others are told to "put it behind them" or "get on with their lives," often by people who genuinely believe that the best way to cope with an abortion is to never look back. Some describe being chided by abortion advocates for putting abortion in a bad light by speaking negatively of their experiences.

Even women who seek professional treatment report that their efforts to address a past abortion are often ignored by mental health care providers. One woman reported being told that it couldn't be the abortion bothering her; it must be something else.

Obviously abortion does not affect every woman in the same way, or as deeply as it has affected the women who shared their stories for this book. But there are millions of women throughout the world walking what the author calls "the lonely road of abortion." This book provides readers with an opportunity to listen to them and acknowledge their needs and concerns.

* * *

As one who has spent over 20 years researching the impact of abortion on women, I think it is important to say a few words about the status of scientific research on abortion since this book was first written and to discuss the impact of these findings.

Most notably, in early 2006, a group of researchers in New Zealand published a paper in the *Journal of Child Psychology and Psychiatry*, an international peer-reviewed journal, detailing the findings of an ongoing survey of some 500 women who had been tracked from birth to approximately 25 years of age. The data was drawn from one of the most long-running and valuable longitudinal studies in the world, and the research team had previously published other well-received papers about the findings from their survey.

This study from Australia's next-door neighbor created an international stir. The researchers had found that the young women in the study who had undergone an abortion were significantly more likely than their peers to experience major depression (nearly double the rate of women who had never been pregnant and 35 percent higher than those who had carried to term), substance abuse, anxiety disorder, and suicidal behavior.[5]

Previous studies had also shown that abortion is associated with higher rates of subsequent suicide, anxiety, depression, substance abuse, sleep disorders, hospitalization for psychiatric care, and other emotional problems.[6] So in that regard, the New Zealand study was not unique. But these other studies had been largely ignored or dismissed by pro-choice advocates for two reasons.

First, pro-choice advocates accused the authors of these studies (including myself) with having an "anti-choice" bias. Second, they argued that the statistical link between abortion and mental health problems was most likely misleading. Abortion doesn't cause psychological distress, they argued, it relieves it. Therefore, if higher rates of mental problems are found among women who have had abortions, it is almost surely due to higher rates of mental health problems that existed among this group of women *before* they had their abortions.

Their theory goes like this: mentally unstable women are more likely to become pregnant in unfavorable circumstances and are therefore more likely to have abortions because they realize they can't cope with an unintended pregnancy. Any subsequent mental health problems would likely have occurred even if these women had never been pregnant and had an abortion, and certainly these women would have had even *more* mental health problems if they had been "forced to carry an unwanted pregnancy to term."

The New Zealand team expected that their study would prove

that this explanation of the link between abortion and mental illness was true. Because they had been tracking and interviewing this cohort of young women for their entire lives, they felt sure that they would be able to identify the pre-existing factors that put emotionally unstable women at greater risk of unintended pregnancies and abortions.

That is what they expected. But their data analysis revealed the opposite. Even after the researchers controlled for a host of other possible factors, *abortion itself appeared to be the most likely cause of higher rates of subsequent mental health problems.*

In interviews with the media following publication of the results, Professor David M. Fergusson, leader of the research team, stated: "I remain pro-choice. I am not religious. I am an atheist and a rationalist. The findings did surprise me, but the results appear to be very robust because they persist across a series of disorders and a series of ages."

"Abortion is a traumatic life event; that is, it involves loss, it involves grief, it involves difficulties," he added. "And the trauma may, in fact, predispose people to having mental illness."[7]

Strong words from a pro-choice researcher. Yet Fergusson is not the first to recognize the trauma of abortion while still believing it should be a legal option for women facing an unplanned pregnancy. Dr. Julius Fogel, a psychiatrist and pro-choice obstetrician who personally performed thousands of abortions, stated:

> Every woman—whatever her age, background or sexuality—has a trauma at destroying a pregnancy. A level of humanness is touched. This is a part of her own life. When she destroys a pregnancy, she is destroying herself. There is no way it can be innocuous. One is dealing with the life force. It is totally beside the point whether or not you think a life is there. You cannot deny that something is being created and that this creation is physically happening. ...
> Often the trauma may sink into the unconscious and never surface in the woman's lifetime. But it is not as harmless and casual an event as many in the pro-abortion crowd insist. A psychological price is paid. It may be alienation; it may be a pushing away from human warmth, perhaps a hardening of the maternal instinct. Something happens on the deeper levels of a woman's consciousness when she destroys a pregnancy. I know that as a psychiatrist.[8]

Indeed, the New Zealand study, with its unsurpassed controls for possible alternative explanations, confirms a straightforward interpretation of many studies linking abortion to physical and psychological complications.

As far back as 1997, for example, researchers studying death rates among the female population in Finland (which has impeccable records due to the fact that all health care is covered by the government under the national health care system) found that women who had undergone abortions were 3.5 times more likely to die in the next year compared to women who carried their pregnancies to term, and seven times more likely to commit suicide.[9] Since the publication of their first study in 1997, the Finland team has conducted additional studies in order to prove or disprove their first findings. The studies continued to show higher death rates for women after abortion, including higher suicide rates and deaths from homicides and accidental injuries. In fact, in 2004 the team published a paper showing that 94 percent of women's deaths related to abortion were not noted on death certificates, meaning that the true death rate from abortion was vastly underreported.[10]

These findings linking abortion to higher death rates were duplicated in 2002 by a U.S. research team (headed by myself), which examined medical records for 173,000 American women for an average of *eight years* after their pregnancies. Our study confirmed that, compared to women who gave birth, women who had had an abortion had a significantly elevated risk of death from all causes, especially suicides and accidents, during that eight-year period.[11]

While more much more research needs to be done to confirm or refute these links, it appears that the best available data supports the view that the stories of the women included in this book are not uncommon. No matter what one's personal beliefs, abortion can be a deeply traumatic experience. It can shatter the lives of both stable and unstable women.

Tragically, however, as Melinda Tankard Reist documents throughout this book, women who seek justice, comprehension, support, good counsel, and some means of finding resolution after abortion are instead often dismissed, silenced, and overlooked both by mental health professionals and those around them.

The experience of Fergusson and his research team bears this out. Before publishing his paper on mental health disorders after abortion, Ferugusson presented the results to New Zealand's Abortion Supervisory Committee, which is charged with ensuring that all abortions are conducted in accordance with the law. According to the *New Zealand Herald*, the committee urged Fergusson not to publish his results, claiming that it would be "undesirable" to publish them in their "unclarified" state.

Ferugusson responded with a letter to the committee stating that it would be "scientifically irresponsible" to suppress the findings simply because they touched upon an explosive political issue.[12] Further, in their paper, Fergusson's team criticized the American Psychological Association for claiming in 2005 that "well-designed studies" on abortion found that "the risk of psychological harm is low."[13] The researchers noted that the APA ignored studies showing abortion's harm and looked only at a small group of studies that had serious flaws—studies which, by the way, were published by researchers with strong "pro-choice" biases.

Fergusson told reporters, "It verges on scandalous that a surgical procedure that is performed on over one in ten women has been so poorly researched and evaluated, given the debates about the psychological consequences of abortion."[14]

The self-imposed ignorance and denial about the real harm caused by abortion isn't restricted to New Zealand. Following publication of the New Zealand study, a member of the U.S. House of Representatives contacted the National Institutes of Health (which conducts vast amounts of research on issues related to physical and emotional well-being) asking if similar studies had been or could be conducted in the U.S. NIH officials responded with a letter saying that a similar database doesn't currently exist in the U.S. Asked what plans NIH had to study the impact of abortion, the officials at this taxpayer-funded organization ignored the issue of abortion and instead responded that they were currently soliciting proposals for studies examining the mental health impact of pregnancy in general—not specifically abortion. It appears that, for one of the leading organizations charged with conducting research to help ensure the health and well-being of American citizens, the health and well-being of American women doesn't even warrant a large-scale study.

In the absence of such research, it is more important than ever that those who *are* concerned about the health and well-being of women listen to the stories of women around the world who have experienced abortion. This book presents a truly compelling opportunity to do so.

*David C. Reardon, Ph.D.*
Director, Elliot Institute for Social Sciences Research

# PREFACE

Amid the maelstrom and clamor of the ongoing debate over abortion, the din of argument, claim, counterclaim and accusation, voices struggle to be heard.

Women's voices. Women bereaved, bereft, desolate, isolated. Women who had an abortion for themselves or underwent it out of deference to others. Women who aborted for self-preservation and found their entire sense of self demolished. Women emotionally disabled by unrecognized and unrelieved grief. Women who feel alienated by the politics of abortion, not "at home" with either side—some who no longer "believe in" abortion and others who still support access—but all agreeing that the cost to them was significant and that the lasting emotional shock after abortion must be acknowledged.

Most public discussion about abortion takes place with little or no consideration of the actual experience of women who have endured the termination of their pregnancies. Painful events need pain-relieving expression. But the response of traumatized aborting women has been repressed—because of the charged nature of the subject; because of shame and the pressure to maintain family secrets ("Don't tell," "What would people think?"); because they don't want to be labeled dysfunctional, deviant, "psycho," hysterical, or a complainer; and because it's not the done thing to talk about this kind of grief.

\* \* \*

It seemed to me the time had come for a book giving space to women who were surprised by the intensity of their feelings after abortion. *Giving Sorrow Words* brings some of these women out of the shadows and allows them to speak.

Many of the stories in this book are bleak and heart-breaking. I make no apology for that; I could not make them less so. The integrity of each woman's story had to be respected, and thus the reader has not been spared their more distressing elements. The accounts are confronting—but we should be disturbed. This is a far more appropriate response than that of abuse—the abuse of denial.

\* \* \*

There are two literary traditions in which the narratives in this book could be placed. The first is "writing as resistance"[1]—writing which gives voice to those who, until the writing appears, have been without voice, either because there has been no one to tell the story, or because "the story" has been consciously or unconsciously suppressed. The pioneering work of feminist writers in bioethics is also part of this tradition, exposing the exploitation of women through reproductive technologies.[2]

The other tradition dates at least from the time of Aristotle, who wrote about the catharsis of emotions expressed in tragedy.[3] Catharsis has been defined as "purification of the emotions by vicarious experiences ..."[4] There is a sense that in the telling there is a releasing of emotions, a cleansing that comes in the articulation or expression of the experience. Catharsis can also come through the commonality of shared experience, when women realize they are not alone in what they have suffered.

The stories told here are intended to be cathartic—for the women who wrote them and for others who are hurting, in whatever way, after abortion.

\* \* \*

Two hundred and fifty[5] women responded to small advertisements in women's magazines, letters to the editor in newspapers, and other notices in various places.

Every woman who contacted me received a letter detailing the project and inviting her to write her story. I was taken aback by how many chose to do this, even though I was a stranger to them and there was no guarantee their story would appear in the final publication. In the end, I could only use 18 stories in the body of the book, with selected extracts from other accounts in the introduction—though every account received contributed in its own way to the book in its final form.

A number of women commented that the small heading on the advertisement for contributions—"Abortion Grief"—in itself had given them permission to open up their grief. They had been stunned by the profundity and complexity of their feelings, thinking they were alone in their grief, that something must be wrong with them for feeling so anguished. For some, sharing their stories for this book was the first time they had spoken to another person about their abortion experience.

The backgrounds and ages of the women were diverse—from teenagers to 70-year-olds. One had had an abortion as a 13-year-old, another was in her forties. A small number had an abortion within three weeks of contacting me (one a mere three days before), others 23 years ago, one woman 45 years ago. Some spoke about one abortion, others about two to five abortions; one wrote of 12.

Some women wrote a single page, others up to fifty pages; two sent 200-page copies of journals (extracts from Lee's and Asphyxia's journals appear here), another a book-length manuscript.

Some asked that their real names not be used and that details which might identify them be altered or removed. Lee, Asphyxia, Maria, Michelle, Jill, Barbara, Marion, Mary, Danielle, Justine, Iris, Carissa and Karen were prepared to use their real first names.

Despite the emotional ordeal it was for most of the contributors, all found the process of recording their stories helpful to them, as reflected in the words of these six women:

Cassie: "So many feelings and emotions, locked in the secret hallways of my heart and mind! But it helps knowing that I'm not the only one going through all this. It helps knowing that other women have the same thoughts and emotions. Thank you for taking the time to listen to women like me, who so far felt all alone in a world that cannot understand the pain, frustration and guilt one goes through after an abortion."

Anita: "Write your book, and please tell the truth, about the pain, the shattered lives. Abortion is an open, bleeding wound."

Trish: "I want you to know how important this story is to me; just telling it to someone has saved my sanity. I hated myself for a very long time ... women should know that they might not get over it."

Iris: "Through putting my story down to let you read it has brought me a certain amount of freedom from my Ghosts. For years I felt that no one could possibly understand or that I could tell anyone."

Jenny: "Thank you for allowing me the opportunity to get it out of my psyche, which was most beneficial to my well-being. I feel I am no longer a victim of the system; you have given me voice and that has allowed me to take back my power."

Linda: "Writing my story has been the best (and only) therapy I have had since I fell pregnant 17 years ago ... I have wanted to cry this out to the world for years."

* * *

Hearing the voices of women speaking through this book, the reader might be more sensitive to the burdens carried by a friend who has walked the lonely road of abortion. The woman considering abortion might gain an insight into what she could face afterwards. The man who never has to contemplate such a decision for himself might more readily appreciate what confronts a woman when she faces it.

These stories are obviously not representative of all women and all abortion experiences. But they are representative of a significant group of women whose voices have been at least stifled, if not deliberately smothered, by institutionalized, systematic denial.

I pay tribute to the openness and generosity of every woman who shared the most intimate details of her life with me. I am indebted to every woman who laid her emotions bare to bring the most intense of pains to light—for this book, for herself, and because she wanted to help other women give sorrow words.

# INTRODUCTION

Give sorrow words. The grief that does not speak
Whispers the o'erfraught heart and bids it break
Shakespeare, Macbeth, Act IV, Scene 3

There are some griefs so loud
They could bring down the sky,
And there are griefs so still
No one knows how deep they lie,
Endured, never expended.
May Sarton[6]

All sorrows can be borne if you put them into
a story or tell a story about them.
Isak Dineson[7]

This is a book about women who don't exist.

The women who tell their stories here have all suffered abortion-related grief: a depth of grief they were not prepared for and which many carry still.

But they go unheard. Emotional trauma after an abortion is treated with disdain, dismissed by abortion advocates as an invention. A number of Australian reports, such as "We Women Decide"[8] and the "Information Paper on Termination of Pregnancy in Australia,"[9] as well as recent books on abortion, such as *The Abortion Myth*[10] and *The Politics of Reproduction*,[11] give the topic scant, almost indifferent, consideration. An international conference of abortionists,[12] held in Queensland, Australia in Nov. 1999, devoted just one workshop to the subject. The workshop's title alone—"Reflections on a Long Cherished Belief: Psychological sequelae of abortion"—indicated a lack of a serious regard for the subject, suggesting it is merely an article of faith, a fondly held myth. The workshop tone was generally dismissive of the research on post-abortion aftermath;[13] indeed, one participant said women were "overwhelmingly overjoyed" and even "euphoric" after an abortion.

Conventional wisdom has it that abortion is mostly trouble-free. Because of this, those who are troubled are made—indeed, often forced to be—invisible.

The grief of the women documented in this book is real. But

their stories, and the stories of women like them, have been disqualified—even by those who say we must listen to women's voices and credit women's experiences.

Attitudes towards women overwhelmed by grief following abortion demonstrate a cruel indifference to women's pain. Their suffering is considered a figment of their imagination, their guilt and remorse a by-product of social/religious conditioning. In short, they are an embarrassment.

There is another constraint on their expression of grief. The politics surrounding abortion have drowned out the voices of women harmed by it.

How free are women to share their anguish when advocates extol abortion as "an act of individual self-determination,"[14] and a "rite of passage into womanhood,"[15] a "positive moral good"[16] for women and "a source of fulfillment, transcendence, and growth"?[17] Women whose lives are shattered by the abortion experience and for whom abortion was not a "maturational milestone,"[18] and who did not feel it made them a "mistress of their own destiny,"[19] are cast aside as oversensitive, psychologically unstable, victims of socially constructed guilt. Their experience is trivialized.

When an article I wrote about women's negative experiences of abortion appeared in *The Canberra Times* in 1997,[20] a Family Planning figure hastily wrote in to dismiss post-abortion trauma.[21] Similar reactions surfaced in a feminist e-mail discussion about my book that lasted several days. The project was treated with contempt by all but two participants. Someone suggested a quick on-line collection of "stories of women not hurt by abortion" be compiled. This reaction unnecessarily pits women's differing stories against each other and, once again, suggests there is only one authentic experiential reality when it comes to abortion.

A woman's abortion pain is discounted and minimized due to the prevailing view that a termination is really no big deal—"just a curette*"—an easy fix. Abortion is promoted by many who dominate the discourse on the subject as a procedure without repercussions. Because of this, attempts to discuss women's abortion suffering have been constrained.

Suffering post-aborted women feel a resentment towards a society which ignores or neglects their suffering. They are not allowed to acknowledge or mourn their loss openly.[22] The disdain for women suffering after-abortion trauma sends the message: you're

*D&C

only upset because you've chosen to get upset. *Herald Sun* writer Evelyn Tsitas epitomizes this attitude: "Abortion can be an emotional subject—particularly for people who choose to get upset about it. There is a movement taking hold called: 'I'll always regret what I did and want to burn in hell for it.'"[23]

This mocking response to women's abortion-related suffering makes them feel they're being melodramatic, oversensitive, attention-seeking. But many women are suffering emotionally from a procedure which was portrayed as emotionally benign. They are filled with feelings of self-loss, daily haunted by their abortion experience. "We live with that regret till the day we die and for some we were wishing we too were dead," wrote a woman who signed her name "Tortured."

These women might have been told "there is nothing there," or that their fetuses look like "scraps of paper" (the description given to one woman by a Queensland abortion counselor). But to them, these were flesh and blood babies; for them, a baby died in an abortion. "I do not think I terminated a 'bunch of cells' but a real human being," wrote Melbourne woman Marguerite, whose story appears here.

Their arms feel empty, they don't like looking at babies, they cry often. They ask: "What would my baby have looked like? Was it a boy or a girl?" Would-have-been birthdays are quietly marked year after year.

As Margaret Nicol points out in her important work on maternal grief, it is a myth that a mother only bonds with her child after birth. A woman never forgets a pregnancy and the baby that might have been. When the baby is lost and there are no memories or visible reminders of the baby, "the feeling of emptiness and nothingness becomes pervasive and it is this uneasy and anxious void that makes women wonder if they're going crazy."[24]

### The History

Women who have been callously treated after losing babies through miscarriage and stillbirth are slowly being given recognition. Women like Glenys Collis: "But at nearly five months it all went wrong. I lost the baby. Of course it wasn't really a baby I had lost, the doctor told me sternly. 'Don't cry, you silly girl. This is all part of being a woman.'"[25]

In 1994, *The Age* published a deeply moving story about an 81-year-old woman, Mrs. Rose, who had searched for 47 years to find the place her stillborn child had been buried. Finally, she learned of a mass grave where her baby lay. She walked around the grave, calling for her lost child. A photo of Mrs. Rose showed her pressing dirt from the mass grave to her cheek. The dirt was, she said, "the first reality I have got."

"It was not the done thing to talk about grief ... I did not cry ... I thought about it privately," she said.[26]

The dirt represented the reality of her buried baby. But the woman who has aborted does not even have a handful of dirt. She has nothing to mark that there was a baby and now there is no baby. As with Mrs. Rose, it is not the done thing to talk about this grief; she bears alone the mantle of silent maternal suffering.

The significance of perinatal* loss[27] as well as the loss of relinquishing mothers in adoption ("Wasn't it enough that women were conned out of their children: were lied to, harassed, intimidated and had taken from them their child in a way that scarred them permanently?"—Marie Meggit, relinquishing mother and advocate); the anguish of Indigenous mothers whose children were forcibly removed under assimilation policies;[28] and the loss of babies "which might have been" by women who are infertile;[29] have now been acknowledged. Grief for an aborted baby is forbidden grief: it remains taboo.

## The Silence

Beatrice, from a New South Wales country town, who underwent a second trimester abortion, describes what this feels like:

> My grief will be unresolved because you cannot grieve the normal way, you can't repeat and repeat yourself. My husband and I never talk about the inner feelings ... although I'm sure he must think of it too. It's just taboo and you put it to the back of your mind ... the regret will always be there.

Katarina, a psychologist from Sydney, wrote:

> My sister has since had two stillbirths—as a family we have grieved and empathized with her and her husband's dreadful pain. Inside of me I felt cheated as no one had grieved with me for my two lost children—not even me. My sister's children died at the same time as both my losses—I felt responsible, guilty and so alone. When my mum says no one in the family has experienced pain like my sister my heart cries out silently—but I have.

*prenatal

A mother of four who gave no name or address, also has no one to whom she can relate her pain as a result of an abortion in 1997:

> I have paid the ultimate price. I have to live with myself. I have to look at myself and know it was my choice—I did it. I hate my husband ... The worst part of the pain is there's no one to share it with; I wouldn't tell anyone and my husband, being a typical man, just shuts down and gets on with things—doesn't know why I'm "still going on about it," but ... not a day goes by when I don't think about it. I can't believe I did it; I wish I could change everything and go back ... I will never be forgiven for what I did.

E. Joanne Angelo, Assistant Clinical Professor of Psychiatry at Tufts University School of Medicine in the U.S., has written about the importance of the mourning process:

> Grief following a death in the family is a universally accepted experience. A period of mourning following the loss of a loved one is a normal expectation in every culture. It is also generally understood that if this mourning process is blocked or impacted, there will be negative consequences.[31]

But there is no period of mourning for a woman suffering grief after an abortion. There are no grief teams, no body for her to cuddle and dress, no footprints or photographs to keep in an album, no ceremony, no grave on which to lay flowers; in short, nothing to acknowledge that this baby ever existed.

Peta, from South Australia, makes this point in an extract from her story:

> [I] silently apologize to the child I lost. The pain and grief continues because there is no acknowledgment of death, except in my heart ... The shadow of my lost little girl or boy will always follow me.

Women are told they'll get over it, that time heals, but find this is not true. Elizabeth had an abortion in 1973:

> The aftermath was a numbness I hadn't anticipated. I was numb, hollow, dead, and so very heavy with sorrow. The feelings didn't "go with time" as my delighted mother assured me they would. I grew morose, bitter, very sad; so heavy with sadness, I can't describe it. I became very different—cheap—I'd sleep with almost anyone. I drank heavily. I didn't care what happened to me and I tried several times to commit suicide. For ten years this went on. I cried every day, I stayed as drunk as I could for as long as I could, and I hated myself and everyone else. I used to dream about the child I'd lost ... I wanted my child. I loved it, cherished it, yearned for its birth, missed it when it was taken from me, and to this day,

26 years later, feel the tragic heaviness of loss. My only consolation is that one day when I die our souls may reunite.

A grieving post-aborted woman faces a conspiracy of silence. She is expected to be full of gratitude and praise that she could access the "right to choose;" to speak badly of her experience makes her seem ungrateful.

Julie, from Melbourne, said a friend told her not to be so ridiculous when she told of her plans to have a little burial service for the aborted baby in her backyard. "What are you whining about? It was your choice," the friend admonished her.

## The Absence of Help

Women often spoke of being unable to get satisfactory help for their grief from clinics or organizations connected with abortion. Karleen said that when she sought help at a women's counseling clinic in Sydney she was told it was wrong of her to speak badly of her abortion experience. Kara, from Queensland, told of posting her personal abortion story on an Internet discussion of abortion. She was told to "get lost"—her story wasn't welcome.

Sue, from New South Wales, went to a women's center and tried to share the grief she had carried for 24 years:

> I took a risk last year at the local women's center and was very surprised to be confronted by the hostility of one woman present— she had every right to her opinion but I made the mistake of assuming that the women's center would be a safe place to discuss it without judgment.

There are few "safe places" for women to share their grief.

Isabelle, from New South Wales and in her late thirties, also felt she could not share the grief over the abortions she had at 21 and 28:

> My guilt was there with me, staring me in the face, laughing at me, and I couldn't share it. Yes, post-abortion grief is a very real experience. It goes on and on. Every time abortion is debated it sounds ten times as loud and it hurts ten times as much.

Women are made to suppress their pain and invent other reasons to explain what they are going through. A woman who shared her abortion pain in a story in *The Age* in 1992 described trying to get help from a pro-choice organization:

> They said the reason (that you are hurting) is that you've got stuff in your background that you need to resolve. But I don't think I've

got unfinished business.[32]

If a woman is depressed after an abortion, she is made to feel it's her own inability to deal with sadness which is the problem. The onus is all on the woman.

## The Lack of Choice

The stories in this book will give the reader a glimpse of the human face of grief after an abortion. They offer other insights as well.

Many of the stories here expose the myth of "choice" in the decision-making process. For so many women, abortion was a marginal choice.[33]

The rhetoric of choice suggests there are lots of choices and all are good and of equal weight. It suggests no desperation, no pressure, no coercion either direct or indirect, such as that reflected in a lack of support.

Many women who contacted me say it was others, usually partners or parents, who wanted them to have the abortion. Abortion was an act of obligation and obedience—pleasing others, maternal sacrifice for the greater good.[34] "Abortion on demand" was someone else's demand.

The experience of too many women was finding that the people they normally relied on for support withdrew it, the people who were tied to them through blood or the bonds of love and friendship were not there for them at this most vital time, and in fact, were opposed to their desire for the pregnancy. These women lost their sense of personal control, surrendering their wishes to others, realizing that the relationship could not withstand a pregnancy. Many women described receiving an ultimatum from their partners: "It's me or the baby."

Zelda, from Melbourne, was under pressure from her husband who did not want another baby:

> My husband gave me an ultimatum: go and get an abortion or he would leave. As the sole parent's pension* was an absolute pittance in those days, I felt that I had no choice ... inside myself I was thinking, "Oh, please don't let this happen—I want to keep this child; I think it will be a boy, a lovely little brother for my daughter. I wish my husband would accept this child too and not make me have it aborted." Each night when my husband came home from work, I begged him, 'Please don't make me have an abortion. Please don't

*government assistance for single parents

make me kill our child. Please, why can't I just have this baby?"

How can a woman be said to be exercising freedom of choice if she aborts because she fears abandonment?

After the abortion Zelda purchased a blue teddy bear and pretended it was her baby. The marriage broke up two weeks before the birth of another baby. Five years later in another relationship Zelda resisted pressure to abort her third son.

Jenna, from New South Wales, also had an abortion for her husband:

> My husband didn't want any more children (he wasn't happy with the first one), but he said it was my decision one way or the other. If I had been a stronger-willed person, and if I'd had support during the first pregnancy, I wouldn't have had an abortion. I knew I was really doing it to appease my husband.

Lena, from Queensland, found herself pregnant at 25 by a man she loved deeply. She wanted the child but felt too emotionally fragile to go ahead without her partner's support:

> He encouraged me to wait until we were married, wait until we had spent more time with each other, wait until we had more money, wait until we did all the things we wanted to do together, and wait until the time was right. I desperately needed some support and agreed out of trust. After all, as some consolation, I had all these other things he wanted with me to look forward to.

The things he told her they would do together never eventuated:

> I have just come to the end of this relationship and I can't help but feel tricked somewhere along the line. We never got to that stage again and at the end of it all I am left alone without the love of either the father or the child ... I feel I have lost something I can never regain.

An unsympathetic husband also featured prominently in Beatrice's story:

> I was married, 38 years old, and my marriage was on the rocks— my husband had affairs ... that broke my heart to begin with, then we went away and I fell pregnant. I had an 11-year-old son and I had not fallen pregnant in all those years. I thought it was a miracle and still do. My husband's reaction was totally different. He made it clear he didn't want any more children, he would rather pay maintenance.* I was in shock, confused ... I don't use the word "choice" because ... when you are cornered there does not seem to be a

---

*child support

choice. I look at my husband as the "judge" and myself the "executioner."

An alcoholic, abusive husband was behind Samantha's feelings that she could do nothing other than abort her fifth child:

I had been involved in an abusive relationship for ten years that ended with a great deal of violence and the police subsequently being involved. Finding out I was pregnant again shortly thereafter was a tragedy ... I knew that I should've been more careful, considering the circumstances I was in at the time, but what can one do when being raped by a drunk man—ask him to use protection? ... Had things been different though, I may well have kept my baby. For it is now two years on and I am still riddled with guilt ... I still "love" and "miss" that child as I would any of my other children, should they be taken from me.

Melanie, 18, in her last year of high school was pressured by her boyfriend and her parents to abort her pregnancy. "I didn't have one person to support me having the baby." Ro had two abortions as a 17-year-old out of fear of shaming her family:

As I had been brought up in a very religious family, I felt that I couldn't embarrass my family, and so had no other choice but to have the abortions.

Jane, 19, also felt she wasn't doing what she wanted when she had an abortion in a Melbourne clinic:

I still get emotional when I see young children, especially young babies. I look at them and think "I killed one of you ..." I've always wish I kept it. Would it be a boy or a girl, what would I call her/him, would he/she look like me? I even recorded the day my baby was due to be born on my calendar. I wish I had done what I wanted to do about my pregnancy, not what everyone else wanted me to do. After all it was inside me, it was part of me. And now I have to live with this guilt for the rest of my life.

A Queensland woman had four abortions out of fear of her mother—three of them after she was married.

Sally found herself pregnant at 16 to a married man twice her age with whom she'd been in a relationship since the age of 11. But she did not choose to have an abortion—her mother determined it for her:

On her arrival [at the doctor's office], my mother's concern was for who the father was. Her next comment was how soon the doctor could arrange "a little scrape out." I was utterly shocked; here was this morally upright, devout woman, a vociferous opponent of abortion, requesting the very same procedure she abhorred for her daughter, without a second thought ... I remember her saying: "You don't want to carry that thing around for too long."

Lisa, 19, from Queensland, had a late-term abortion to please her boyfriend:

> My boyfriend told me if I kept it, it would break us apart. I loved him and I went and destroyed a life which I wanted so much. I was 18 weeks pregnant; it took me three days for the operation. Men don't understand what you go through and I wish they did. Throughout the three days I had needles all the time and nausea. This was all because of love. I always think of other people before my own feelings, but look at where it's gotten me ... I felt empty, like I had no soul in me ... My boyfriend said to me a couple of days afterwards that we might end up being married and we could have a family together. I said I couldn't marry someone that made me destroy a baby.

A teenager, Anne underwent an illegal abortion in 1961. Her sole motivation was to save her father—who held an important position in the town where the family lived—from shame. After years of depression, drug abuse, and a suicide attempt, and following the accidental death of her adopted baby daughter, she made a confession to police. "I confessed to murdering my baby. But the confession was for the baby I had killed by abortion."

A 1956 Royal Women's Hospital study concluded:

> Society condemns illegitimacy and frowns upon fatherless children; if in inducing an abortion the unmarried woman committed a crime, she nevertheless took the course which, she thought, would give least offense.[35]

Giving the "least offense"—to others and to society at large—continues to act as a significant influence in the lives of pregnant women.

## The Exploitation

Many of the stories received highlighted exploitative relationships and the inability of many, particularly younger women, to negotiate sexual relationships. One appalling example of this was the experience of 16-year-old Adria, from New South Wales, who, after the death of her parents, was placed under the guardianship of a couple who were family friends. Within a short time the male guardian, 20 years her senior, had begun a sexual relationship with her. When she became pregnant, he dropped her off at the abortion clinic and went to buy his wife flowers for Valentine's Day. She knew that by having the abortion she was "saving him."

The language of "choice" also meant little to the small number of incest and rape survivors who shared their stories. For them, it was even more difficult to share grief over the loss of a pregnancy which was the result of sexual assault.

## The Social/Cultural Factors

The lack of choice is reflected not only in pressure applied by others, but also operates through social and cultural factors.

The decision to have an abortion is often made under conditions of reduced freedom. Inequitable workplace treatment, struggles to receive appropriate welfare and child support payments, class and cultural biases in family size, attitudes toward "older" women and toward disabled women and disabled unborn babies, along with the social subordination of women in general, all conspire to direct certain women in a certain direction.[36]

If the conditions for continuing an unplanned pregnancy are not considered perfect when judged against socially accepted criteria, women often feel a sense of duty to abort. Germaine Greer wrote in 1992:

[T]he fiction of the right to "choice" masked women's real vulnerability in the matter of reproduction. It is typical of the contradictions that break women's hearts that when they availed themselves of their fragile right to abortion they often, even usually, went with grief and humiliation to carry out a painful duty that was presented to them as a privilege ... Abortion is the last in a long line of non-choices ...[37]

Greer elaborates on this in her book, *The Whole Woman*:

What women "won" was the "right" to undergo invasive procedures in order to terminate unwanted pregnancies, unwanted not just by them but by their parents, their sexual partners, the governments who would not support mothers, the employers who would not employ mothers, the landlords who would not accept tenants with children, the schools that would not accept students with children ... If the child is unwanted, whether by her or her partner or her parents, it will be her duty to undergo an invasive procedure and an emotional trauma and so sort the situation out. The crowning insult is that this ordeal is represented to her as some kind of a privilege. Her sad and onerous duty is garbed in the rhetoric of a civil right. Where other people decide that a woman's baby should not be born she will be pressured to carry out her duty to herself, to the fetus, to other people, to the health establishment, to the state by undergoing abortion. Her autonomy is the least important consideration. In both cases she is confronted with other people who know better than she what she ought to do.[38]

Jael, from Victoria, highlights the structural issues which make women feel they have little choice other than abortion, in her account of her two terminations:

> The financial strain in my life was too enormous to even consider having the baby ... there is a grieving—I wished I had been given the "body" to bury—this would have made me sit down and think for myself, but I felt so railroaded by "the system"—the alternatives seemed worse, as anybody who is involved in the vicious cycle of homelessness, domestic violence, unemployment, low incomes, welfare and public housing, knows. My grief was more at being out of control of the situation—no woman would kill her unborn child if there were suitable, decent alternatives. We are offered a pittance and some women grab at this rather than abort. I grieve the loss of woman-centered society, where abortion would never exist, except only [on] purely medical grounds. I think public space should be given to women to bury their dead and let them finalize their grief and maybe the male-rule system will bend a little to be less cruel to us when it sees the thousands and thousands of tiny graves, that they, not women, have created.

Sherryn, a ward of the state at the time of her abortion in Queensland at the age of 13, had no say in what would be done to her, though she did not want the abortion: "I didn't understand how they could do that. Basically, what they're saying is: 'We can murder your child because you're a state ward.'" Sherryn suffered months in institutions after the abortion and engaged in self-mutilation. When pregnant a second time, she went on the run so as not to be forced to abort again.

Liz, from Tasmania, felt a sense of shame about a pregnancy in her forties, when the youngest of her three children was ten:

> Seeing my distress, my doctor assumed that I didn't want another child and reminded me I was middle-aged, as if I didn't know. I went for an ultrasound in order to discover whether there might be an abnormality that would give us a valid reason for terminating the pregnancy. Instead of rejoicing with me in the signs of new life there was silence and my questions went unanswered under my

doctor's orders. The risks of being an older mother were well known to me ... I pictured myself old and gray by the time this child was in high school. Even harder to bear was the remark by my husband that he felt he might be ridiculed by colleagues at work. Looking back I needed encouragement and offers of help as I felt almost alone with an impossible decision. I cannot describe the torment of the following months and years. My experience of a miscarriage some years before had been nothing compared to this overwhelming grief which engulfed my life after termination. A few years later when the older children left home I went through a period of deep mourning again. On every visit to the shops I was searching for my baby ...

Laurel Guymer, a former abortion clinic nurse, left her job in a Melbourne clinic partly because of the pressures she saw being applied to women judged unsuitable for motherhood:[39]

Women who were poor, unemployed, too young, too old, working in the sex industry, not married, had no steady partner, or suffered any mental instability were reassured by the clinic staff and society that it was best they have an abortion. It is clear that society fears a certain type of woman having a baby and I found that many of the doctors and nurses I met in the abortion clinic were not any different despite their supposed commitment to feminist principles.[40]

## The Inadequate Counseling

The stories contributed for this book also raise questions about pre-abortion counseling. Most women who submitted stories felt poorly treated in the pre-termination process. "Counseling," for them, was non-existent, token or over-directive. Their ambivalence was either dismissed or exploited to secure a "yes" decision, while risks were either not mentioned at all or downplayed if they were.

Sue, whose abortion took place in Adelaide when she was 15, recounts the following experience:

I was sent to the Family Planning Center for help; well, they helped me all right, so much so they had me booked in for an abortion the next day. Their reasons were I could not take care of myself let alone a baby. I had no permanent home, and to even think of keeping "it" was totally selfish on my part. They gave me no options and no information; my rights as a human being were not valid because of who I was, just another stupid teenager who got pregnant. I wanted so much to talk to someone, maybe someone would say, "Don't do it, I will help you through," or maybe, "You can keep your baby, there is help available and there are people who care," but instead I was herded into a room with about ten other girls like cattle and spoken to like I was a piece of dirt and treated as such.

Katarina, the Sydney psychologist quoted earlier, also had a negative experience with a family planning counselor:

The lady who met me there [at the local Family Planning Service] treated me as rudely as anyone could treat someone; there was no caring or concern in her manner. No options were presented to me. She said I was stupid to get pregnant and as I was 18 and at university she "presumed I wanted an abortion." I remember asking about the difference between local and general anesthetic and she said, "Have [a] local as then you will know it has happened and never make this mistake again." Her negative and unsupportive attitude is something I will always remember. I asked her at the time about other options, and she said, "Do you want to finish uni?*" I said, "Of course," and she replied, "Well, you can't have a child." ... I don't remember making the decision, just that this is what I was expected to do; from the little information I had been told it seemed there would be no support and no future for me if I was to have the child ...

Sam, from Melbourne, also felt her emotional needs were not properly addressed in the pre-termination process:

I had to stumble through a system which was not supportive of my emotional needs, and I certainly did not make an informed decision. At no stage did [they] discuss the alternatives, or the procedure, possible effects or how I felt for that matter ... when I made it to the clinic I had to go through "counseling," which was basically me justifying why I wanted an abortion. This wasn't really counseling at all, and my guess was it was to satisfy some legal requirement ... no professional created an opportunity for me to discuss anything, really ... no one that I came across ever said to me, "Why is this happening to you, what is wrong, why have you had more than one abortion, what can we do about it?"

Linda, a New South Wales college student, also felt alienated by the counseling process:

[My family doctor] ... was more concerned for [my parents'] respectability in the community than for the life that was inside me. He asked what I thought mum and dad would say. I said they would kill me. So he gave me the phone number of a termination clinic. That was it, as simple as that, end of consultation. No trying to find out what I really wanted to do, no suggestion for any alter-

*university

native or the option of me and Henry being able to get married. No, absolutely nothing, just a phone number ... I did not even know there was government financial assistance for people in need, such as social security, single parents' pension etc.

Jasmine, from Melbourne, was given a pamphlet but no counseling:

I was nine weeks pregnant. There was no counseling offered, just a leaflet telling me that I might feel a little upset, but that it was hormonal and would pass ...

A Queensland teenager's experience of counseling was to be put in a room on her own with a tape recorder and cassette tape to listen to.

Kerry, who was a teenager at the time of the abortion, felt put down in the counseling process:

The counselor who saw me a few minutes before the procedure was rude to me, treating me with no compassion, talking to me as though I was a slut and a brat.

Amy, 15, from Queensland, wrote: "I didn't really understand what the lady was saying but I just agreed with basically everything she said."

Laura, from New South Wales, was asked by the counselor "if this is what I wanted to do. I said I didn't know. She said, 'Well, you are here so it must be.'"

Kathy, from Western Australia, who became pregnant 20 years ago after her birth control failed, was told that if she was carrying a male fetus and didn't have an abortion, he would be homosexual.

Many women expressed feeling desperate for just one person to suggest they pause and think a bit more about the decision. Peta, from Southern Australia, quoted earlier, wrote:

I wish at least one of [the doctors and nurses] had tried to make me think seriously about the reality of what I was doing, rather than saying, "Don't worry, dear, we'll fix you up."

The woman cited earlier who called herself "Tortured," is a West Australia mother of two children she had difficulty conceiving. She wrote about her abortion experience as a 31-year-old in 1995:

I told both family and friends that I had become pregnant and not one of them were at all pleased about it. They said I was "mad" to bring another child into an already unhappy household ... I didn't want to go through with it but I had no support; I felt so alone. The night before the dreaded "abortion" I must have cried myself to sleep, holding my stomach and saying, "I'm so sorry," over and over ... [The next day a nurse] took some particulars. Although she was very sympathetic to my very distressed state, she did not ask me to perhaps think about it a bit more, which, looking back now, was all I wanted someone to say ... I was allowed to go home a little later in the afternoon but what I really wanted to do was throw myself off the nearest bridge ... I look back now and wish just one person would have said, "If you don't want an abortion, don't do it." Why didn't anyone hear my cries for help? Why didn't the staff at the hospital not ask me if it was what I really wanted to do, after they saw me in such a distressed state?

Winnie, originally from Hong Kong, had been told as a teenager that she would never have children due to hormonal problems. She accepted her infertility; she and her husband "made their lives outside of having children." Her hormone imbalance was treated with the Pill. Naturally she was stunned to find herself pregnant. "I panicked. I was traumatized. It was like finding out I had cancer," she said.

Despite the remarkable nature of the pregnancy, the likelihood that it would be her only opportunity of having a child, and the fact that she was "hysterical" in the days preceding it, an abortion was arranged. Not a word of caution was spoken by anyone, including the "counselor" she saw at the clinic in Adelaide:

I was not prepared for what I would feel. There was no information on the emotional effect of the operation. There was some clinical explanation and the whole process was presented as not as complex as it has been. Given what I know now, I would not have gone ahead with it. Now I know what downs feel like. I feel very empty. My life is black and unhappy.

Criticisms were leveled at the state of counseling back in 1985 by Kerry Peterson, writing in the *Australian Journal of Sex, Marriage and Family*:

Two major criticisms can be directed at the present system. First, abortion counseling is not readily available to all women seeking abortions; and second, it could be argued that some of the counseling that is done in the private sector is more concerned with "appearances" and evidentiary matters than the genuine well-being of the clients ... counseling should be independent of the abortion service in both the public and the private sectors.[41]

The accounts told here suggest there has not been much improvement since those criticisms were made.

The more recent publication, "We Women Decide," also

acknowledged the reality of coercive or judgmental counseling.

> [I]t was surprising and alarming to find that such information [held by women to be appropriate and helpful] was quite commonly absent or inadequate ... there were disturbing accounts from some women about the superficial pre- and post-operative information that was received from one clinic.[42]

Unfortunately, superficial information is not the preserve of only one clinic. Yet it appears that little is being done to change these practices.

The lack of care described by the women above often carried over into the actual abortion procedure itself. Many women describe feeling uncared for by the doctor performing the abortion.

## The Procedure

Jenna, who described earlier having the abortion to "appease" her husband, wrote:

> I recall the woman performing the abortion being less than patient, she clearly didn't wholly agree with what she had to do (what a horrible, horrible, horrible job). I hated her because she didn't attempt to create a relationship with me even if it was for 10-15 minutes. I felt cheap and wrong ... She went away with my little one ...

Lee, from Canberra, whose abortion took place in Sydney, felt the staff were callous towards her:

> I remember that the doctor who was to actually perform the D&C was an unpleasant person—he seemed to be eaten up with anger (no wonder, what a ghastly lot in life was his if that was his main occupation) ... the staff involved seemed callous—callous people, callous in their approach—not that they were rough with me; they strongly impressed me with their indifference to a woman in pain ... Inside I screamed protest at their treatment of me—the lack of attention when I awoke with severe pain; the looking through me as if I didn't really exist; the fact that they weren't interested in me, as a person, [enough] to hear my story or to help me make sense of it all. I remember that, after the pre-med had been administered and I was waiting on the cot* outside the theater** doors for my turn, I actually managed to lift my heavy head from the pillow to look through the windows in the doors to try and see who and why the surgical staff were creating such a ruckus—they were hooting, and laughing, and regaling loud and apparently hilarious

*stretcher    **operating room

stories to each other while performing these abortions.

Sue, whose experience of trying to talk about her grief at a women's center was cited earlier, felt she was being punished for having the abortion:

> The abortion was performed at a small private hospital. I remember going into the theater hearing a radio playing—it didn't seem right. I felt sad and they didn't care. I felt isolated from the other patients knowing what I had done and I felt one malicious staff member wanted to take advantage of this—she asked me to get up and clear up the other patients' lunch things because I wasn't sick.

Serena, from New South Wales, felt she was just a number when she had her abortion at 19:

> I felt ripped off ... as about 20 other women were "done" in the same session. It felt cheap, so utterly foul. To my great disbelief, to save money, they bundled us all in together—yuck! "Mass Abortions." So one then carries the loss of not just one, but 20 babies.

Genevieve of Canberra also felt insensitively treated by the response she received after the abortion: "One nurse yelled from across the room 'Congratulations, Genevieve!' I felt like a rape victim being raped over and over again by the system. All I wanted was to get out of the hell hole."

Adria, described earlier, who was pregnant to her male guardian, said she was told, "Quick, you're over; get off the bed, we need it for someone else." A 23-year-old single mother (who supplied no name or address), did receive a card from the clinic after her abortion. "They kindly let me know it was a male fetus. It really topped things off. I think I may have coped better without this information," she wrote.

### The Aftereffects

Many women were not aware of the potential physical and psychological complications of abortion. For them, abortion was, in the words of the 1994 United Kingdom inquiry into the effects of abortion on women, "an irreversible act chosen without sufficient knowledge."[43] Most women said they were totally unprepared for what they would go through during the abortion—and after. They felt cheated that abortion was presented as something quick and easy and over with when the reality for them was very different.

Melody, 32, from New South Wales, felt totally unprepared for the experience of the abortion she had in 1990:

The doctor and nurse ... didn't prepare me for the horror of termination ... I thought my uterus was being sucked out ... I could hear them saying it was a healthy nine-week-old fetus and everything was intact ...

Carol, of Melbourne, describes her experience:

It has been ten years now, almost to this day, and I can still remember, clearly, those fatal few minutes that I will regret to my dying day. The abortionist did not speak or look at me except to growl, "Be quiet and keep still," when I began to shake and cry against my own will as I felt his cold, sharp instruments cutting out the life that had been growing inside me for the past three months. The sound of the fetus dropping into the plastic bucket held between my legs is a sound I cannot erase from my memory, and to this day my throat feels choked and my stomach tenses, as I fight back tears for the baby I allowed to be killed.

Some women wrote of experiencing a sort of psychic trauma immediately after the abortion. Patricia, from Melbourne, pregnant to a married man she loved deeply and for whom she later relinquished custody of her other children, only to see the relationship collapse, wrote:

I felt like I was committing the worst crime when I went into theater. When I came out of the anesthetic I began to panic. I was dreaming or imagining where have they taken the soul of my baby. I felt robbed; I felt something hideous, terrifying. I was in a state of fright and shock. All I remember is thinking, "Where have they taken my baby?"

A significant number of respondents suffered physical side-effects, ranging from heavy bleeding, sometimes for months, to infection and incompetent cervixes. A surprising number had to have a second procedure to remove "retained products."

Mariah, from Melbourne, woke from the abortion in "excruciating pain."

I began crying in pain, and as I lifted the sheets there was blood everywhere. The pain was unbearable, it was like a knife kept stabbing me in the stomach over and over again ... The nurse gave me an injection for the pain, but it didn't help. About 15 minutes later she gave me another shot; it still didn't help. After the third shot she was so worried because I was still in pain that she called the head doctor who operated on me to take a look at me. When the doctor took the folder from the end of my bed and looked through the pieces of paper, he was shocked. He called the nurse over and asked if it was correct the amount of pain killer shots she'd given me. Because I was still crying and holding my stomach in pain, the doctor had no other choice but to inject me again ...

Deb, from New South Wales, describes the physical aftereffects of her abortion:

It feels as if someone has got a knife and scratched and scraped around inside your lower belly area ... two days after the procedure I couldn't walk: I was in terrible pain, and hunched over almost crawling, which I didn't experience with my miscarriage ... four days after the procedure, I started bleeding heavily and I was changing a sanitary napkin every hour and I could not sleep, as the bleeding was too bad ...

She had to undergo a second procedure: "They had trouble inserting the thing they had to insert, and tore my cervix a little bit."

Jael, the Melbourne woman quoted earlier on the structural reasons compelling women to abortion, also experienced severe bleeding:

I must have copped a real woman-hating doctor, because something went wrong—I rang the hospital and told them I was passing big clots and they told me to take a couple of Panadol*—that's all. I eventually passed out from blood loss after passing a clot that at the time seemed the size of a football, and ended up back in hospital for a D&C.

Lara, who underwent an abortion in Queensland at the age of 21 in 1996, also suffered physically.

I began to have pains in my stomach and I rang the 24-hour hotline where they told me to go back. I did this and I was given a course of antibiotics and treated for an infection in the womb. I was not really impressed with the service, as it appeared that they had no records of my procedure. A week later I was still suffering pains in my stomach and they were getting to the point I could hardly walk. I was rushed [to the hospital] ... I was told I was not the only one who had gone through this after a termination ... I remained in hospital for four days ... I broke out in hives from the medication ... My condition was only getting worse ... I was now unable to walk ... [I was] told that my body was probably just in shock. [A few months later] I found myself still going through the emotions of a pregnant woman, and close to the day I would have had my baby, I had labor pains. I lay on the floor in pain, crying and alone ...

Ginny, a Melbourne mother of two, also says she was not made

*a painkiller

aware of the implications of the abortion she underwent a decade ago after a vasectomy failure. She was told only that the abortion was "similar to a curette." Ginny has been hospitalized on psychiatric grounds a number of times since the abortion and has not been able to return to work. She suffers stress-related skin conditions, self-mutilates and experiences terrible nightmares.

> I would hear a baby crying in my sleep or I would get up thinking I had to breastfeed or just getting up to check on the baby, but it was hearing a baby crying that was the worst. No one prepared me for the years of nightmares, the guilt and the pain.

Ginny was, at the time of writing, undergoing shock therapy.

A number of women wrote or spoke of subsequent problems with infertility. Katarina, from Sydney, quoted previously, wrote:

> I was told I may not be able to have children because of problems with my ovaries and ... fallopian tubes. If I cannot have children—after aborting [one] and miscarrying another—I will die of an unfulfilled heart.

Theresa lost four babies as a result of miscarriage and stillbirth. She attributes these losses to two abortions six years earlier.

Trish, quoted in the preface, wonders if there is a connection between abortion and cervical cancer, having had three procedures to remove abnormal cells. She had two abortions, forced by her previous husband and, though having two children from that relationship, is not able to have any with her new husband because of the abnormal growths and related problems. Karen from Western Australia is infertile and part of an IVF support group. She has had a prior abortion. "Did I have my chance [and] then go and blow it?" she asks. Andrea, 36, who had an abortion at 15, has learned she suffered a "silent infection" and that her tubes are blocked by scar tissue. She suffers excessive bleeding, painful ovulation and cyst problems.

The more common abortion aftereffects experienced by those contributing to this book include uncontrolled crying, dreaming of babies, grief reactions on the date the baby would have been born, fantasizing about the baby, depression, emotional numbness, sleep disorders and anger.

A woman in her sixties wrote anonymously about the abortion her husband made her have almost 40 years ago:

> I tried to live with having an abortion, but I lost my confidence in life and have been a very frightened person inside. The veneer that I parade in front of family and the world is very false.

Julie, from New South Wales, wrote of the "deep inner pain" she experienced daily following an abortion in 1993.

> I am tormented ... I've lost self-esteem, inner peace, find it very difficult to find joy anywhere in life, am always depressed. I'm taking Luvox [an anti-depressant] and use alcohol ... and marijuana to cope with the pain of living. I always feel sad and ashamed ... He or she would have started school next week.

Cassie, from Melbourne, had a desperate need to know what happened to the body of the baby conceived as a result of an extramarital affair, and aborted "to save my family."

> I often wonder what happened with my baby. Where did they put her? Sometimes I wish I could have seen her, although I know that it would have been not only painful but I think I would have gone out of my mind! Still, most of the times I wish I knew what became of her; was she buried or just thrown away like some piece of rubbish. Sometimes I think of just ringing the clinic and ask them what they do with all the babies, but then, what am I expecting they'll tell me! ... All through the day I wonder how she would look, and how it would have been having her around with my two sons ... Whenever I'm asked how many children I have, I refrain from saying three! Nadia is always on our minds.

## The Replacement Child

A number of women became pregnant after their abortion to try to make up for the loss they felt—what is referred to in writing on the subject of abortion loss as the "atonement child" or "replacement child" phenomenon.[44] It was often the birth of a subsequent child which triggered the severest grief reactions.

Renaee, who had her abortion in Victoria at the age of 17, wrote:

> I had such a deep sense of betraying the baby who clung within me; it trusted me and I was its only love ... After I gave birth to my first child, the reality of pregnancy kicked in. Now I could see the end result and I felt very sad for my lost baby.

Melanie, who said there was no one who would support her having the baby, describes the devastation the abortion has wrought and how she hid her next pregnancy so as not to be pressured again.

> ... Over the next three months I suffered so much pain, anger and loss that I stayed home from school and slept and did nothing day in, day out. Every night I would cry myself to sleep praying that

God [would] send my baby back to me ... The pain inside me is so
unbearable ... I feel so out of control ... The one memory that
I have of my baby is when I was at the clinic I saw the ultrasound
photo and every hour, every second of every day I have flashbacks
to that photo and it feels as though my heart is crumbling ... I have
been trying so hard to be strong but I am losing hold of my life ...

Four months later Melanie was pregnant again—she told no
one until she was 12 weeks along "so no one could take him away
from me."

Every time I look into my beautiful son's eyes I think of how I
took the life of an innocent baby earlier ... I really believe that
when I had the termination a part of me went too ...

Some women felt they were at risk of harming their other children. Jenny, from Queensland, who had an abortion more than 40
years ago, felt this way.

When [the new baby] was a few weeks old, one night I got this
terrible feeling about what I had done. I just couldn't get it out of
my mind and thought I'd go crazy and do something to harm the
new baby.

Three women wrote of having to resist snatching other women's
babies from their strollers.

Belinda, from New South Wales, felt she needed to "atone" for
her loss:

I needed to show the world I was a life-giver, not a baby killer. My
children literally were my life. They defined my life as a loving,
maternal female—not a female aberration or mutant-life killer.

After two children and four abortions, she underwent a sterilization reversal to have a third child, in an attempt to make up for
the abortions.

Jasmine, from Melbourne, quoted earlier, finds herself wishing
for another baby:

[After the abortion] the grief set in. It was like nothing I'd ever felt
before, far worse than the grief after my miscarriages and even my
father's death. Along with the grief was guilt, such as I'd never
known before ... [it] never left. It turned inwards. Many times I felt
like committing suicide but never did because of the children I do
have ... I have a longing to turn back time so that I might undo
what I did. Often at night, I'll dream of the child that might have
been. The last one I had, I dreamt of the abortion and that after-
ward I was covered in blood that would not wash off. I find myself

wishing for another chance, another baby.

The births of her subsequent children intensified the pain of a woman who wrote anonymously.

It was eight years ago and I still think about it every day—feelings of grief and loss, anger and self-hatred. After the birth of each of my children, the grief was enormous. To see their beautiful little bodies and personalities growing fills me with pain at the loss of the first child and with fear of losing them ... my mind is obsessed ... I notice other children around the age mine would have been. I have confused my wedding anniversary with the termination anni-versary. I have confused my firstborn's birth year with that year. My life is divided into two segments—before and after the termination. Sex reminds me of pregnancy and grief and I feel like crying and have to stifle that emotion. I feel we don't deserve to enjoy our-selves as a couple, such as going out together without the children ... I feel depressed, useless and isolated ...

## Giving Sorrow Words

Unlike the Maori woman in Perth who took the remains of her aborted baby home and kept them in a jar in the fridge prior to burial,[45] the women in this book did not take their baby remnants home to grieve. But they understand what Bob Ellis wrote about "the aborted child arriving in dreams at her bedside, tugging at her sleeve, calling Mummy, Mummy."[46] Many women feel their sleeves being tugged. Many hear babies crying in the night, calling for them. They feel the shadow of a baby following them. They have a need to mark the event, something to acknowledge the reality of the life that was inside them, and to farewell it: a pair of booties or a teddy bear or doll bought after the abortion; a tattoo; the grave of another dead child visited as though that of their own child; pictures of an unborn child drawn; set aflame and "cremated."

This book is a way for a few of them, at least, to give sorrow words.

# MARGUERITE

*I open my arms and embrace the air*

I realized the other day that my grieving for the dead has come to overshadow my love for the living.

What brought this realization about? Failed relationships? Disinterest in family and friends? Living without hope for the future? Well, it really doesn't matter. What is important is that I have finally admitted to myself that the Ghost of Grief is ruling my life and I have not said "no" to it yet. Not so far.

I wanted my baby. I unequivocally wanted my baby.

I was a 23-year-old student living with a man who was prone to violence, resorted to violence, loathed violence, was violent. I had recently suffered a breakdown. My friends and my family were absent. He said that I did not need them. He took hold of my hand and said that he would be there for me always. But now, we must act responsibly. He said he was not ready for children. He said I was not ready for children. If I had the baby, he would have to leave. There would be other children one day. Truly.

A week later I was in the hospital for the abortion.

I remember the preceding week fairly well. I spent most of it in bed dreaming of my baby. Pretending to myself that if I lay there long enough, I'd give birth before the abortion took place. My body felt soft and roly. My nostrils were overwhelmed by the smell of lavender (I had been packing bags with lavender for extra money).

Protocol had me meet with a doctor. My partner was present. I could not speak. Were they going to ask me if I wanted the abortion? I waited. No questions asked. The day drew nearer and panic set in. I remember one night being so alarmed by pain in my womb that I was convinced I was miscarrying. I ran to the hospital and burst in, tears streaming down my face. "What does it matter?" a nurse scolded. "You're going to have an abortion anyway." I slunk away.

The day of the procedure, my partner fell asleep on the hospital bed while I sat and waited to be taken into theater.* He was tired and exhausted and upset. I was feeling ill-fated. They took me

*operating room

away. On the operating table they proceeded to administer the anesthetic. I looked into the anesthetist's face. I said "no." But they performed the operation anyway. No last minute absolution in this place.

The day after the termination I recorded in my diary a conversation which took place between two nurses prior to my going into theater.

> How many ABs today?
> Eight.
> All we need is one more to beat the other night.
> I know. It must be the heat.
> It must.

And I dreamed for many weeks later of human beings copulating indiscriminately in the sweltering heat of infra-red streets and alleys, just like animals. The cities were filled with clinics where impregnated women could abort, only to walk back on the streets to begin again the senseless game of conception and murder.

I remember also before the operation, recalling part of Judith Wright's poem *Women to Man*:

> The eyeless laborer in the night,
> The selfless, shapeless seed I hold,
> Builds for its resurrection day—
> Silent and swift and deep from sight
> Foresees the unimagined light.
>
> This is no child with a child's face;
> This has no name to name it by:
> Yet you and I have known it well
> This is our hunter and our chase,
> The third who lay in our embrace.

Oh, I felt so betrayed.

I tried to see things this way—this nameless, faceless being which I could "put on hold" for a while and create again when the time was more "appropriate." But there was always a face and a name. From the very beginning I felt connected to my baby and believed that I could see him. I even named him but I do not care to repeat that name these days.

For many months after the termination I woke during the night to hear my baby screaming. Sometimes, confused, I would get up and look for him. Other times I thought, this is my penance, and lay awake and forced myself to listen until he settled down. Eventually, after many months, the screaming turned to crying, and

then to whimpering and then to sniffling. One day it stopped altogether. But this was not the end.

To this day, I feel him around me. Sometimes he is more present than at other times. Sometimes I open my arms and embrace
the air as if I am holding on to something tangible. Mostly I just
talk to him with my hands—making gestures in the air to demonstrate a thought or a sentence or to share an interesting view. Or I
might run my hands around the smoothness of his face. I know
that there is nothing there, but these are impulses which I carry out
without thinking.

While riding on trams I drift off into a fantasy. A magic genie
has offered me a wish. One wish. And I am transported back in
time where I am swollen and sleepy and so incredibly happy. In this
world, my partner is not violent and does not threaten to leave. In
this world, I pack my bags and return to my mother until such time
as he feels ready to be a father. And that time comes soon.

I lost my child and my relationship broke down. I felt so
betrayed I could no longer sleep with him. I see him around (we
are in the same profession). He once told me that he was devastated that I had listened to him then. He holds this wish that I had
said "no" to him and continued with the pregnancy. We both
grieve. But we do so alone.

The guilt? There is certainly some of that. I wrote in my diary
about a year and a half later:

> I sit like Theseus in my chair. Unmoving. I'm doomed to never
> sleep but to think think think—to regret the failure of my king-
> dom, the death of my son, the loss of my honor amongst the
> gods ... for once, you know, I was a favorite ...

This shame is all-consuming. Yet, I am not a religious person. I
believe that women have the "right" to have an abortion. That
does not stop me from feeling like a murderer for terminating my
child. I did not terminate a "bunch of cells" but a real human
being. And yet, I do not expect to be shamed by my community.
This is not an issue for the moral majority. I have fought the stig-
ma of the majority—on both sides—who talk of my abortion as
if it is a "right" or a "wrong." These are simplistic terms which
cannot convey what it means to me: a regret and a grief. Abortion
is an issue which every woman approaches differently. I have spoken to women who have terminated and who have never looked
back. This is not how it is with me. I have looked back and am constantly remembering and grieving. I grieve and see no end to the

grief because what I did, rightly or wrongly, was irreversibly and irrevocably permanent. Do you see? I cannot, for all the riches in the world, get my child back.

I was in the Northern Territory recently, at a place called Simpsons Gap, with a man who was my fiancé but is no longer. I had this sudden urge to draw on the sand. I drew a child encased in a kind of aura. My then-partner looked at the picture. "Who is the golden child?" I shrugged. But we both knew who it was. And he is a golden child. The least I can do, after having created and then destroyed him, is to embalm him in a warm and golden light. I thought then, for a moment, I could step aside after the pain, guilt and grief, forgive myself, and, perhaps create again.

The desire to conceive again is overwhelming. To somehow bring back what I have lost; to attempt to fill the void. I wrote in my diary:

> ... There are babies being born all the time—there is no way to escape or deny—my womb opens up like an empty yawn. I want to conceive ...

But I have not conceived again. I cannot. Will not. I am disabled by the very ability which brought all this about in the first place. I have not recovered my desire for lovemaking. I have not recovered my love of children. I have not discovered the joy of that selfless giving which is parenthood. Is six years of grief penance enough? Perhaps not. Perhaps the grief is the only way I can keep my child alive in my heart. But with him beckoning daily, I have left no space for anyone or any thing else.

If you ask me what grief is, then it is all that I have described above. It is a mixture of loss and desire, guilt and shame. It is palpable. It permeates waking and sleeping hours. This is the kind of thing every woman considering termination must be aware of before the procedure, not after. In my mind, I have a son I cannot touch and cannot feed and who follows me about like a ghost. He grows with me. I sense him around me all the time. I love him with all my heart yet I do not have the power to bring him back to life.

There is a face and there is a name, but there will not be a resurrection day for the selfless, shapeless seed that I held.

# JANE

*It blew my soul apart*

It was 12 months ago and I was 31. I wasn't in a committed relationship with this man; however, we had been good friends for many years, and I knew him well. We were in a relationship five years previously—we maintained our friendship, and had been supportive of each other through hard times.

He had been away, come home, and we decided not to continue our relationship. I hadn't expected sex, but that's what happened after a few wines, and I got pregnant. I was glad to know I could get pregnant; I was quite proud of that. But I was also panicking about what lay ahead.

When I told Andrew he took the news well, really, and was quite calm. He thought things through over the next few days and decided that I should terminate the pregnancy. I was always pro-choice when it came to this issue, however, many years previously I decided that once I finished studying, if this ever happened to me, I would keep the baby.

I was old enough, mature enough, and financially able to have this child. I have a supportive family (although a mother who worries a lot) and some close friends. I was wanting to keep the child.

Andrew started to put more and more pressure on me to have a termination. I would wreck his life completely; he would hate me forever; I would be wrecking this child's life by bringing it into the world; the child wouldn't have a good life; this would be my fault; it would be extremely selfish to have this child; how could I do that without taking into account the effect it would have on him, on his family and on my family; it would devastate everyone. He said.

It is supposed to be a joyous occasion, but the birth of this child for him would be a tragedy. He would seek custody of the child (he would take this child from me one way or another); I have a choice available to me, so I should take this choice, and not bring another unwanted (by him) child into this world; there is enough suffering as there is without adding to it; I should be responsible, not selfish, and terminate the child. It would be the best decision for everyone. He said.

Andrew stayed with me for a week and I took time off work. He would say these things to me all day, every day, saying he had my best interests at heart. I felt powerless by the end of it, so unsure of what to do. It was like I was being brainwashed. Why I didn't talk to my mum or some close friend—I ask myself that every day. I needed some people to stand by me, so I could tell Andrew that I was having this baby. It is my baby, a part of me, and it isn't right to kill it. I knew that. He would get angry—and that frightened me. "Mustn't make people angry." "Mustn't wreck other people's lives."

I went to see two counselors—both were pathetic. As a counselor myself, I can honestly say the counseling I received was crap. I asked what happens to women who have a termination when they don't want one. One of the counselors said: "Some women get a little bit depressed afterwards." A little bit depressed! This was the biggest lie I have ever been told. The counselors did not give me any help; they were abominable.

So I thought I'd go along to the clinic to show Andrew that I would go that far for him, but then I wouldn't actually go through with it. And I didn't the first time. The clinic counselor suggested I lie to Andrew and tell him I would have the termination. She should have supported me in ways to tell him that I was not having this termination for him. I was left with nowhere to go. I still hadn't told him I wasn't having the termination. I was also getting very worn down by this stage—I hadn't slept and was feeling the physical and emotional effects of the pregnancy—while trying to maintain the appearance of a perfectly normal life to others.

We get home. Because of the operation, I hadn't eaten or drunk anything all day. Andrew goes completely berserk at me—and I have nothing left. So I agree to have a termination. He stands over me while I ring to make the appointment—there is a time at 8 a.m. the next day. I go in, I cry and cry, two nurses take me to the room and I want to sit up and say STOP—but I went under the anesthetic immediately and it was over.

And I just have no words to describe what I went through when I woke up from the anesthetic. I cry as I write this. I wanted to slice myself up, to get a gun and blow my head off. I wanted to do something violent and bloody to myself—I wanted to literally blow myself apart. How could I have agreed to an abortion? How did I let that happen? I ask myself those questions every day.

I did not feel I deserved to live. All I thought about was how I would kill myself, when I would kill myself. I wrote goodbye letters to my family, my good friend and my flatmate* and researched the

*roommate

most efficient and effective way to kill myself—I wasn't going to make any mistakes. After all, if I can kill my baby, I can sure as hell kill myself—and I deserve it. Because I couldn't even look after my baby when it was right there deep inside of me. Couldn't even do that.

If my mother hadn't been going on a trip to Antarctica, which I knew meant the world to her, I would have killed myself. I am quite sure of this. But I thought I would wait until after her trip. If I killed myself beforehand she wouldn't go. I still feel enormous guilt and shame and God, do I miss my baby. I dream a lot about my baby. The pain is indescribable and I did it myself. It was my choice, my doing; I went there and I had my baby killed.

Before I had the termination, I looked in the Family Planning library for books about how a woman might feel afterwards. But there was nothing. Nothing that describes what can happen to you.

Two days after the abortion my brother rings and says: "Guess what, you're going to be an aunty!" Their baby was born early— two days after my baby was due to be born. My nephew will be a constant reminder to me, all my life, of what I gave up. And my brother and his wife don't have any understanding of that, but just think I'm not a very good aunty—and I'm not, because it is all just too painful.

Andrew promised me he would be supportive. I haven't heard from him since Jan. 1998. The whole thing is nicely over for him.

I ended up resigning from my job and pulling out of the post-graduate study I was doing. Now I'm thinking about getting out of my profession altogether because there are too many reminders of what I've done.

Around the time my baby would have been born the "abortion debate" began in Western Australia. And I found hearing all the news about it and it coming up in people's conversations, extraordinarily hard. It's horrible, and I regret my decision with every bit of me. I regret it every day. If someone had told me that I might experience this much pain, there is no way I would have done it. I didn't realize how deeply attached I already was to my baby—until it was too late and it was in the rubbish bin. No one tells you that, and I don't know why. The abortion has blown my life apart, blown my entire self/psyche/soul/belief in myself apart. It has devastated me and I don't know how long this goes on for.

# CELESTE

*In my culture women with illegitimate pregnancies*
*are despised and seen as whores*

When I was 16 years old I moved from a country in Asia where I had been born and raised, to live and study in Australia. My main aim was to go to university and study a "prestigious" course like medicine. I was an average to above-average student in my own country, but for many years had a dream to become a doctor. In a country of super-achievers, to get into medicine required excellence. I was not exceptional in any way. Vast sums of money were required for me to try and fulfill my dream but my parents were prepared to sacrifice their life savings for me.

I lived in a student hostel affiliated with the college where I studied. Early that year I met and fell in love with David, a Chinese guy two years older. Our relationship started out platonic, but soon evolved to become a physical one. Both of us were virgins, but I was more naïve about sex than he was. In my strict Christian household, sex was never discussed.

About a month after we began dating, I was pressured into sex. I felt that the relationship had been going too fast too soon, but was unsure of how to handle it. I was torn between the conflicting emotions of guilt for having sex before marriage, and desire. In the early stages we were using condoms. What little I had heard of the Pill seemed to indicate that it was a bad and dangerous thing. After a few months of using condoms, I had a pregnancy scare, but the home test kit was negative. Shortly after, I got my period. The one thing I learned from this episode was that David would not have married me, pregnant or otherwise. His father is a well-known professional in his home country and the shame would have been horrible.

Unfortunately, around this time David began to complain that he did not enjoy using condoms. To be honest, I didn't either as I was very dry and knew nothing of lubrication. Somehow we ended up switching to a combination of withdrawal and the rhythm method. When my period did not come the next month, I was initially too terrified to do anything. But eventually I bought a home pregnancy kit. I was horrified and thought that I was going to be sick when the test came back positive. I think that deep down I already knew. A second pregnancy test performed at the doctor's surgery\* meant that I could no longer fool myself. The female doctor was very nice but did not offer me any alternatives or discuss my choices with me. She only asked me what I thought I would do.

My mind was in a whirl and I was too confused to think straight. I knew that my boyfriend had already said that he couldn't marry me. If he had shown even the slightest bit of support, I would have given everything up to have this child—my dreams of going to university and becoming a doctor and ties with my family. I was too ashamed of what I had done and too afraid of their reaction to tell them. Illegitimate pregnancies are especially shameful in the Chinese culture and women who have one are despised and seen as whores.

I had nowhere to turn and no alternative. I requested a referral to an abortion clinic. I went to the clinic the same day and made an appointment for a termination, which was to be the day after my final exams. On my return home, I sobbed my heart out and begged my boyfriend not to make me do this. To this day, I still blame him. But some of the blame does lie with me. I was not strong enough and did not have the courage to face up to what I had done. Somehow I managed to make it through the exams and somehow to score exceptional results.

The morning of the termination, I had to see the doctor first. He was elderly and a total bastard, neither understanding nor sympathetic. He spoke to me and looked at me in such a way that I felt I was on trial. I almost got up and left, something I now wish I had done. He explained the procedure and gave me antibiotics to combat any infection. No other complications were discussed nor was I given any form of counseling. Nothing at all was mentioned about my mental and physical health after the abortion. He also said that I would have to take the Pill. When I raised my concerns over what I had heard about the Pill, he dismissed me, saying, "That's nonsense!" He did not explain the risks or benefits of this form of contraception and seemed only keen to ensure I take it, no matter how I felt about doing so. I felt very pressured and uncomfortable that whole interview. It was the worst day of my life and the doctor did nothing to alleviate the agony. Instead, he contributed to it. I will never practice medicine the way he did.

Following the abortion, I developed a severe case of infection and, though treated with antibiotics, I now carry the fear I will

\*office

never have a child.

I was in shock for two weeks after the abortion. I didn't talk about it and carried on life as normally as I could. But the veil of denial lifted and I sobbed uncontrollably for days. My emotions were a mix of sorrow, anguish, regret and shame. For five years after, I continued to have periods of sobbing that lasted hours.

Following tremendous social and professional pressures, I fell into a deep depression and attempted to take my life. I am now seeing a private psychiatrist and we have explored this issue after it has lain hidden for so long. It was really only after counseling that I have managed to cope with the grief and loss. This has helped me very much and I recommend it to any other women who have ongoing emotional trauma from a termination.

The psychiatrist, David, and myself are the only people who know about the abortion. I would have no hesitation taking my own life immediately if my parents ever found out. I never meant for things to turn out this way. I am ashamed that after sacrificing so much for me to realize my dream that I could let something like this happen. I also have a lot of guilt to deal with because I believe that abortion is murder. The taking of a defenseless life is the worst sin I can think of, and I am guilty of it. This is something I will have to carry for the rest of my life.

Following my suicide attempt I finally had the courage to break off with David, after having been together for almost five years. I realized that although we both love each other, the memory of this child, and not our relationship, was the thing which kept us together. I have not seen him for months now and this is fine except that I worry about having another boyfriend. Will he want me if he finds out the terrible thing I did? As a medical professional I see many patients and get envious when I see other women enjoying their children. I think, "That could be me." The pain is especially great when I see children the age my child would have been if he or she had lived. My only consolation is this: I believe with all my heart that when I die and go to heaven my child will be there and I will see him or her again. That is the hope that keeps me going.

Writing this has been extremely painful for me but I think that if I can help just one person by what I've written, it would all be worth it.

# BARBARA

*Won't anyone save me?*

I was the 39-year-old mother of four children aged ten to 15 years. I had had a second Copper 7 IUD inserted after having my older one removed. Prior to this I used the Pill but was taken off it due to my age. I asked the doctor if IUDs worked as an abortifacient and was assured that these newer copper devices were purely contraceptive, unlike some of the older IUDs.

I had always wanted six children, but had promised my husband that if I could have four I would never burden him with more. Because of this promise I had always been very careful with contraception, never missing a Pill in 11 years except to get pregnant with children three and four. I was not—and still am not—a Christian. However, I fully understood that abortion was the deliberate killing of a human being. But on the usual grounds of "it's my body" and the plight of the unmarried mothers and the poverty-stricken, I felt quite proud to be a South Australian because of our liberated abortion laws. Abortion was for other people, the poor, the uneducated—it would never be for me, healthy, educated, reliable, married, and financially secure in my own right.

I had one normal period after the new IUD. The second began at the right time but started and stopped over 23 days. During this time my emotions started to change and I had great delight in fantasizing that I might be pregnant again. However, as this feeling got stronger, I became worried about the awful promise made to my husband that I would never have another baby. I mentioned the possibility that I might be pregnant. He did not take much notice, just mumbled, "Get rid of it." I began dreaming every night about blasted bloody babies, squashed baby birds, and dead pups and would wake up crying. During the day I was hopelessly emotional and felt like dancing in the sun (this is not the usual me). At last I decided to make an appointment with my family doctor on Aug. 22, my 39th birthday.

My doctor was slightly amused, said I might be lots of things, but not pregnant. He reluctantly took a urine sample, wished me happy birthday, said how young 39 was, and told me to call in two days for the result. I went home happy. I had experienced this happy fantasy and that was the end. The next afternoon the phone rang. The doctor said the test was positive and to come back the next day. My world collapsed. I stood in front of the bedroom mirror screaming and crying and telling my baby how I loved it but how it must be killed (recalling this moment after 19 years has just started me crying again).

I thought things over all night and decided I had some chance of talking my husband into keeping it. But I was very worried what the fresh copper from the IUD had done to the baby. The doctor said he did not know about the copper but it was definitely a poison. This aside, he said I was a very "unusual" woman wanting a baby at 39—it was unfair to my husband, the doctor would expect his wife to have an abortion under the same circumstances, it would ruin our social life and be detrimental to our other four children.

The doctor referred me to the specialist who had inserted the IUD. I told him my story, said I did not want an abortion, that I was worried about the copper, had a reluctant husband, etc. He examined me and stated that he did not think I was pregnant, but if I was, the IUD would need to be removed and this usually caused miscarriage. Home I went, unsure if I was pregnant, but feeling that I could at least cope with a miscarriage if this was inevitable.

I lost a bit of brown mucus here and there over the next week but no baby. Back to the specialist at the end of the week, I had an internal examination and was now no doubt pregnant. I was still worried about the copper. The specialist yelled at me that it did not matter—I had two children already (actually four), I was 39 and I had no right to do this to anyone. I was "odd." My husband would probably beat up all the children (he did have a history of violence). I signed the abortion papers with tears dripping over them and was booked into hospital for the following week. Things were made even more difficult for me because I would not consent to a tubal ligation at the same time.

The final week at home before hospital was hell. I cried constantly and begged my husband to change his mind, but all he did was hiss, "Get rid of it." I was in a totally confused state. I felt the doctor knew something I did not about damage from the copper.

I had expected the doctors to have said, "Don't be so silly, you're a very healthy woman, people like you do not have abortions; go home and wait for your husband to get used to the idea." (I have certainly learned a lot since then.)

The time came to catch the train to the hospital. My children waved me off.

Once in hospital I began to get some fight back. I decided that once and for all I would insist on information on my copper problem and would just go home if all seemed okay.

Eventually a doctor came into my room, took my blood pressure and remarked how healthy I was for my age. I said I did not want the abortion but had husband and copper problems and could he give me some info. He said I would have to speak to my private specialist who would not be in until the next morning. He then left the room and walked down the passage. All of a sudden he stormed back, put his head in the door and said: "It is just not done to have children at your age under your circumstances."

That night I thought it through. I had been told my doctor always spoke to his patients first thing in the morning and I was anxiously waiting for him to turn up. At about 9 a.m. I asked a nurse when I would see him and was informed he was already in theater.* I was to be prepped immediately because I was the first to be done. I was shocked. I was given a pethidine injection and after 11 weeks of avoiding aspirin, artificial colorants, and insecticides, this was the final blow. I was wheeled crying through miles of corridors to the theater, feeling defeated. There was much joking about whether I was related to a well-known doctor at the hospital (I wasn't) and how nice the new blue theater hats looked. I thought of getting off the trolley** and running and have often wondered if anyone has ever done this. While I was still crying they said they would just give me an injection into my hand. I said "Won't anyone save me?" The specialist laughed and that was the end.

On returning home from the hospital, I could not stop crying. For three days I felt if I killed myself I could catch up with my baby and have it back. After this time I felt I had lost it forever which made me even worse. At last my husband started to become alarmed. He got back to the specialist and asked if this sort of behavior was to be expected. He was told some women are upset but I would be over it in a week or two.

The weeks went by. I followed women with babies in prams*** trying to get up nerve to run off with a baby. I was obsessed with babies. I hated my other four children, seeing it as unfair that they had been allowed to live and my last baby had been killed. I jostled pregnant women. I contemplated killing my husband and the

*the operating room    **stretcher    ***strollers

doctors, but most of all I wanted my baby.

Time dragged on. At the end of November I stopped taking the Pill with the idea of having another baby. I did not get pregnant and went back on the Pill for one month. Deciding I could not live without a baby, I stopped the Pill again and after two months my period due on April 1 did not arrive. This was the due birth date of my killed baby.

This time I progressed with care. I kept away from all doctors until I was 16 weeks pregnant. I felt we were both in danger while there was any chance of being mentally intimidated into another abortion. Even though I was pregnant I was still aggressive to other pregnant women and was very sensitive to seeing a baby and hearing one cry. I had come back to loving my other children after a car accident one month after the abortion. One of my children was thrown forward against the windscreen* and in that instant my hatred disappeared.

I had a very easy pregnancy. My little girl was born with her father and three brothers present and was loved and spoiled by all of them. My eldest 16-year-old daughter was like a second mother to her.

Even though all seemed to go so well, I was still very tearful and depressed. It was only when my eldest daughter got married at 18 and I was forced to think about wedding receptions that I started to pull out of my depression. However, I was still worried about how other unsuspecting pregnant women could find themselves faced with an abortion they did not want. One day I saw an ad on a church notice board where I went to playgroup wanting counselors for Birthline. I went along and eventually became a counselor.

In Oct. 1988, my 20-year-old youngest son was killed in a car accident and it was this that made me realize the terrible trauma and guilt I had been through with the abortion. I loved my son as much as any other mother but compared to the abortion, the effect of my son's death was nothing. I had the ears of understanding friends at Birthline and personal friends and grief counselors and a supportive husband and family to listen, share, and help through the grief process. This was in total contrast to the lonely helpless feeling I experienced before and after the abortion.

The beautiful flowers I received when our son died meant a lot to me. When, a few months later, a pro-life group organized a

---

*windshield

march to place a flower for an aborted baby on the steps of Parliament House, I took the opportunity to make a beautiful flower arrangement with a letter to my baby enclosed, saying how much I had loved her/him and how terribly sorry I was for what had happened. Since then I have moved on. I am recovered from this experience; I have learned from it and become a much more rounded, compassionate person. I hope that over the years as a counselor I have managed to save the lives of at least a few other babies who may not be here now if all this had never happened.

# DANIELLE

*The doctor told me I was too young and incompetent to raise a child*

When I found out I was pregnant I went into a state of shock and denial. I had my whole life ahead of me. I was only 16. I had a study and career path all mapped out. My parents would freak. I'd always wanted children, but not just now. My boyfriend was 17 years my senior, with three children of his own who lived with their mother. He was the first person I told and his exact words were, "So? Just abort it." Like it was so simple. I asked if maybe I should keep it. "If you do, I will deny being the father and won't help you out in any way," was his blunt reply. This was not the man I thought I knew.

I went to a counselor at the local community health center and told her my predicament. She asked if a child fitted in with my plans for the future. I told her that it didn't. She then questioned me vigorously about these plans, my life so far, my life experience and whether I thought I could bear the responsibility of a child. I answered as best I could that I didn't know as I had never tried before. She told me that adoption was one option but that it was more emotionally painful than abortion, which would be easy and effective. She also told me I needn't feel guilty as the child was not really a child yet.

I went away with all she had said spinning through my mind. My boyfriend kept hounding me as to whether I had had the abortion and continually reminded me that I did not have time to dawdle.

I became irritable and would fly off the handle with little provocation. I stopped attending school regularly and began drinking heavily every day. I would sleep for 12 hours at a time to try not to have to face the day. Eventually I went to my doctor and he put me on anti-depressants. He then told me I was in no condition to raise a child and would never cope. I told him I was only so depressed because people kept telling me to abort the child and he said that was an effect of my depression, not the cause itself. He told me straight out I was too young and totally incompetent as far as raising a child was concerned.

After a painful night of thinking I came to the conclusion that the professionals are trained in these matters and know more than me who hadn't even finished school yet. I chose to get an abortion.

I lay in a bright, sterile room which smelt of antiseptic, surrounded by steel trays. I lay, still and calm, giving my permission to these smiling professionals to murder a life I created.

Once it was all over I walked out into the slightly overcast world. Men and women were going casually about their business. The sun warm, the breeze cool, leaves on the trees rustling. But I was a murderer.

Slowly I walked to the bus station, hopped on a coach and settled down for the ride home. When I got there I crawled straight into bed and curled up in a fetal position where I lay until I fell asleep.

The next day I went to see my boyfriend who told me he was proud of me and he loved me. He tried to hug me but I shied away. Over the next few weeks I got to the point where I couldn't stand his touch, let alone sex. The doctor kept me on antidepressants and told me to see a counselor. But I refused. After three months my boyfriend moved out as I refused sex. The idea of committing an act designed specifically for reproduction repulsed me.

I withdrew, rarely talking to anyone, barely leaving the house. I quit my part-time job and left school. I continued to drink myself into a stupor every day. I couldn't look at myself in the mirror. I felt as though a part of me had died. I felt guilt at destroying what I had created. I stopped eating, guilty at wanting to when my baby couldn't. I cut off all my long hair I had loved so much and began to slash my arms and legs with a razor blade. I felt I should suffer for my actions and I hoped the physical pain would draw my focus away from the pain and anguish I constantly felt inside. It gave me something else to focus on.

I felt I didn't deserve to have any semblance of a good life, as I had taken the opportunity for life from another. I became severely suicidal and once tried to overdose but a friend found me and took me to the hospital. She has never known of my abortion but we became close and our friendship turned to love as we formed a sexual relationship.

I am now single and gay. I am searching for a new job and house and am getting on with my life. I still take antidepressants and occasionally at night when I am alone I want to throw up with revulsion at the thought that I couldn't even sustain a human's life. But I cope because my death would not solve anything. At least now I know that only a conscious decision will result in my becoming pregnant again; but the thought of sex with a man is something I still can't even think of.

# ANNE

*Finding Hope*

A little over 10 years ago, I had an abortion. The reasons why aren't complex or confusing. I was young and inexperienced, pregnant and very scared.

Fear is a great motivator. It prompted me to seek a solution to my problems that proved to be devastating.

The day I found out I was pregnant seems like a bad dream. I had the sense that my connection with reality was broken. My chest was tight; my face felt numb, like a mask. I found it hard to speak or think clearly. My movements were slow and clumsy like a sleepwalker's. Externally, I must have appeared drugged. Inside I was panicked and very afraid.

What did I want? I wanted the terror to go away. I wanted to be accepted and loved by my mother. I thought my decision would help me live; instead I wanted to die.

A baby. Something couples dream of. Something couples spend fortunes at fertility clinics trying to conceive. A baby. Growing inside me. I should have rejoiced.

I was 18 and unmarried. I had an invalid mother, younger teenage brother and stepfather. They had enough trouble holding their lives together, let alone supporting me through early parenthood. My boyfriend was six months older than I and a university student. I was working as a secretary.

We wanted to be married and had realized we would have to wait. My family thought it ludicrous that we would consider marriage. We knew all the arguments by heart—we were too young, we had no money, we should live together first. Only my boyfriend's parents would listen to our hopes and dreams for the future. Now I clung to the hope that they would understand and help me; reassure me that I would be all right. I was desperate to see them. I had been to my gynecologist with my mother. She told the doctor that I would be having an abortion.

I barely registered what was happening. Abortion. The word played through my head over and over like a recording jumping at the one spot. The doctor looked at me and told my mother to leave the room. She went, reluctantly. He told me that there was no reason why I could not successfully have this baby. I was young, strong, and healthy. He asked me what I wanted to do. I cried, like I'd never cried before. I seemed to be drowning in fluid. I grabbed a handful of tissues and managed to gasp that I wanted my baby. But I was terrified. Terrified because there was no one who would support me. Terrified because my mother refused to allow me to remain under her roof and have the baby.

On the way to the surgery* she had kept up a steady stream of muttered conversation. Through lips drawn tight across her mouth, words issued forth that felt like tiny knives digging into my heart, every one of them loaded with the poison of bitterness, anger, rejection, and threat, every one of them designed to wound, humiliate, torment, and feed my fear. Not one word failed in its purpose.

The doctor looked at me. He said again that I could have this baby. There were places I could go, people who would help me if my mother would not. He didn't understand. I knew all about those refuges for women. I knew they would probably be able to help me. Help me with everything—except my mother. My mother. You had to be there. She was someone people thought was so nice, genteel. A real lady. But that was the facade. She was physically weak, but emotionally strong. Mum knew how to wound for maximum effect. No lumps, bumps or bruises—never anything anyone could see. But the wounds and the pain are still with me.

I had a choice. Have my baby and be rejected by my mother. Abort my baby and have a roof over my head. To my eternal regret, I chose the latter. I make no excuses. My decision was based on sheer terror. The paralyzing fear of what my mother was capable of if I defied her was my motivator. I had defied her to my great cost before.

I had 24 hours to make a decision. I managed to get away from mum for awhile. My boyfriend and I went to his parents' place. Visitors from overseas had just arrived. We drove frantically around to our minister's house. He had just left on two weeks' holiday. My hopes of a last minute reprieve lay in the dust. Without the immediate support and reassurance of anyone who loved both of us, I knew what I would do. We looked at each other, tears running down our faces. Defeated and demoralized, we drove back to my place.

Waiting. In hospital admissions with my mother. Uncomfortable, tense, my mask of numbness on again, I waited. My baby waited too. Soft, warm and vulnerable inside me. Unaware it was

*doctor's office

on death row. Not guilty but condemned anyway by its mother's fear.

Already, I was sentencing myself. Some time ago I had become a Christian. Fat lot of good my faith was doing me now. Suddenly, my number was called.

I hate hospital corridors. I hate hospital trolleys.* Lying on one and prepped, I began to panic. A nurse brought me a consent form to sign. I became hysterical. "I don't want to do this ... Oh, God, sweet Jesus, help me; I DON'T WANT THIS!" I signed though. I don't remember how, but I signed that paper and my baby's life away.

Another needle. It hurt. Hurt because I was writhing around like a demented woman. Then, nothing.

I floated in a drug-induced abyss while my baby was systematically dismembered and pulled from my body.

Consciousness hit me like a fog rising from nowhere. I felt a sudden pain and asked for a bedpan. As they raised me over the pan to a sitting position, black blood poured out of my body like a river. After filling two pans with it they injected more medication. I slipped into the abyss again.

I woke to find a nurse watching me. A kind face. Why was she looking at me with sympathy? I deserved none.

Nothing could ease the guilt and condemnation that I meted out to myself. My boyfriend came. It had taken him two days to see me. My mother visited. At last I had some measure of power over her. I could justify ignoring her and telling the nurses to make her leave. She brought presents like I'd had my tonsils out. I'd been her good little girl after all. The only person I hated more than her was myself.

I went home. Empty. Without a baby. Without a life. Without reason. Without myself. I didn't know who I was. I had dismembered myself out of solidarity with my baby. I went to work. I came home. I went to bed and dreamt of death and ruin and blood. Oceans of black blood with bits of baby floating in it, like dolls with their arms and legs off.

I refused to look at myself in the mirror for fear of confirming that I still lived and breathed and my baby didn't. I didn't want to exist because my baby didn't exist anymore. My boyfriend refused to give up on me. I didn't realize that he was crying too. My internal screams engulfed every waking moment. My self-hatred

---

*stretchers

swallowed everything else. Eating me alive. And I wanted it that way. I went through massive bouts of depression. Waves of guilt washed over me, relentlessly drowning any hope or positive thought.

Then the pains started. Then the bleeding. Blood again. More blood. I went to bed and began to feel strange. The room kept going away and coming back again. I was hot, so hot, then freezing. Mum came in to check me. Ten minutes later I was in a taxi, back to hospital.

In casualty,* they put me in a wheelchair. I left a nice little trail of blood for them so the doctors would know where I was. A gynecologist was passing through and followed my trail. Instead of the torture of waiting, this time it was the torture of an internal examination. I began screaming out loud this time: "Don't take my baby; oh, God, where is my baby? I want my baby." Another needle, another abyss.

I went home; I didn't talk. I just did what I had to do. Work, home and sleep. I talked with my doctor. I had developed an internal infection. Pain, fever, another operation. So what, it didn't matter. Nothing mattered anymore.

My mind and emotions were locked into that event and while outwardly I functioned as I needed to, inside my thoughts revolved like a train on a circular track that stopped at the same stations.

My boyfriend and I drifted like two shipwreck survivors, clinging to our relationship to keep ourselves afloat in a sea of misery. We nearly didn't make it. In desperation, he went to his dad and told him what had happened. He was devastated for us and very kind and understanding. The only snag was that he felt my boyfriend's mum should not be told. My sense of shame deepened. We had never kept anything important from her before. I could see now just how others were affected by my choice.

I could not cope with relating to my boyfriend anymore. In the middle of his final exams I dumped him. His mother was confused and angry with me. I broke down and told her that I had murdered what would have been her grandchild.

She wept, [and] told me she would have helped me as much as she could. With her help I began to heal a little. My boyfriend and I started taking slow steps towards each other again. We became engaged and married in Sept. 1987. We are still together and still in love. We have three fantastic children, two sons and a daughter.

*the emergency room

My healing is by no means complete, but two events stand out as beacons of hope in my progress from depression to freedom.

The first was realizing I had nearly died in hospital. I hadn't known then how close I came to getting my wish. The staff had told my mother to stick around as I may not "make it through the night." I was still here; I had a second chance.

The second event occurred in 1997.

I had been plagued by questions about the spiritual state of my baby. Had I sent my baby to hell because of what I did?

What I describe now came to me as a kind of vision or dream. I choose not to debate or question its validity or try to prove its worth to anyone. It is enough that it was, firstly, real to me; and, secondly, gave me an enormous sense of release and healing.

I was reliving the whole abortion experience, the pain and anguish in my heart were overwhelming. I began to pray and cry out as I had done so often over the years. This time a friend was with me and she gently suggested that I ask the Lord to heal me once and for all. I cried out at this, saying that was impossible. How could God want to heal me when I had not only murdered my baby but also sent it to hell?

She was appalled that I had labored for so long under this mis-conception. It took time but she convinced me that I was wrong. She confessed her own abortion to me and revealed how the Lord had reassured her that he had her baby. She encouraged me to pray and ask for healing and reassurance for myself. With tears blinding me and pain like a vise in my chest, I did just that.

As I waited in silence, eyes closed and hands clenched, a warmth came over me and I saw bright light. The pain was forgotten as I saw Jesus holding a baby in his arms. I heard him say, "This is your daughter. She is now mine ... She always was mine." I found myself asking: "What is her name, Lord? What have you called her?" The answer came back, "Her name is Hope."

Since then, I've had a measure of peace that has enabled me to think about the whole event, and even write this down, without crippling pain inside me. Sadness and regret remain—abortion vio-lated my body, soul and spirit. But there is no more crushing guilt and depression.

It was through Jesus alone that I found Hope.

# JUSTINE

### *My adopted grave*

At 21 I had graduated from my real estate licensing course, was raising a perfectly wonderful five-year-old daughter and had just returned home from five months living in America. My dreams were coming true. I was young, happy, healthy and everything was going pretty much to plan.

The day after returning home a doctor confirmed I was pregnant. I was shocked. For days after I kept looking for my period and for it all to be a mistake. The period never came so I called the baby's father in America.

I was devastated and confused but as far as he was concerned there was nothing to be confused about. He told me I knew what I had to do. But the truth was I didn't. I couldn't imagine having to live with myself after having an abortion so I came to the conclusion that I just wouldn't do it—I was going to keep the baby or put it up for adoption.

Adoption was pretty quickly ruled out, mostly because of the impact it would have had on my daughter. So I was having a baby—yes, it would be difficult but we would make it somehow. Soon all my friends and family knew. No one was exactly happy for me.

Although things were pretty serious between us before I left, Charlie and I had made no definite plans to have a long-distance relationship. When I called to tell him I was going to keep our baby he informed me in no uncertain terms that he wanted no part in its life. He never wanted to see a photo of his child or know his name or even be named on the birth certificate ... But he still loved me!

All of a sudden I had no choice. No way to make a "right decision." I was thrown into a depression, crying all day and night, unable to get out of bed and barely able to respond to my daughter's concerns for me. If I have discovered anything from this experience it is that I am loved unconditionally by one person— my daughter.

How could I give up a chance at having that kind of relationship a second time? But how was I going to answer this baby's questions when he asked, "Where is my daddy?" and, "Why doesn't he love me?" I had no answers because I don't know how anyone could not love a child of their own whether it was planned or not. And I love my children too much to do that to either of them—but is he better off dead?

I used to believe that I was a strong, determined person and all of the problems that would come with another child could be overcome. Except for this one—a father who refuses to acknowledge his own child. I know myself, far too well, the pain a child can go through when your own father wishes you were never born.

And still people believe that I had a choice. As far as I was concerned there was no choice, no support, nowhere to go and no one to help.

The hardest phone call of my life was making an appointment for the abortion. The hospital would only do the operation at nine weeks so I had to have an ultrasound to confirm exact dates.

The last time I had an ultrasound I was so happy and excited. I couldn't believe that the best thing to ever happen to me and the most tragic could be the same.

My depression worsened and my confusion escalated. I didn't want to kill my baby, that much I was sure of, but I didn't see any other way. I called the baby's father again. He was obviously pleased I was going to do the "smart thing."

Getting out of bed was harder every day. I felt like I was plotting the murder of my own child. I refused to take pain relief tablets because it could harm the baby, even though the days were slowly ticking by and his chance at life was fleeing anyway.

I drove myself to the hospital to book in and see the social worker and the doctor. The social worker was barely the same age as myself and from all indications had no experience or way of understanding what I was going through or how hard it was for me just to be there. It seemed more of a formality as she asked her standard questions. I cried in spite of myself. She wrote my referral to the doctor, and wrote down all the reasons why this was okay for me to do. But where was the sheet of paper telling me it was okay to let my baby live?

The great "right to choose" has changed public opinion from abortion being a dirty secret to an intelligent way to resolve an unfavorable situation—with no emotion expected at all. I felt and had been told that I would be looked upon in a much worse way if I kept the baby and became a single mother to two children with different fathers, than if I had a termination and just "got on with my life."

Leaving the social worker's office distraught and feeling hope-less, I went to my car instead of to the clinic to see the doctor. But I didn't leave the hospital car park—there was nowhere to go, no way to make it okay ... no choice.

Showing emotion publicly or even with close friends is not usu-ally the way I deal with anything. But waiting in the clinic with heavily pregnant women and others who had newborn babies obviously waiting for post-natal checkups was more than I could handle. It was only hopelessness that kept me from leaving.

The doctor was also routine (it was routine for her anyway). She did offer to answer any questions but my quivering voice gave me only options of screaming, or silence.

I was asked questions about my health—to answer that I was perfectly healthy and had already been through a trouble-free pregnancy and birth that resulted in my little girl seemed unfair. I wanted there to be some reason beyond my control for being there, some way to absolve me of guilt or fault. I was handed a form that I could not see through my tears, but I knew I was sign-ing my baby's life away. The operation was scheduled in six days. I could now count down the hours he had left to live.

I didn't feel I had a choice but I do feel it was my fault. The guilt starts from letting it happen in the first place—not being careful one time. I know I wasn't alone then but I have been ever since and in some ways always will be; after all it was "my choice."

Leading up to the abortion I was plagued with nightmares—on the nights I could sleep. I would dream that I had lost my baby because someone else had caused me to have a miscarriage. Waking up in the middle of the night halfway through a scream or in tears—or both—is now part of my life.

Calling Charlie in my lowest moments begging him to just give our baby a chance did no good. Trying to convince him that it may not be so bad only seemed to make his position firmer. I was still not convinced that I would have the strength to go through with the abortion. Now I see that my strength should have been to not listen to Charlie and all the other people who knew what was best for me and everyone in the situation. I should have had faith in my abilities as a parent to raise another child on my own. I know it wasn't fair for the baby to pay with his life because he came along at an inconvenient time for his father.

Before I knew it, it was the night before the operation. One last phone call to Charlie to warn him that it may not happen. I still couldn't believe that I would be the one responsible for making this decision. I was the mother of this child—isn't it my job to protect him from any harm and to provide the love and basic needs for life—at the very least? Not to take it away altogether. Do I have the right just because he cannot defend himself?

Being told by friends, "it's just a D&C," hurt me. I am jealous of that attitude now—to be one of the many who believes that it is not a life or a baby and not a heart-wrenching decision to have to make and live with. I heard from so many people who had never been in my position that "they knew exactly what they would do, if it were them." I had thought so too, before it was real.

The night before the abortion, I was alone. I had no intention of trying to sleep. I spent the time apologizing to my baby. Saying goodbye to someone you have never met is hard for others to understand.

I drove myself to the hospital. Others had offered, but I didn't want to have to deal with anyone's opinions and I didn't want anyone to see me like that anyway. All the way there a part of me was silently wishing for a car accident or some kind of natural disaster to intervene and stop me from getting there so it wouldn't be my fault—I would have to keep the baby.

For hours I was left to sit alone and think. I had read a lot while pregnant with my daughter. I had wanted to know everything and be prepared for the pregnancy and birth. I knew that the baby was quite large in comparison to the long thin tube used to "vacuum" the uterus. And I knew that at that stage he had basic reflexes and would recoil from touch. Sitting in that hospital, all I could see in my mind was my baby flinching as that thin tube came towards him, then broke up his tiny body and sucked him away from me.

If anything were to happen to my daughter and I lost her, I know—as I have since the moment she was born—that I would not be able to live without her. How, then, could I expect to live with myself after killing a child of my own whom I know I would love just as much? I was also afraid that I might not be able to go on and be a good mother to my daughter after doing this to her baby brother who she would have loved also.

From the hospital, I tried to call Charlie. It was Sunday afternoon and he was not home. I had visions of him at a baseball game or a barbeque and not giving a second thought to what I was doing for, or because of, him. Defeated and upset, I went back to the ward to wait my turn for theater.*

*the operating room

When the orderlies came to collect me, once again I could not control my tears. A nurse saw how upset I was and asked the orderlies to leave us. She spoke to me for a moment and sympathized. She knew I was unsure but that I did not want to talk to the immature and unhelpful social worker again, so she got the doctor out of surgery to come and speak to me. Essentially I was told that I should forget about the father because he did not love me or the baby and the real reason I wanted to do this was because I did not want to raise the child alone. I could go home if I wanted but the hospital only did terminations at nine weeks (I was already nine-and-a-half) and if I left it it would be too late.

They left me alone with my tears. I dressed to go to the phone once more to beg Charlie for our baby's life and my sanity. He was home this time. As I sobbed into the phone that I could not do it, he reaffirmed that I had to. The money for the call ran out and with it my hope. I walked back to the ward again, changed into the hospital gown and waited once more, but this time I knew I was not leaving until I was no longer pregnant. I said a silent sorry to my baby. Sorry that I was not stronger. Sorry I was not enough of a parent or person to save him.

In the operating theater, a different doctor from the one I had previously spoken to introduced herself, asked my name, date of birth and what procedure I was having done. The answer that came to mind was, "I am here to kill my baby," but I looked her straight in the eye and was unable to say anything. Silently I begged her to refuse to do it because I could not answer: she just answered for me.

I cried until I slept and woke up in recovery screaming. Reality hit me like a ton of bricks. I had actually done it. I could feel instantly that he was gone. I was still groggy from the anesthesia but could not get out of there fast enough. I began pulling off the monitoring equipment attached to me. As soon as I was transferred back to the ward I dressed and discharged myself. I couldn't face who I was and didn't want to be near anyone who would ask me how I felt.

In the only two brochures on abortion I had found, the word relief was used to describe how I should expect to feel after the operation. I knew I would never be relieved but I had no idea that I would grieve as much as I have.

As soon as I got home from hospital I called Charlie again. He was afraid to ask whether I had gone through with it. As soon as I told him that I had, he told me that he was wavering—he was going to change his mind! I had done it all for nothing. If only I had waited, just gone home to think it over ... but then I don't really believe he would have said the same thing. I will never know for sure if he would have come around. He still tells me he would have. That only adds to my guilt—if that's possible. It's too late for my baby now anyway—he truly did die for nothing.

I wanted to know what they would do with the fragments of his body, but did not ask for fear I would break down again at the answer. Instead, on the next day when my daughter went to visit her father, I went to the cemetery. I found the grave of a baby boy who had lived only three days. I imagined that it was the name I would have called my son and the date he was due to be born on the headstone. I have kind of adopted that grave since.

I think of the mother of that baby and I am jealous that she got to see her son and name him and hold him and bury him. I am sure no one has told her, "It was for the best" or, "Well, now you can get on with your life." She is allowed to grieve for her lost child.

I hate myself for having such thoughts about a grieving mother whom I know nothing about. I know it was my own fault and everyone believes it was my choice, but this is not what I wanted. I am now the mother of a dead baby and it is no fault except my own.

A good friend of mine had a son two days after I had the abortion. I cannot visit her and I am not sure when I will be able to. There is one thing I am sure of, though. I can never go through this again. I no longer feel I should have the right to "choose" to have more children. So I decided that I want to have my tubes tied. At 21, the doctors refused to do the procedure. When I am in my thirties, I will need my partner's consent to have the operation. I am outraged that they can make it so easy to get an abortion of a baby that already exists but can refuse to save future heartache of women who have been through enough.

My baby died ten days ago. He was due to be born on my 22nd birthday. I am sure that is an extra punishment for doing what I did. For the rest of my life it will be a day of grieving and I will never want to celebrate my birthday again. Instead I will visit my adopted grave.

# CATHERINE

*A meaning denied her in life*

My child was aborted in Nov. 1989. I was 28 years old, and it was my first (and only) pregnancy. I became pregnant in the early—and, as it would eventuate, the latter—stages of a relationship. We were only together for three months.

I believe I became pregnant when he forced me to have unprotected intercourse. I had a filled prescription for the contraceptive Pill, but was waiting for my period so I could begin taking it. In the meantime we had been using condoms and I was, on many occasions, a consensual partner to protected intercourse. However, on this occasion he held me down, ignored my pleas of "no," and forced himself into me—because he wanted to see what I felt like without a condom. It took a long, long time for me to acknowledge this and call it what it was—rape. I think this was, in part, because after the abortion I felt so guilty, so responsible, that I was unable to even contemplate trying to share the blame.

My menstrual cycle is usually very regular, so on one level I suspected pregnancy a couple of weeks before it was confirmed. On another level, however, I denied it—despite morning sickness, indigestion and breast tenderness. I didn't tell anyone of my concerns, as if verbalizing it would make it reality.

By the time my period was three weeks overdue I could ignore it no longer. Even though [I knew] I could be pregnant, it was still an enormous shock to have it confirmed. My feelings were ambivalent and contradictory. I felt guilty and ashamed of being an intelligent single woman in this situation. This was the sort of thing that was supposed to happen to other people, such as irresponsible teenagers. How naïve.

I felt betrayed by my body and angry that it had let me down. I felt hostile towards this child that had invaded my body. I felt I was being punished for enjoying a relatively casual sexual relationship. (In fact my feelings about him weren't casual ... but it soon became apparent that his feelings for me were.)

I was repulsed by the thought of getting fat, developing stretch marks, and of my breasts sagging. However, I also felt secretly proud that I could get pregnant and felt strangely protective towards the baby. Such contradictions. Even as I was plotting to

71

kill it, I was also nurturing it. I stopped smoking and drinking, was careful about what I ate and what I lifted.

My pregnancy was confirmed by a urine test at the local community health center. Before being given the result I was asked whether I planned and wanted to be pregnant—to which I replied that I didn't. They then told me that my test was positive and—without my asking for it—proceeded to give me a letter of referral and a list of abortionists detailing addresses, costs, etc. Their immediate assumption seemed to be that an unplanned pregnancy should be removed. They offered no information about options other than abortion. No mention was made about adoption or single parenthood. It seemed that in their minds there was no decision to be made: the obvious course of action was to terminate the pregnancy. They seemed oblivious of the fact that they had just thrown me into the middle of a major personal crisis.

I made an appointment to see the doctor who had previously provided me with contraceptive advice. I told her I was pregnant and that I wanted information about my options as I had not yet decided what to do. She proceeded to tell me that she could terminate my pregnancy. She explained the surgical technique and demonstrated it (using a plastic uterus and a suction catheter—no blood, no fetus in sight). She did tell me that in her experience it was better to continue with the pregnancy if I was unsure after thinking about it. She didn't elaborate on why it was better—and it was beyond my experience to imagine what she could mean. She also offered no information about alternatives to abortion, or advice about where I could get this information.

I had only been in Australia for a little over a year. I had no family here and limited support. I knew I would not be entitled to maternity leave from work but didn't know whether they would be flexible with my work hours if I had a baby. I also didn't know whether I would be entitled to any government assistance, as I was not an Australian citizen then. I really needed this information to help me make my decision, but if I was going to decide on abortion then I didn't want anyone to know that I had been pregnant.

My two closest friends were overseas. I spoke to one of them on the phone and confided my dilemma. She was confident I would do the same as she would. She said she didn't think I should go through it alone and that I should make my boyfriend come with me and pay something towards the cost.

I also told one friend here—though retrospectively she was a poor choice of confidante. A widowed sole parent of two children, she has found the going very tough at times and told me it wasn't a situation she would willingly have entered. She sounded very bitter as she painted a picture of struggle and hardship. She didn't directly suggest that I have an abortion but she did tell me that another friend of hers had one and seemed to be okay.

I didn't tell any of my family or ask them for help. I was too unsure and scared of their reaction, which I wasn't confident would be helpful or supportive. I felt that I had let them down by getting myself into this situation. I had some turbulent times in my teenage years and felt that me being pregnant would confirm my place as the black sheep in the family. I was afraid that they would say, "Oh, Catherine, we are so disappointed in you." I was already disappointed enough in myself without having the responsibility of disappointing others.

Last, but definitely not least, was my boyfriend. The day my pregnancy was confirmed we met. Before I could tell him my news he told me that he wanted to split up for a while. Not permanently, he said, but just for a while, as he needed some time to think things through. This turned out to be a lie and we never got back together.

I kept quiet about my pregnancy then. However, a few days later it became clear to me that I could not make a unilateral decision. I contacted him, told him my predicament and made arrangements to meet with him.

He was my last hope. No one else had expressed any confidence that there were realistic alternatives to abortion. Certainly no one suggested that I could manage (or even thrive?) if I had the child. I couldn't imagine coping on my own and so abortion did seem like the solution—unless my boyfriend offered some support.

Sadly, he did not. I didn't expect an offer of commitment to me, but would have liked an offer to be an involved father to our child. He, however, made it quite clear that he wanted me to have an abortion. He had rejected me once and I hurt from that. I couldn't risk a second rejection by voicing my desire for support and help.

Even as I was making my decision to abort, I was also imagining what the child would be like, what it would look like and act like, what its life would be like, etc. I hadn't known if I wanted children at all. But it is one thing not to want an imaginary child, quite another to deny a child that is a reality.

I did consider seeking help and information from places offering pregnancy counseling in the Yellow Pages. I recognized that I was in a vulnerable state so didn't pursue this for fear of being pressured by radical pro-life or pro-choice people. I didn't trust these places to put my well-being ahead of their own ethical, social or religious beliefs. I worried that they would try to sway me—not realizing that I had already been swayed and subjected to pressures. I wanted the decision that was best for me—yet in the end made the decision with little regard for myself.

I guess everyone wants the best for their children and I was no exception. It seemed that having me as its mother would be a pretty poor deal and I hurt at the thought of my child having a father who wanted her aborted. I doubted that I would cope emotionally, physically, or financially. These factors seemed to stack up and suggest a difficult future for the child and for me. It didn't dawn on me that the only thing abortion offered my child was death. And I had no idea that life after abortion would be so hard for me. However, even though I suffered in the aftermath, my child remains the biggest loser.

Abortion is sold to women as the great solution. I thought I was going to have a minor surgical procedure which would solve a major problem. Instead it unleashed a host of problems for me. My abortion experience has, I believe, predisposed me to a lifelong vulnerability and fragility that I would not otherwise have had. Even the happiest events of my life are now shadowed by a secret sadness.

Retrospectively, none of these problems seem insurmountable. But that's not how I imagined them at the time. And so it was that I phoned and made the appointment to have an abortion.

The pre-procedure counseling consisted of the previously described demonstration with the uterus and suction catheter. On that earlier occasion, I was reassured that the risk of infection was lessened by doing the procedure in ten minutes and by providing antibiotics. She also told me there was a small risk of cervical incompetence, which could lead to miscarriage in subsequent pregnancies, but this was dismissed as unlikely.

When I arrived for the abortion, I was seen by a nurse and told to get undressed. I was then given a leaflet detailing information about when symptoms of pregnancy would resolve; what to watch for and what action to take in the event of complications; general hygiene and lifestyle measures; when a follow-up appointment was required; and—the one that would become most important for me—"that you may feel emotional, teary or feel a sense of sadness following the operation and if this feeling continues you may have to talk to us."

There was a lot of information to absorb on this sheet, yet it was given to me five minutes before the abortion and at a time when I was dressed in a flimsy gown and feeling sad, ashamed, anxious, nauseated and hungry. Hardly the optimal physical or emotional state to receive and absorb such important information.

Was my consent informed? Now I don't think so, not truly. The only complications I was informed of were infection or cervical incompetence. Although I was warned that it would be better to continue with the pregnancy if I was unsure, this information was so vague that it was meaningless to me. I didn't realize at the time, but I now recognize that I was deprived of information that was crucial for me to make a true choice.

Certainly I knew theoretically that there were alternatives, but the facts about them were withheld from me. Before the abortion, I allowed myself to think in terms of "products of conception" or "blobs of jelly." Yet afterwards I knew with absolute clarity that I had killed a child. My child.

At the time of my abortion I had no idea what the laws were in Australia or Victoria. I knew that in my country of origin, abortion was granted if the woman's mental or physical health was at greater risk if the pregnancy continued. I was never told on what grounds my abortion here was being granted. I don't remember signing a consent form.

Immediately after the abortion, I felt disgustingly well physically. I had virtually no pain and only moderate bleeding. I remember that this felt wrong somehow. I thought that my body should have objected more fiercely. I had killed my baby, so surely I should have suffered more, have had more physical punishment.

Mentally, it was another story. In the weeks following I had extremes of feelings that at times seemed contradictory. I had expected to go back to being the pre-pregnant me—not realizing that person was gone forever. The anticipated sense of relief never happened. Instead I felt terribly empty inside and had a sense of horror at what I had done. I felt empty, my breasts were returning to normal, I was bleeding; and yet somehow I was also fantasizing that I was still pregnant; hoping I was still pregnant. I remember thinking that if my baby really wanted to live and really wanted me as its mother, then it could have escaped the suction device and might still be there.

At other times, I was filled with anguish and despair. I cried with body-racking sobs. I felt like an injured animal, which just wants to curl up and lick its wounds. I felt incredibly fragile. At work I felt cut off from everyone, as I was so preoccupied with my thoughts. I also wasn't sleeping well, having disturbing dreams, and waking up crying, with my heart pounding. Once I was woken by a plaintive wailing—and then realized it was coming from my mouth.

I wasn't eating and lost a lot of weight. My home life was also far from calm (I was sharing a house with two others). I was tense, secretive, and antisocial. My whole life felt like it was disintegrating around me. I felt I was losing my mind. Yet insanity would almost have been a welcome escape.

I was also very distressed my ex-boyfriend had made no contact. He came with me to the abortion, but I hadn't seen him or heard from him since. How could he be continuing his life without a thought for me or the baby we had killed? How could he have been so intimate with me one week, then appear to have no concern, even as a friend, the next week? I longed to see him, hear him, touch him. I don't think it was so much him that I wanted, as the link he would have provided to the baby.

Inside I was screaming and angst-ridden, yet outside I was composed. I remained tired, lethargic, and disinterested in everything and had no enthusiasm for life. My depression became all consuming. I was irritated with myself and irritable with other people. I was disturbed by the sight and sound of babies. I felt repulsed by them. It was as if I was trying to convince myself that I hadn't given up anything that was worth having.

I did visit a couple of general practitioners in the few months after the abortion. I purposefully selected medical centers from the Yellow Pages which advertised the presence of a psychologist. When I was at the GP's, I complained of not feeling well, tiredness, tearfulness, not sleeping, and loss of appetite since an abortion. I knew that there was a psychological cause but couldn't directly verbalize this, for fear of being pronounced mad. Yet I wanted them to realize and give me help. However, after physical examinations and blood tests failed to find a cause, I was dismissed and told that nothing was wrong.

Yet I knew something most certainly was wrong. I was starting to think that suicide was the only way to stop this incessant hurt. I knew this wasn't normal and it scared me. Yet the thoughts were accompanied by a feeling of conviction that this was the only way I could assert my control over the situation.

I had struggled on my own for about five months when I decided to avail myself of the service offered in the post-operative instruction leaflet. I made an appointment at the clinic where my abortion took place—ostensibly to get a prescription for more contraceptive pills.

I started to cry, said how depressed I felt, and pleaded, "When is this going to feel better?" The doctor told me that I may never feel better and that I had made my bed so would just have to lie in it. She said I couldn't expect to feel better when there were pregnant women and babies everywhere to remind me of what I had done. She then told me that "life sucks" and proceeded to tell me about her own problems with infertility and her difficulty getting pregnant. She implied that I deserved to feel rotten for having an abortion and said that I should be glad to be upset because it meant I wasn't a hard bitch like some of "them."

But there is no gladness to be found in a state of depression. I was well aware that I had made my choice, but I was having great difficulty living with it. Yet that was the response I received at a center supposedly familiar with the problem of post-abortion depression. I knew I had done a terrible thing without her telling me. Yet she was right. Of course I deserved to suffer. Her attitude increased my already considerable guilt and shame.

She made no attempt to assess my depression or to arrange appropriate follow-up care. Yet inadvertently she did help, because my anger was now partially directed at her instead of myself. My suicidal thoughts faded for a while.

I stopped fighting as much after that encounter. I accepted that this was where I deserved to be. The days of feeling sad, confused and depressed spread into months, and then it was a whole year since the abortion. I must have cried a lifetime's ration of tears in that year. Everything still felt so fresh to me and I was acutely aware that time—that supposed healer—had not in fact healed me. I did have brief periods of remission when I felt better, but then I would relapse. I continued to think about the experience virtually every day. If I realized I had missed thinking about it for a day or two then I felt guilty for forgetting.

I tried to take my mind off it and reinvest in life, but was still struggling terribly. I took foreign language lessons, met new people, had a holiday, but was still filled with anguish. The holiday actually accentuated my fears. I realized that my visa allowing me to return to Australia was "subject to the granting of a re-entry permit." If this wasn't granted, then I would be forever parted from my child! The thought tormented me. My initial motivation in later seeking citizenship was to ensure that no one could make me abandon my child again. (I didn't realize then that my "ghost child" could travel the world with me, for she now exists in my mind.)

It was about a year after the abortion that I saw an advertisement for the organization that would eventually become my salvation, on a railway station billboard. It read "Abortion and miscarriage can be a lonely and emotional experience. It is natural to want to talk it through. A skilled and caring listener can help you resolve these feelings." It then gave a phone number for Pregnancy Action Center [now Open Doors Counseling].

It was such a huge relief to know that help was available and that perhaps I wasn't abnormal. It was a bit like being thrown a lifebuoy. I was able to keep treading water for a while longer with the knowledge that help was near at hand.

That sustained me until I was overwhelmed by fresh waves of grief on the day that would have been the baby's first birthday. I felt panicky that I was spiraling out of control again. I couldn't stop crying and felt desperate and helpless; I couldn't continue like this any longer. I made an appointment with the Pregnancy Loss Counseling Service [at Open Doors].

I would like to be able to say that everything became easier from then on—but this would be a lie. In many ways things became even tougher. I just wanted someone to stop the relentless pain I was feeling. I had a notion that there would be a formula to follow, that if I did A, B and C then I would feel better. I could never have envisaged that it was possible to start feeling even worse.

I ended up having two and a half years of professional grief therapy and eventually a long course of antidepressant medication. I had carried my dark secret for one-and-a-half years with no outlet for my feelings. The friends who knew of my abortion never mentioned it again. I think they considered it to be over the day I had the surgery. Not that I blame them—I had expected it to be over then too.

Initially, as I was helped in therapy to explore and express my reactions, I became even more despondent and bogged down in my prolonged and profound grief. They tried to provide a safe haven where I could unburden myself, but I just felt as if I was being sucked into quicksand and suffocated. I despaired of ever having any sort of catharsis or resolution. I was so afraid of being judged. Yet the truth was that no one could have judged me as harshly as I judged myself in reality or as harshly as I let others judge me in my imagination.

I had had an abortion because I thought that having a child

would be too hard, would ruin my life. Yet, because I had killed my child, how could I ever hope or deserve to feel better? How could anybody help me to resolve such a contradiction? Even though I now had someone to talk to, I still felt very alone and totally undeserving of sympathy. I continued to ruminate on the thought that I was a murderess who deserved to be punished. I withdrew further and became even more introverted, irritable and intolerant. Sometimes I felt like a brittle shell, while at other times I felt so filled with evil that I thought I would contaminate people if I touched them.

However, I ached to touch my child. My womb, my arms, my heart all felt so empty. I longed to hold my child and tell her I loved her and was so sorry for what I had done. I felt so possessive towards her. When my therapist asked me to share my thoughts about the baby, I was filled with panic, as though sharing would somehow leave less for me. This misery was awful, but it was all I had left of my child; relinquishing my misery risked leaving me with nothing.

I continued on my progressive decline and was unable to visualize any solution to all this ... until the night when the thought of suicide returned. It came from somewhere outside me and lodged in my brain. Welcome thought! It was like a religious experience— its presence uplifted me. I felt as if I had found the great answer. To splatter myself on the front of a train seemed perfect. I had splattered and dismembered my child, so now I would splatter and dismember myself. Then be reunited with my child and tell her how sorry I was and try to atone.

Now I had hope. I had the trump card; the power and means to end the pain. It would have been the perfect plan—except that I was too slow in carrying it out. The nature of suicidal ideation is such that it doesn't last forever and I was too much of a perfectionist. I studied the train timetable, looking for the express trains that wouldn't slow down at the station. I spent hours on the station platform trying to work out where to jump from, the timing of the jump to get the maximum impact for me and minimal impact for the train driver. It took me so long working this out my suicidal urges receded.

I still had a strong need to punish myself however—to punish the woman who had killed my child. So much inner tension and conflict remained, and hurting myself seemed to help reduce this. I used to sit and hit myself with a hammer or bang myself against a wall until I was covered in bruises on my arms, legs, pelvis and ribs. I then gained comfort from looking at these bruises and feeling that I was doing something to avenge my child's death by punishing the person responsible.

Food was another way to punish myself and express feelings that had few other outlets. In the first few weeks after the abortion I lost my appetite and lost weight. It wasn't a conscious thing, it just happened without my noticing it. When it finally did come to my attention, I concluded that hunger was an emotional need rather than a physical need—a weak emotional indulgence. Subsequently, when I was depressed and suppressing or denying other emotional needs, I also suppressed and denied the hunger need.

If, as usually happened, the physical need for food asserted itself, then I despised myself for being so weak and felt compelled to make myself vomit. Forced vomiting by sticking my fingers down my throat was a way to reinforce my self-revulsion, to demonstrate to myself that I really was a disgusting person.

All these psychological problems arose for me because I was so constricted by the lack of a suitable outlet for my grief. Abortion is such a secret loss and there is nothing tangible to grieve for. There are no mementoes, photos, memories to share, no grave to visit, nothing recognizable to anyone else. It all takes place in your imagination.

For the first couple of years after my abortion, it was possible to think of "the baby." But when that baby became a toddler and then a young child in my mind, it was no longer possible to imagine it in gender non-specific terms. This was another source of distress and conflict for me. I thought it would be letting my child down if I thought of it as a boy and it was actually a girl—or vice versa. Eventually, though, I listened to an innermost feeling about this and allowed myself to think about and grieve specifically for my daughter.

Marking the anniversary of the abortion and the baby's would-have-been birthday has always been, and remain, hard. There is no grave to tend or take flowers to—and yet I have the need to mark the day with a symbolic gesture. I visit a cemetery on these dates. I walk among the graves, read the headstones, imagine these deceased people and ask their spirits to look after my child. The gravestones with photos on them are good for this—I look for the kindly faces and then imagine them with my child.

Christmas is also a hard time. I deal with it by buying a gift to leave under a charity tree. I select, with great care and love, something for a little girl the same age as mine would be. Then I think of another little girl being happy as she opens her presents.

Another thing that saddens me is the thought that I am probably the only person who grieves the loss of this child. I doubt her father mourns her passing. Others, such as pro-lifers, may grieve for the collective loss of aborted babies, but not specifically for my child and not specifically on the days I consider significant and worthy of remembering.

A couple of years ago, on the anniversary of my baby's death, I went to the cemetery and wandered among the graves for a while, then sat on a bench to contemplate and cry. I saw a little girl skipping through the grass. She came to me and said, "It's okay, Mum, let me go." I don't know whether I actually saw her ghost, whether I imagined her, or whether I hallucinated. I do believe it was a message of forgiveness from my daughter. That brings me comfort, especially at those times when I am not sure if I have forgiven myself.

Most of the time now my abortion experience occupies only a small part of my consciousness, but even after all this time, I am sometimes hit with a pang of guilt or sadness. Guilt if I feel happy—am I betraying my child by feeling happy when she is dead? Guilt if I feel unhappy—didn't she die so that my life could be happier? Guilt if I respond in the negative to the question, "Have you any children?"—does my "no" answer deny and betray my child again? Sadness that I may never have another chance at motherhood. Sadness that I may not be able to fully commit my love to a future child. Could any future child live up to my idealized ghost child?

I liken my abortion experience to a kite on a string. Sometimes I am happy to let it soar and float far away in the sky, let it go almost out of sight as it mingles with the clouds. But other times I feel compelled to reel it in close again, to examine its details and confirm its existence. To make sure that I am not just holding an empty string; to make sure that I didn't imagine it all. Perhaps the time will come when I will feel safe enough to release the string from my grip and let the kite and myself be free.

Having an abortion took me to a dark tortuous place and left me plummeting into an abyss. And yet that place showed me a depth of love that I never knew existed and I have used that to claw my way back. My ghost child lives in my heart as a legacy of that love. If my story can increase awareness, change attitudes and give support to other women, then that will help to provide a reason for it all. Perhaps in death my child can have a meaning that I denied her in life.

# MICHELLE

*A cradle in my heart*

There are a lot of things in my past that I would rather forget. But I guess that in order to fully let them go I need to speak of them.

I come from a small town in Victoria, the younger of two children. My childhood was fairly happy up until the age of six when I began to realize there was something wrong and I thought it was me.

My father was an abusive alcoholic, my mother a passive but somewhat manipulative co-dependant. But I had my brother, my protector and soul mate, to look after me and stop me from getting hurt.

Unfortunately, my brother died of cancer when I was nine years old. I was not told of this. The door of his room was closed and he was never really spoken of again. I had never felt so alone and frightened and I was so angry with everyone for all the secrets and lies. At 11, I began making plans to leave.

I became determined to do things my own way and was quite unruly at school. I discovered sex, found out that boys liked me, thought that I was popular, and I admit that it felt good to be wanted. However, I was very naïve.

I was still very unhappy at home. After much persistence from a relation who married into the family, I went up to his place one day for a coffee and a chat and finally thought that I had found a friend that I could talk to about my problems at home. He was like a brother, I thought, until he and his brother-in-law raped me. I never knew things like that happened. They continued to taunt me, driving up and down the street tooting and waving. I tried to commit suicide.

I never received counseling for my rape, as I didn't feel that anyone would believe me because of my past. I felt dirty and the police gave me a taste of what it would be like in the courtroom. Back then you weren't always seen as the victim; they virtually interrogated you about your personal life.

Sometime later, after attempting to complete my nursing training, I fell for a boy who used to go to school on the same bus as me. He seemed "safe." I remember thinking as he drove past one day that he was going to take me out of that place and he did—to Perth.

I was with my partner from the age of 18 to 23. His job took him away a lot and he thought that money would make me happy, but all I wanted was love.

In 1987 I fell pregnant to him. I spoke to him on the phone and we discussed what we should do. He suggested that we should not bring a baby into an already unhappy relationship and suggested that we should try to make our relationship work. So two days later I had an abortion. Unfortunately, I woke halfway through the procedure with a burning sensation to my lower abdominal area. I remember screaming "No!" but I think that it was too late. I remember floating back to sleep. After the procedure they got me to hop off the table and told me just to grab my knickers* out of the kidney dish on the bench which I had to find. I found that quite hurtful and humiliating.

I remember crying afterwards and a friend consoling me by saying that it was better to be crying then than for the rest of my life. But I have not stopped crying.

My friend stayed with me at home until I fell asleep, as my fiancé was still away. Later that night I awoke and tried to ring him but he said that he couldn't talk, that he would ring me later. He never did. I cried myself to sleep, I felt so alone.

About a week later I tried to ring him. Instead I ended up talking to a woman who he'd been having an affair with. He is still with her today. I never forgave him for that, nor have I forgiven myself for what I did.

I tried again to commit suicide.

Wherever my child is, I hope he understands that it didn't mean that I didn't love him. I did, but I made a terrible mistake. My boy would be ten this year. As I am now a nurse, from time to time I get to see miscarried fetuses. Every time I know that something like that has happened on my ward I have to see the fetus and I always think of my baby and wonder what it would have looked like and what size it would have been.

I just hope that wherever he is he knows that I loved him and I hope that he can forgive me. I hope I will see him when I die. I just wish that I could hold him. There will always be an empty space in my heart for my baby that I never knew. But in that space there is a cradle surrounded by love. If only I could have touched him and held him.

*underwear

# ASPHYXIA

*A house built from tears*

**July 6, 1996**

Something terrible has happened. I don't want to write about it. All I want to do is run away and escape. I feel that if I write about it I'll get swallowed up in this huge wave of nausea. It's all just unimaginable. And somehow it's real. God—I can't bear it.

**July 13**

I've done no work on the house this week. I'm so sick I can't believe it. Is there no respite? Went to hospital on Thursday and got bundled home again. I told them I was homeless and didn't have anywhere to go, but do you think they cared?

**July 22**

I seem to be healthier physically now. I went to the hospital the next day, after my last diary entry, and they gave me a prescription for antibiotics and sent me away. I don't know about my emotional health though. I have this feeling like I'm skating on thin ice. I don't want to think about it. I'm using all my think-power for my house now. I've rented a run-down flat* to live in while I'm building. I can't believe how wonderful it is to have a space of my own again. All the exhaustion of being homeless is pouring out of me now. It feels like my whole dream is really going to come together. When I first thought of building a house it was in a liberating moment when I felt so strong and capable of doing anything, of learning how to do anything ... At first it was nothing more than a dream—I didn't think I'd really do it. But it grew on me, kept on growing, until it consumed me and I knew I just had to.

**August 14**

Most mornings I wake up with this sinking feeling in my stomach, this horror of what I've done ... I am crying. I have to face the fact that I have some sort of problem.

**August 18**

We've started building! My friend Mace and I got up all the

*apartment

supporting posts yesterday. A woman I was talking with at a party last night asked me,

"So, Asphyxia, what do you do?"

"I'm building a house," I told her.

We talked about that for a little while, and I began to realize that she thought I meant I'm having a house built for me. It wasn't until about ten minutes later that I said, "No, I'm actually building it myself." I mimed hammering and drilling and bolting. [Asphyxia is deaf and communicates through signing or miming. When making a phone call, she uses a relay service for the hearing impaired.]

She looked most amazed.

## August 20

I feel lousy. It feels like everything is just too much at the moment. I feel exhausted and like I'm heading for burnout. There is something so very wrong with me. It's like everything I do is mechanical. I can't feel things properly, not the way I could before. I mean, I get excited about my house and everything, but there's something inside me that isn't there. The part that is really me, that part that lives.

## August 26

On Saturday I was laying bluestones around the bottom of the house. I was working by myself, and at first I was having a great time—the buzz of discovering a new skill I had, but then I got all introspective. I started thinking of how things could have been and felt all the tears welling up. I cried into the mortar as I laid the bricks, and when it got too hard to see I lay in the grass and cried some more, until it subsided and I could keep on building.

## August 27

It's been a great day. We put the roof on! My friend Cath showed up. She came in the gate and looked up in amazement at all our progress. "Wow! It's a real house! The windows are incredible—they are so beautiful," she said. Gothic arched and churchy, they really do make the place look like a little chapel. She raved about the bluestones, the fact we'd passed the inspection, the fact that the roof was so stable that I was actually sitting on it.

## August 31

I'm sinking. Everything's going downhill and I feel like I just can't bear it. I woke up this morning feeling like I was drowning.

The tears started and I cried in bed for hours. I finally dragged myself out and had a bath and cried there too. I can't see how I'm going to be able to do anything. I want to turn to someone, have them hold me and comfort me, but I can't think of anyone.

### September 1

I woke up at six and couldn't get back to sleep. I'm losing touch with reality. I get so far away in my fantasy world and then when something touches ground again I realize that it's all pretend and everything comes crashing around me. All I can see ahead of me is this gray desolation.

### September 2

I got my act together a bit today. I woke up in the same terrible state but I dragged myself out of bed anyway, determined to go and do the loft floor. It was sort of meditative. The weather was gray and it drizzled all day, but with the roof on my house I had shelter, which felt like such a luxury. I wish I could immerse myself in my house 24 hours a day, then I wouldn't have to face the rest of my life or my feelings. I'm glad I got myself there today—it made the biggest difference. It's much better than lying in the bath crying for hours on end.

### September 4

God, what a day. I spent most of it in hospital. When the bleeding began I grabbed my bath towel and used that to stop myself from getting blood all over the floor as I hobbled to the bathroom. In the shower all the blood clots filled the plughole and the water mixed with all the extra blood and rose in a gruesome red bath. I turned off the shower and sat there for ages in the blood bath, trying to get my act together and work it out. Since the first time I was in hospital, I haven't stopped bleeding. Eventually I got out of the bath, using two towels, one to try and contain all the blood, and the other one to dry off the water, and I went into the lounge* to ring the doctor. She told me: "Go straight to the hospital." I wanted someone to take me there but I couldn't think of anyone. I drove myself, packing my shorts with two tea towels and hoping that would be enough to survive the ride. I spent the day lying on a bed in emergency. I got examined twice and they kept giving me white towels for all the blood. I couldn't think of a more impractical color.

*living room

At the end of the day, the doctor gave his verdict: "Go home and come back in a week if it hasn't improved." I protested. He insisted. After quite an argument, I talk him into authorizing an ultrasound.

### September 5

I went back to the hospital today for the ultrasound. This time I had to wait in the area where all the pregnant women were getting theirs done. I could feel all the emotions building up inside me, the agony of it, the unfairness that I'm sitting there, skinny and flat, waiting for an ultrasound that isn't going to hear any heartbeat at all, and they're waiting for a murky video recording of their babies swimming in gray womb waters. The more pregnant women I saw, the more I started to shake. When I went in for my turn, finally, I had to go into this cubicle to change into hospital clothes. Two white gowns, one forward and one backwards. Putting them on brought everything back to me, what happened last time. I put them on, and I started crying. When I came out of the cubicle there was another woman in her gowns, pregnant and looking very calm. I lay obediently on their table, shaking and crying, and made a lot of noise when I was told to remove my undies. Blood spilled on everything. Finally the doctor who was doing the ultrasound pointed to the screen and said, "Can you see that?"

I could see a screen full of gritty gray stuff moving around.

"The doctor missed that. It needs to be removed."

I started crying even harder. I could barely get my words out.

"So ... do I ... need ... another one?"

The nurse just said: "Your doctor will tell you what's best to do about it. Just go back to"—she checked the form she was holding—"Emergency, and he'll discuss it with you."

### September 7

I'm writing this in hospital. I wish I could stay here for a whole week, rather than having to go home and face the misery I've been in the last few weeks. I was wearing two white hospital gowns and was bleeding into the bed. After a while I gave up trying to keep the pad between my legs and just let myself bleed ...

(Later) I'm at home again now. I have to do other things for a few weeks, because I can't build my house. The nurse told me my uterus is very soft after all this stress, and I mustn't do any heavy lifting or difficult exercise. Nothing acrobatic. This puts a slant on my life because all I am right now is a builder and an acrobat. What am I without those?

## September 9

Since the hospital I have been so cut off from my grief. It's almost as if I have gone past it, but I know it's just a numbness and that I'm shutting it all off. Some friends joined me tonight and we ended up having a conversation about being gay and lesbian and coming out to parents. It was great. I was talking about myself as a lesbian but sometimes I feel as if I must be lying. All my main relationships have been with men. It feels as though I'm somehow not a "real" lesbian. No more penetrative sex. That finished a while ago and I have no intention of doing it again for a long long time.

## September 21

I'm reading a terrific book. It's called *You Take The High Road* (Mary K Pershall), and it's about the grief a girl goes through when her baby brother dies. It's touching me deeply. I can see her grief. The book talks about when the baby was born and Sam looking after him and how sweet he was, and then suddenly he dies. There came a point in the book where Sam starts being ready to face it, to talk about him and remember him. Perhaps guided by strength from Sam, I thought maybe I could be ready to face a little bit too. I was pregnant. There was a little baby inside me. It had a heart beating and its own bloodstream, and hands and fingers and toes, and a brain, and a respiratory system.

I had an abortion and I killed it. I feel so sad. I never gave it any love—I didn't put my hands on my tummy and stroke it, I didn't give it anything. The sadness within me is just overwhelming. I can't turn back the clock. I should be four months pregnant but I'm not. I can only think of that song:

*Oh, my darling; oh, my darling,*
*Oh, my darling, Clementine.*
*Thou art lost and gone forever,*
*Dreadful sorry, Clementine.*

## September 22

My sister Evie is staying with me tonight and she will be with me all day tomorrow. I drove home with her and I couldn't stop watching her sweet, sleeping face at every red traffic light. She is so beautiful—it is hard to comprehend how much love I have for her. I think I would make such a good mother. I can't help wondering what a child of my own would be like. I wonder about my baby. Was it a boy or a girl? Or twins? I really, really wanted to ask the doctor if it was twins, but he was so utterly mean to me before the abortion that I didn't dare.

## September 24

Went back to the hospital today. I started bleeding again a few days ago and didn't want to leave it two-and-a-half months like last time. I had a swab. I hope I don't have an infection—it seems like everything that can go wrong with me is going wrong. I wouldn't be surprised if they make me have a third abortion. I feel bad enough that I don't have the baby, let alone having to go through the whole procedure a million times because they can't get it all the first time. The doctor told me to go back next Tuesday if I'm still bleeding then, and to go back before if it gets heavier. The other morning, after I wrote in my diary about the baby, I woke up wanting to cry. My friend Lucy suggested, when I mentioned my tears later, "Maybe you need to do something to say goodbye to your baby. Have a funeral or something like that." Somehow, since she said that, I've felt so much calmer. I'm not ready to say goodbye yet, but that somehow brings a bit more of a purpose to it. It makes the ache less intangible ... I'm not sure about a funeral, in the conventional sense, since that's usually a social thing in which several people participate. It seems to me that my baby has only come alive for me, but not for anyone else. For them, it is a piece of fetus, like the doctor said. But it seems I am the only person who can project my pregnancy into a real baby, a real person, growing and changing, and it doesn't seem appropriate for people who don't feel that way to be there. So maybe it would just be me. My own private little funeral. I started thinking, maybe in the garden at The Hill, somewhere hidden amongst the trees in the orchard, I can make a small grave. A little rectangle of bluestones with a small wooden cross planted in the ground. I am not religious, but I like that shape. I can plant something nice in front of it, to grow up over the cross. I started envisaging a day when I plant my cross, wear a nice dress, and then kneel in front of my baby's grave and silently read it the letter I've written. And that would be my goodbye. The thing I like about making the grave is that I can go back and sit there and think and feel and say goodbye as many times as I need. I thought perhaps Feb. 17. That is the day my baby was due to be born. And maybe by then I will be ready to say goodbye. I'd quite like to be living in my house when I make the grave too—so it's not a grave on a building site, but a grave that's a little place, a part of my home.

**September 28**

Last night I was lying in bed and the pain hit me all over again, as acutely as ever. In a way I welcomed it because I'm not ready to stop caring about the baby yet. But at the same time I can't believe how much it hurts. There is such a big part of me that wishes I was still pregnant. I like to daydream about what it would be like. The most important thing would be to finish my house before the baby is born. I also imagine if the baby was born while I'm still living here, in the flat. The baby could sleep in a nice wooden box that I'd sand and paint. An old fruit crate or something. And I'd dress her or him in black and purple and dark red and dark green. At night she could sleep with me. In the day, in the wooden box. Oh, it's so confusing. Sometimes I'm really glad I'm not pregnant. Life is so much easier without a baby. But then on the other hand there's that sense of inevitability—that I should be pregnant because I was pregnant before. I can't get away from that. I can't seem to be able to go back to how I was before it all happened: not thinking about babies, not caring, and definitely not entertaining the possibility of having one myself. I think part of me was scared to fantasize about having a baby in case I started wanting one and then stupidly decided to have one. I was so cut off from my maternal instincts and I didn't want to get in touch with them or awaken them ... Today, I want to get pregnant again. I'm scared of it but I also really want it.

**October 2**

[I dreamt my brother was to be killed.] I knew they were going to kill him soon, and I wanted to say "I love you" to him before it was too late ...

**October 3**

I had counseling with a friend's mum. She was very warm and reassuring. She told me she thought I needed long-term counseling because I have so many issues as well as the abortion that need dealing with. I'm glad she could see that in me. She has organized for me to see a woman at Open Doors in Ringwood. I hadn't mentioned anything about wanting to have some sort of funeral for my baby, but Mama Yates said, "Perhaps we should have a burial ceremony, and you can give your baby a name. Tell me when you are ready."

I told her about how I'd thought of writing a letter, and how I also wanted to make a place for the baby—a place I can go to to say goodbye, as many times as I need to. "You need to put your baby in a safe place. And if you name it then you have even more to hold onto. Something real, not imagined."

Later, I went to Open Doors and the woman there gave me a few leaflets. There were some words in them which struck me strongly. "It is a myth that women only bond with their child after birth." That's what it was—I felt a bond with my child—but I wasn't aware of it until after the abortion. And: "A pregnancy loss, be it a miscarriage, termination or stillbirth, leaves a woman in a state of physical and emotional readiness for a baby that will never be." That describes how I feel so perfectly—simply by becoming pregnant, I got ready for it, whether I wanted to or not, and now there's nothing to be ready for.

## October 4

I suppose now is a good time to start my essay about why I had an abortion.

### Why I Had An Abortion

I thought I had the flu. I woke up in the morning and thought about getting up. I thought about throwing up. I decided to stay put. Nausea overwhelmed me and I kept wondering if I was going to vomit. I tossed and turned and dozed until my bladder got the better of me. I dragged myself out of bed, and was halfway along the hall when I suddenly, for no reason at all, thought of the pregnancy test. I went back to get it. It was more to reassure myself that I wasn't pregnant, and to give me peace of mind, than anything else. But a red line showed, and then, very quickly, the other red line came up as well. I stared in horror—it couldn't be right. I checked the packet, but it was very, very clear that the test was positive. Or you could say—I took a pregnancy test and failed, miserably. I tipped the urine down the sink and hurled everything across the room. I started crying and kicked the bath and smashed at the door. There wasn't much else I could do because I didn't want to damage what wasn't mine. After a while I gathered my things together and went back to the room where I was sleeping. It wasn't my house. It wasn't my room. I was homeless and hating it. Crying, I woke my brother. The best he could do was to offer me some practical advice about how I should have an abortion, be done with it, and if I wanted he'd organize for me to talk with his friend's girlfriend, who has had about five of them. They only cost around $500. Only.

The condom had come off and Dan and I had found it inside me afterwards. I worked out that it was around the wrong time of month for me to be likely to get pregnant, so stopped worrying. It had been at the back of my mind though, and I got a pregnancy testing kit a week later and tried it, but it showed up negative. I left the other test in the box on my shelf, and didn't think about it after that.

Dan and I performed together in an acrobat show. It started off as a gorgeous romance, with lots of dancing, and spinning fire in his backyard. He was full of life, always doing something creative and physical and that's what drew me to him. But after about a month, things weren't going so well. I couldn't deal with his bad moods.

And then suddenly, that morning, knowing I was pregnant, everything was completely, and horribly different. I lost interest in everything. I had to make a decision, and fast. My body felt as though it was invaded with a hot, red, expanding pressure. Like my blood cells were expanding until all my skin was so tight I thought it would explode. My whole body was taut, and my head was spinning. There was nothing else in life except the fact that I was pregnant, and I just couldn't believe this could have happened to me. I was so careful—always used contraceptives. And I had never thought about the fine print on the condom packets. "99 percent effective." So for every hundred [times you had sex] you could get pregnant. Great. Aren't there millions of people all over the world, getting pregnant by accident on average, every hundred times they have sex? Why didn't I know about this before? My whole body was hurting, my head hurt, my heart hurt. I had heart-burn, and a constant tummy-ache for the whole time I was pregnant. I could barely eat for all the nausea and I was so, so tired. Did I want a baby or not? What about all those people who would be asking, who was the father? What would I tell them? What if Dan had these ideas that we could bring up a child together? I couldn't imagine myself in a long-term relationship with him. I felt like I was going to explode. Could I be a single mother?

I told Lucy about it.

"The trouble is, I just don't believe in abortions."

"Does that mean that there might be a mother-Asphyxia?" she asked me. "So, I'd be an aunty to something other than plants, dogs and furniture? I know you don't watch TV, so I'd have to make sure your child didn't miss out and was well initiated into the joys of *The Simpsons*. And also, from a very young age, I'm going to train it to

like hot food. I'll feed it chilies from the moment it is old enough
to start eating."

We made up scenarios all afternoon, and then her housemate
Clare came home.

"Are you going to tell her your news?" Lucy asked me.

I looked at Clare flatly.

"I'm pregnant."

"Oh," she looked at me meaningfully. "And are we keeping or
discarding?"

"We don't know," I told her.

And then it was time to go to the doctor. I think that's enough
of my essay for now.

## October 8

I've got back to my house now. I've decided I can't keep giving
up in the face of no motivation.

## October 17

My house is, finally, going really well. If I keep making this sort
of progress I could be doing the final inspection in one month,
and moving in in two. I'm so happy and excited about it all. There
was a moment, a little while ago, when I was walking with someone and for a moment I actually got a grasp of an overview of my
life, and felt quite happy about it. It's the first time this has happened for a long time, that I've been able to get past the precise
minute in time that I'm actually in, and see my life in general, and
have a feeling about it.

Sometimes I go for a while (but probably not more than a few
hours) without thinking about the baby at all, and life feels nearly
normal. Except there's something funny happening underneath so
I know it's not normal. Sometimes I pretend that I was never pregnant and never had an abortion. Or that I had an abortion but it
was no big deal and hence of no consequence for me. But if I start
thinking that I immediately start feeling awful again. One thing
that's helping me feel a bit better now is simply the acknowledg-
ment that it's a humongous thing and it's really traumatic for me
and will take me a while to get over. With that attitude I can get on
with things better.

I have been thinking about a name for my baby. The only name
that ever comes to mind, and that always comes to mind, is
Clementine. If she was a live baby I don't think I would name her
that. I don't especially love the name, though I don't dislike it

either. I think it sounds a little pretentious, though I'm sure a lot of the names I'd consider for a live baby would sound far more pretentious. I think it's starting to get to the point where I couldn't give the baby any other name and feel like the name belongs. So maybe I should say that she is a little girl and name her Clementine.

I wish I could be telling people I was pregnant and happy about it, rather than that I had an abortion. I would be more than four-and-a-half months pregnant by now. More than halfway. I feel so flat and skinny, where there could be a baby growing. My little Clementine.

## October 21

Today, when I was working on the house, a terrible thing happened. I can hardly bear to write about it, I feel so bad. A bird has been trying to make a nest in the roof of my house. I've been removing the bits of straw periodically because I don't want the bird thinking it can live there. I always check first that there are no eggs in the nest. Well it's been a while since I last evicted the bird, and she's been really persistent. I felt around as carefully as I could and didn't feel any eggs. I felt so sad taking the nest out—the poor bird who went to all the trouble of making it. But she can't live in my house. The nest was so very soft inside, and so delicately made. I had finished taking it all out, when I looked down and saw blood. There had been an egg in the nest! And it was broken. Cath said there was another one that fell to the ground and I hadn't heard it. I couldn't believe it—I thought I checked so carefully for eggs first, but I couldn't feel them. I felt so devastated. I cried and cried. The poor little bird—I've killed her babies. If I'd known the eggs were there I would have left them and the nest alone and shared my house anyway. I wished desperately I could flick time back by ten minutes and bring those eggs back together again. I felt I had aborted two more little babies. I don't know what birds feel, but if it's anything like how I feel after what I did to my own baby, my heart hurts. I just wish I could write in bird language, "I'm sorry— I'm so sorry."

Cath gave me a hug and held me for a little while as I cried. She didn't try to tell me it didn't matter or wasn't important. She put down the trowel and came into the shed with me and said, "Okay, we're making a bird box." I thought it wouldn't help much— nothing can help that poor bird with no babies growing in their eggs. I put the nest back together in the box and we taped it just outside the house. I don't know if the bird will use it. I put one of the broken eggs in it. I didn't know if I should have done that or not, but I figured how lost and confused the bird would be if it went back to the house and there was just nothing there. It should have the right to at least know what happened to the eggs—that they broke. I also filled the gap with newspaper so the bird can't make another nest. I felt so heartless and cruel.

## October 27

Sometimes I feel I'm going crazy. At times it's directly because of Clementine, like yesterday when I was working on the house and feeling as heavy and miserable as hell with grief and anger. Since Antonia, the counselor from Open Doors, told me that it's okay to feel anger, and that it's in fact very common when you are going through grief, I've started to notice and feel how angry I am. Especially with Dan. I'm furious with him. I think, why should I have to go through all this grief, when he played as big a role as I did in causing it, but he gets off scot-free? I have to go through mountains of grief and he doesn't. He never carried that child inside him, its heart beating determinedly. He never had to make the decision to kill it either, and he doesn't have to live with it. Cath told me yesterday that a girl we knew from ages ago has got married and has a baby daughter who is already one year old. I became angry with her for having a little girl—it's not fair that she has her little girl and I don't!

I've been doing my homework that Antonia suggested. To think about my plans for me and the baby—what could have happened. So many plans for me and her. I was wondering last night if I would send her to a co-ed school or an all-girls school. A school with a uniform or without? I figured co-ed definitely. As for the uniform, I'm not sure. I don't believe in uniforms, but if there was one it would make matters a lot cheaper for me and there's less pressure to have the trendy clothes. I can imagine Evie coming to stay the night. All three of us sleeping squashed up in the loft in my new house. Then waking up in the morning and Evie holding Clementine, playing with her, picking out her clothes for the day. Then the two of them playing outside while I cook breakfast and tidy the house. Evie and Clementine traveling around the garden on an adventure trek while I plant some more veggies ...

## October 29

Yesterday I worked for nine-and-a-half hours of solid bricklaying—lifting, mortaring, toweling; it's very physical. My body is starting to feel like it's made of rock. Today and yesterday, as I was working, I've felt quite cheerful and content, and I haven't been thinking about the baby quite as much. The day before that I cried all day, and it was so difficult to work. I'd stop between mortar loads and lie down in the grass to cry, and sometimes I'd just drip tears while I was working. I wonder how I would work if I was pregnant. Two days ago I would have been exactly five months pregnant. Very visible, but not yet at the time when it starts tiring me down with the weight. Would I still be lifting heavy bricks all day?

## November 2

I feel exhausted to the very core of my being. I have done a lot of dreaming today about a lot of things, mostly concerning my future and Clementine. I dreamt about her and me packing up my car with enough things to go and live with Mace for one year, when Clementine is about seven. She would go to school in Bendigo. We would live in the beautiful medieval castle that he will have built by then (with lots of my help). We'd walk around in medieval clothes, eating food grown from our permaculture* farm, tending to the animals ...

I finished a book called *Children of the Dust* by Louise Lawrence. It was about a nuclear holocaust. It got me thinking about the world as I know it and as I want it. I want to live in a place that is environmentally friendly. A place where we are living from renewable resources, and not creating rubbish and pollutants. I want to live without fear of a nuclear war. I want to live close to people and in a supportive atmosphere, rather than the alien and anonymous atmosphere of the cities and suburbs. When I feel so frustrated and sad about the state of the earth and the society we live in, I think, at least I'm doing something about it. I'm building a house now which is completely environmentally friendly. I am taking active steps to be the kind of citizen I wish everyone would be. If everyone did this then our world would be such a lovely, safe place.

## November 11

I wish so much I was still pregnant. I would be almost five-and-a-half months by now. She'd be heavy and kicking around, and I'd probably be doing a lot towards getting ready for her birth. I'd probably be as scared as hell too, really nervous of what my life

*organic

would be like with a baby to change every aspect of it. I wonder where I would be planning to live? I would hope it would be in my house, equipped with a washing machine and dryer in the shed for all her nappies* and burped-on baby clothes.

### November 13

It's been a grueling couple of days. After my last entry I couldn't stop thinking about Clementine. I've been hurting so much I can hardly stand it. This morning in counseling, I cried like I haven't cried before, over Clementine. Antonia was really good. She held my hand and she felt for me so much that she started crying too. She told me she lost her 18-year-old son, who went skiing and was lost in the snow and never came home. That must be a million times worse. My heart goes out to her. I came home and went to bed, lying there, unable to believe that it could hurt so much.

### November 17

It's late and I feel tired, fragile and vulnerable. I'm craving some affection—I want to feel warm and loved and safe. I met Millie for the first time—my new baby cousin. She's six weeks old. I had been thinking about what it would be like to meet her and in my mind there was a fairly big build up to it. I didn't touch her. The adults were all in the kitchen, and the younger children were sitting in a circle around Evie, who was holding Millie. It was very quiet and peaceful. Millie was sucking her thumb and making slurping noises, and Evie was watching her calmly. The adults seemed quite content and trusting to leave the baby with the children. I went and sat with them, and said hello to her. I sort of wanted to hold her, just to feel how she would feel in my arms. But there wasn't another right moment. I can't think about Clementine. It's like I have raw wounds inside me, and thinking about it is like starting the gush of blood all over again. I threw in my work today after an hour or so because I'm just tired right through to the bone.

### November 18

I don't think things could get much worse. I've got that feeling where I want to take a handful of sleeping pills and sleep for a week to run away from life.

### November 24

Last night I started thinking maybe I was strong enough to start

*diapers

thinking about the baby again. I still feel so raw and sore, but it's a little bit better now. I finished reading *The Mourning After* (by Terry Selby). It has helped me understand a bit better what is happening to me and why. And it's given me a language for a few things. I think I'm a lot better off for facing it all now rather than in ten years after I've [ruined] my life in the process of not grieving, which is what the book talks about ... I found one thing which hit me really hard—"mechanical rape." That's the part I have completely blocked out because I just couldn't deal with it. Even now, just writing about it, my whole throat is getting all blocked up and it feels hard to breathe. Before the abortion, I was absolutely terrified of the idea that I would be unconscious while someone was "mechanically raping" me. I expressed that fear to a couple of people before the abortion, and they both said it was most definitely nothing like rape and not to worry about it. When the book said the word rape it summed up exactly how I felt. Someone must have put my legs up and inserted lots of instruments inside me and dug around and scraped and so on. The idea of that upsets me so much that I couldn't even think about it. And the poor little baby. What happened to it? To think it was a little person, fighting for its life, and losing against these great big instruments, squashing and killing it.

## December 4

My poor little baby. I know it's impossible, but it would be nice to go back and find out I was pregnant, and then actually let myself listen to and feel that tiny little person in there. I was so busy blocking it out. I didn't want to let myself love that little baby, because if I loved it, then I wouldn't have a free choice; I'd be forced to have her. I thought that if I didn't let myself love her that I could decide freely and more logically. But now I can see the feeling was there, struggling away inside me, wanting to love her and cherish the thought of her growing inside me. I can see my maternal instincts were there all along but I blocked them out so forcefully that I could easily believe they really and truly weren't there. I've got so much love to give that little baby. I wish I could have been able to stroke my tummy and talk to her, and enjoy the feeling of her growing within me. But I didn't touch my tummy at all. I couldn't bring myself to touch it. I think that for me to put my hand on my tummy was like saying hello to the baby. And if I said hello, I couldn't possibly say goodbye and just kill it. Once my hand was there, accidentally, when I was going to sleep at night. And as soon as I realized I snatched it away, feeling terrible. I never said hello to her. I never gave her any love. Sweet little Clementine—she was in there, so determined to live and do her best and be healthy and strong, and I just ignored her, got rid of her as fast as possible.

I think it's time I wrote about what happened, the abortion itself.

## The Abortion

Lucy and I caught the tram* to the hospital. I was shaking with nervousness, terrified at the thought of what they were going to do to me. I was completely shut off from the baby. It was as if it didn't exist. I couldn't allow it to exist, couldn't think about it, because the decision arena was closed. My terror was of the pain, the vulnerability of being so exposed to the doctors, the fear of the general anesthetic, losing consciousness. I couldn't forget my pre-abortion interview with the doctor, who looked down his nose at me like I was a stupid and careless little girl for getting myself pregnant. I explained that the condom had come off, accidentally, that it wasn't like I hadn't bothered with contraception at all, but that didn't seem to make any difference. I asked him, "When would the baby be due?"

He glared at me over his wide mahogany desk and snapped, "It's not a baby! It's a piece of fetus!"

(I looked it up in a chart at the back of a pregnancy book later—Feb. 17.) After that I was too scared to ask the other question that was going round and round in my mind—what did they do with the baby, after they'd scraped it out and killed it? I've been wishing that I asked anyway. How long did it take for the baby to die? Did it die instantly, when their metal instruments started knocking it around? Did it die from being crushed, while it was still in the womb? Or did it die when it was pulled out, dumped in one of those kidney-shaped silver bowls?

I asked instead about the hospital procedure for the abortion. Apparently it would take about 20 minutes to do the operation itself, and then I could stay in the recovery room until I felt well enough to go home.

"How long is well enough? And is it possible for me to stay overnight? I don't have a home to go to. I'm homeless."

"No, it's not possible to stay overnight. You should be fine to go after an hour or so, and take it easy for the rest of the day. The next day you'll be fine."

I looked at him skeptically. He made it sound like having a tooth extracted. I didn't believe it could be that simple, especially after a general anesthetic, and all the chemicals that knock your body out. But that was the end of the information I was getting from him. He was devoid of compassion, full of contempt for us stupid girls who come to see him, day in and day out, to deal with their "accidents." The thought of having him touch me in a place where I felt so vulnerable, while I was completely unconscious, made me feel sick deep inside. There were forms to fill in at the hospital—form after form.

A lot of waiting. Then I had to go through a series of interviews. Every time a nurse or doctor interviewed me, the first thing they asked me when they realized I was deaf was if I could read or write. They were so patronizing.

First was a nurse, who weighed me, checked I hadn't eaten, told me to take off all my clothes, including my underpants, and supplied me with two regulation hospital gowns. I had funny little socks to put on that looked like shower caps, and another larger shower cap for my head. My earrings had to be removed, which was stressful since I couldn't get them off by myself. The nurse impatiently covered them with a large piece of masking tape, which pulled at the skin and made it itch until I yanked them off and spent the next 15 minutes fighting with my earrings. When I was appropriately dressed, she asked me, "What form of contraception will you be using?"

I blinked at her, unsure what I was supposed to say.

"We can prescribe the Pill for you now."

She waved a prescription pad and gestured towards a packet of pills on the table.

"I don't need the Pill," I mumbled.

"Well, you don't want this to happen again, do you? What are you going to do about it?" I stared at her and said, "I'm not going to have sex."

She pursed her lips and swallowed, trying to remain patient. I'm sure it was one of the answers she found most ridiculous. Her voice sounded strained when she said, "Yes, but it's easy to get carried away in the moment."

I knew perfectly well I would never be getting carried away again. I had already thought about it pretty hard, figured that I wasn't going to have penetrative sex with any guy unless I'd figured that if I did become pregnant, I'd be able to deal with it.

I refused to answer her and clammed up, staring at the floor until she gave up, and went to get the anesthetist. This was another interview, the third degree all over again about my entire medical history, any allergies I may have, any past operations. I couldn't even remember! I didn't like this man any more than I had liked the nurse, and was becoming increasingly sullen and afraid. My answers were monosyllables and I stared at the floor for most of it.

Then he left, and another nurse came in. She looked rushed, picked up my clothes, dumped them into a calico bag, and steered me out into another waiting room full of nervous looking women, all different ages and ethnic backgrounds, all wearing the tiny shower caps on their feet and two hospital gowns. No one looked at each other. No one smiled. I joined them, mute and miserable as well. I asked the nurse how long it would be until I went into the operating theater.* She checked my name, consulted her list, and finally told me that I would be the first one, quite soon. "Quite soon" felt like a long time to me. Eventually another nurse came in, called my name, and led me into a corridor. She was young and pretty, with soft eyes and a gentle smile. She had her hand resting lightly on my shoulder.

"I'm scared," I confessed to her, softly.

She put her arm right around me in a warm hug.

"Don't worry sweetheart, you'll be okay. It doesn't hurt. I'll hold your hand."

She was still steering me along the corridors, turning corners, keeping her arm around me and distracting me with questions about what I did for work. Eventually we came to the operating theater and she led me in. There were several people in there, a tiny room with one operating table, and they looked busy but I had no idea what they were all there for. I saw the doctor and the anesthetist among them, and quickly returned my eyes to the floor. The nurse helped me onto the bed, untied my outermost gown, and smiled at me as I lay down. She went to the other side of the bed, away from all the doctors, and stood close, smiling at me and holding both my hands. It was the most warmth and affection I had received in a long time and I wished I could disappear with her to a safe place, bury my face in her neck, and go to sleep. The anesthetist extracted one of my arms from her grasp, tied a black belt around it and started prodding, looking for veins. When he was satisfied, I saw him lift an enormous syringe, filled with a milky substance. I realized that all of this was going to go into my arm and knock me out. I felt a terrifying wave of nausea wash over me. Then he was jabbing at my arm with it, the nurse was squeezing my

*operating room

hand really tightly, her eyes staring into mine, smiling, and I was trying not to scream. The nurse's face started to fade, the room went white, shook, wavered out of view, and then my eyes were open and someone else was talking to me.

Another nurse. I was somewhere else. I was lying on my side, not my back. I felt completely disoriented. I found out later that I'd remained unconscious for twenty minutes longer than I was supposed to. Another nurse came in and said I had to go now. I was almost howling, miserable and overwrought. I shouted, choking on my breath as I did so, hiccuping wildly, that I couldn't get out of bed and there was no way I was leaving yet. The first nurse came back, took my arm gently, and said, "Okay, you can stay for one more hour."

I cried for the whole hour. A different nurse again came in and said I had to leave. She dumped the calico bag with my clothes in it at my feet, and told me to get dressed. I wanted to lie there all day, shut out from the outside world, and hide deep inside myself, but they kept on wheeling in more women and I could tell they had to get rid of me to make space for them all. I had four visits from the nurses, trying to hurry me up. When I finally stood up, the room spun for a moment and I promptly sat down again. I was still sitting there when I got my fifth nurse-visit, and she took my arm, steered me down the corridor to another waiting room with chairs, and sat me in one of them. That was it. I had to wait for my mum to come and pick me up. Some of the women looked fine, eating biscuits,* reading, talking to the people who'd come to get them. Some of them looked terrible, leaning their chair back to lie with their eyes closed. One woman was wheeled in, sitting in a wheelchair. I couldn't believe the nurses had thrown her out when she still didn't even look conscious. She was propped there with her head flopping to one side. Later, when I was leaving, I saw someone else wheeling her through the car park. What sort of hospital can let a patient leave when they haven't even come good after a general anesthetic?

## December 6

It's been an awful day. I woke up feeling miserable and the feeling hasn't stopped. I have been deciding between two kitchens. The guy there tells me to get my father to measure the fridge for me and come in with me to approve the quote. Why can't I get

*cookies

some ---- credit? On top of all this there's Clementine. I feel like I just can't hack it any more. Why can't I be pregnant now? I have to stop writing 'cause I'm crying too much ...

## December 7

Finally a big achievement today. After eight weeks of work (the last two being rather slack) the walls are finished!! Every last brick has been laid! It's done! Finished! And I just can't believe how good it looks! It's still light enough inside (I was worried it would be too dark) and it looks gorgeous. My bedroom is stunning. The window is exquisite, and from the outside with the window it looks incredible. The bathroom is really sweet and looks like an old-fashioned attic, because it's darker down at that end. I can't get over it. It really hasn't sunk in yet.

## December 8

I don't think that I could ever just get on with my plans the way I had them laid out before. I think I have to make a new set of plans for my life, that accommodate the abortion and all the pain I've gone through since. Now I want to be more settled, whereas before I didn't. I'm not interested in flings and short relationships for "fun." I just want a calm and steady lifestyle. I suppose I would be adjusting my life like this if I was pregnant—"nesting"—to make it easier for me when the baby is born. But even not being pregnant, that's how I feel. It's not like I'm really hanging out to have a serious, long-term relationship, although I would like that for one day. I don't especially like being single, because so often I'm craving affection. And yet, the Catch 22, I don't want to meet a new lover. I'm just not in the mood to do the whole courting ritual, to try and get to know someone, and feel all the anxiety and stress of, "Do they like me; are they interested in me?" I wish I could get together with someone I've known for ages, nice and comfortable without anything scary. But there's no one in that category either, so I guess I'm stuck as I am for now. It's not something that bothers me much. Mace told me that another of his friends had a miscarriage a while ago; she had always wanted to be pregnant, and then lost the baby. But Mace didn't think she was ready to have a baby. I said, "I never thought I was ready to have a baby either. But since I got pregnant, I've got ready too." "Oh, I think you're ready to have a baby," Mace said straightaway. "I think you would make a wonderful mother."

It was so good that he said that. I have held those two statements close to me since he said that—I'm ready to have a baby, and I would make a wonderful mum. When I say ready to have a baby, I don't mean ready to have another baby, I mean ready to have Clementine. I have to deal with Clementine before I can be ready for another baby. Born or unborn she is still one of my babies.

**December 9**
My thoughts of Clementine have been with me all day today, at the front of my mind, but in a more gentle way. I seem to be able to endure the painful times for longer before I go into automatic blockout mode.

**December 15**
Two days ago, I was walking through a shopping center where a lot of construction work was taking place. I was wearing the same dress that got me crying at yoga on Thursday night, because it makes me look pregnant. One of the construction workers asked, as I went through, "Oh, are you pregnant?"

I was really angry and upset. Upset because people should think I'm pregnant when I'm not, and angry because regardless of whether I am or not, it's none of his business to comment on my body. I stared at him scathingly and said, "What?!"

He just repeated the question. I shoved past him and didn't answer. I keep on crying about Clementine. I woke up this morning feeling shattered about it.

**December 17**
Last night I had a really horrible dream. My brother killed Evie. It was me who found her. Evie was lying there, a small child with hollow black eyes. I guess it's another dream about the abortion.

**December 19**
Last night I dreamt I was in hospital, giving birth. I was lying on my back, and pushing hard but nothing was happening. Then I remembered from all my reading that being on all fours should help because of the gravity pull, so I turned over. Instantly the urge to push and the entire labor seemed to disappear. What would it be like to give birth to Clementine? Less than two months to go, now. What would she look like when she's first born? How would I react, how would I feel? Would I hold her and be overwhelmed; would I need a while to recover from giving birth, before I could connect with her? I'm not afraid of giving birth. I'm not afraid of

the pain. I think I could relax and go with it. If I meditate and con-
centrate hard I'm pretty good at dealing with pain, especially if it's
positive pain, like when I got my tattoo. Having a baby would have
the same sort of outcome, I think. The only situation in which it
would be absolutely unbearable, is if I found out that the baby had
died, and would be born dead. I want Clementine to be alive and
growing, so badly. I want to experience it all for real.

## December 23

I woke up feeling ---- awful. I want my baby back. How could I
ever have imagined I wouldn't want it? I read a book about a
woman who was going to have her baby adopted out. At the end
there was the scene where she gave birth in the middle of the bush,
and at the very last minute she changed her mind about the adoption. The whole time I was crying out to her not to give her baby
away. And when she changed her mind she was so happy. The birth
sounded incredible. The baby was exquisite. I have such a clear picture of it in my head and I want it for my baby too. I'm feeling so
desperate this morning I could do almost anything to run away
from the pain. I even feel tempted to find someone to have sex
with and get myself pregnant again. But I know, logically, that
won't take the pain away. It will just give me another baby. It's ago-
nizing! I woke up crying, wanting it so bad. I still want it so bad.
How can anything be this painful? Today is the day my family cel-
ebrates Christmas—gotta go and have an all-day lunch with the
whole family. I couldn't think of a worse way to spend the day. I
better go. But how can I drive when I can't see for all these tears?

## December 27

I was imagining, after I read that book I was writing about in my
last entry, what it would be like for me to give birth to Clementine
out in the bush. In the end the best place I could come up with was
Elands, where [ex-boyfriend] Kel and I went when I first got inspiration to build my house. Elands has become a sort of magic place
in my memory—a shrine to something that has given me years'
worth of energy, purpose and inspiration. And there could be no
one there with me but Kel. I imagined that Kel and I were stuck in
the house, without transport or phone and half an hour's walk
from our nearest neighbor. And then Clementine decides to be
born, maybe one or two weeks early, but completely developed and
healthy. Kel would be glowing with excitement, and very capable,
organizing everything and preparing a space for her to be born. He

would hold me and talk with me while I pushed through the contractions, and catch her at the end when she finally made it out. He gently puts her onto my stomach, and helps me rest back onto the couch. She has black hair with tiny wet curls around her face, and very pink skin and dark blue eyes.

She is covered with all sorts of muck and blood, but Kel wets his lungi* in warm water and carefully strokes some of it off. Eventually she would be wrapped in another of his lungis, and he would bring his futon downstairs from the loft for me to sleep on. And propped up in the futon, cuddling Clementine, I could finally rest. Kel would lie with me for some of the time, cuddling both of us and then after a long time he would get up and make us both some food. Well, that was my fantasy.

I've got a really clear picture in my head of Clementine with her black hair, and sweet open mouth. Ever since I thought my way through all that, several days ago, Clementine has been with me, like a dark cloud at the back of my mind, reminding me that she is dead. I don't want another pregnancy. If I got pregnant now it would just feel like I've gone through seven months of pregnancy, and now I have to start all over again, at the beginning. I want Clementine. I wonder, if after the date that she ought to have been born, I will feel freed from this phantom pregnancy? Or will it just get worse because I should have a baby in my arms?

## December 31

I have written this on a piece of paper ready to burn it because it is New Year's Eve. But I wanted to keep what I wrote just in case I want to read it again.

Dear Clementine,

It's nearly new year and I'm supposed to write my year down on this piece of paper and then burn it to let go of it. When I think of this year all I can think of is you. And I'm not ready to let go of you. I don't want to accept you as ashes to dust, like this paper will be when I've burnt it. This year is clinging onto me, and I can't see that I could lift the weight of it from my shoulders to walk freely into next year. I'm carrying you with me, sweet Clementine. Ashes to dust. Ashes to dust ... You came into my dark womb, and I didn't give you enough love. I didn't give you any. I'm so sorry, little one. So sorry.

Can you forgive me? I love you now with all of me. I wish I was

*long piece of cotton material

cradling you in my huge belly now, loving you and waiting for you to be born. Do you know how much I want you, little child of mine? I want you so bad, and I love you so much. I tried my hardest to do the right thing—can you love me even though I failed you? Please? Who were you in there? How would you have grown? I want you back, Clementine. I'm hurting all through.

Love, cuddles and more love, from your mother,
Asphyxia

## January 1, 1997

Last night when I was writing that letter to Clementine, my feelings got pretty intense and I went very quiet. I sat with my wall of silence around me, and leant against it and felt comfortable to feel what ever I wanted to feel. I didn't look at anyone when I put the paper into the fire. I just sat and watched it burn. Over my writing I used my fingers to paint colors all over the page. I suddenly felt angry and miserable, and I painted Clementine, a thick black dot, amidst smears of heavy red blood, smashed across the page like a broken bird's egg.

## January 2

I went to bed and dreamt, again, that I was having a baby. After a while I half woke up, realized I was dreaming about the baby, and deliberately went back to sleep and stayed asleep for a long time, wanting the baby to stay with me, not wake up and find it didn't exist.

## January 13

Wow! Today has been a really good day. The house is amazing—absolutely amazing! It feels like it's all coming together. Suddenly everything I have been worried about I no longer have to worry about. Today I have actually felt joy welling up inside me, with excitement about the house. I haven't felt truly happy from all the way within, for such a long time. I have been dreaming and working towards this day for one-and-a-half years. It's a house! Am I ever proud of myself! The end is really in sight, and I'm still on schedule.

## January 15

I feel ---- terrible. Just got home and kicked the wall on my way in. The house failed the final inspection. I know I should be rational and just accept it as another hitch along the way, see that building is a difficult task and setbacks are to be expected. But I feel like the biggest failure! I've put everything into the house, so much so that it feels like it has become me. And for it to fail is like I personally have failed. That glorious bubble of excitement has abruptly deflated into a terrible emptiness. I'm in a foul mood. I feel like smashing up everything. There's this black hole inside me, threatening to swallow me up.

### January 16
My new friend Imogen has been helping me fix the things in the house that caused it to fail the inspection. Something really great is happening with her. I think we're systematically working through our entire life stories with each other. I'm beginning to have the most wonderful warm feelings towards her.

### January 21
Imogen's and my latest schedule has a day by day listing of what we need to do between now and Feb. 7. I want to move in on the weekend of the 8th and 9th, so that I have some time to wind down and also get ready for the 17th, the day that Clementine was due. I couldn't bear to move in any later than that. Clementine's birth day is crucial. I couldn't bear to have my ceremony for her on a building site. I have to be living there. I just have to.

### January 30
I was still really worried about the inspection today, but it was so easy. The house passed!! Yes, it really passed!

### February 2
Less than two weeks left for Clementine. My tummy would be bulging. Or perhaps she would have been born early. I get this gut feeling that I'd be telling her to hang on, don't get born until you're due, and we're safely in the new house. I'm imagining what it would be like to be with my new baby in the new house. I would like to make a beautiful baby sling with all my scraps of material.

The baby can sit in there, snuggled up against my front while I cook, work in the garden, clean up, go shopping, and so on. Oh, I want her so much. It's not fair that she isn't around—that she just doesn't exist any more.

### February 5
Tomorrow I start moving in. My head is full of moving house things. Realistically, it would probably be better if I hung on

another few weeks and finished off a lot of things properly before moving in. But I can't hang on any longer. It's good enough for me to live in. I can't work any more. I need a break.

## February 7

Moving day today. I don't feel great. I think it will take me a little while and then I will love living there. It's a big change, I suppose, when a dream you have been longing for, for so long, is finally realized.

## February 8

Well, here I am, writing this in my new house. I'm not afraid any more. My house is gorgeous. I have set it up beautifully and it feels amazingly sweet. To think that I worried so much! Now that the change has happened, it's exciting and fun. I stood in the middle of my veggie garden today and held the hose above my head as a shower. The water wasn't too cold, and the day was hot, so it was quite comfortable. I started thinking about how I have eaten, slept, walked, talked and breathed this house for the last six months. That's only counting the time I was actually building. Before that I was working for the money, burning myself out. It's over. It's really over.

## February 17

Today is the day that Clementine was due. I had the ceremony for her this morning. Antonia was really nice, organizing to come in to work this afternoon, even though she doesn't normally work on Mondays. That meant I would not worry so much about "losing it" because I knew I would see her afterwards—it was like a safety net. I got up and actually took some care in getting dressed, for the first time in months. Normally I just throw on anything (usually the jeans, old singlet* and flannel shirt). Today I still think I looked awful, but at least I tried. I wore a long black dress and my red and white stripy top underneath. The black dress for mourning, the stripy top a symbol of liberation. I brushed my hair, which took a while because first I had to find my hairbrush and then attempt to unmat it.

For breakfast I ate a mango. I couldn't bear to eat anything more than that. And then I couldn't put it off any longer. I'd spent the whole weekend preparing for this. On Saturday I bought some plants and selected a large bluestone. I made a cross out of timber

*tank top

and painted on it:

*Clementine, 2/17/97*

On Sunday I spent the day preparing the garden, weeding, digging and planting both the cross and the plants. I put them under a big tree, behind some bushes, close to the fence. It's fairly private and shady in there. Just to make sure though, I erected a couple of the pallets left over from the mudbrick deliveries, so that it can't be seen by anyone walking past. When I went there this morning it was a grave that was green and beautiful in the speckled light, and very private. I brought a red flower and put it at the foot of the cross. Then I sat on the bluestone and began writing.

Clementine, little baby daughter of mine,

How can I tell you what it's like for me, sitting in this garden I have made for you, on the day you might have been born? You are so much to me and I don't want to say goodbye. I want to hold you close, alive and warm in my arms. But I'll never be able to do that, because you are dead. And that's my fault. I did the wrong thing and I'm so, so sorry. I know now you were such a small baby, but with such a will to live. I can still feel it—your battle to stay there inside of me, struggling so hard for the freedom to live out your life. But you were powerless, tiny and hopeless in your war, and you lost. Sweetheart, I would do anything to undo that now, but it's too late, and I am powerless too. I keep hoping that somehow, something I say or do will bring you back. But nothing will. Nothing will. Little one, can you somehow forgive me. I feel you must hate me, with a fiery anger, but can you let it lie in peace, because I am so sorry. I have suffered enough. Can you see how much I love you, how much I want you? I just didn't know it at the time, that you would grow on me, grow in me, and my wanting you would grow too. Everything would've been all right, but I didn't know that then. I had no way of knowing and I was just trying to do my best.

*I am stretched on your grave*
*And will lie there forever*
*If your hands were in mine*
*I'd be sure we'd not sever*
*My apple tree my brightness*
*It's time we were together*
*For I smell of the earth*
*And am worn by the weather*

I love you. Thinking of you always,
Your mother, Asphyxia

By the time I'd finished, I was crying, just a little. Softly I sang *Stretched On Your Grave*, and then I sat there quietly, rocking myself backwards and forwards for comfort, soaking up the feeling of being there. Before I left I took a photo of the grave. It looked so beautiful, especially with the red flower. I'll put it in a box along with my letter to Clementine, and the only photo I have of me when I was pregnant.

**February 22**

Today I walked to the park and thought about Clementine. My one-week-old baby. I imagined sitting there with her for a whole hour, just holding her and marveling at her. Enjoying the warmth of her small delicate body in my arms. I was remembering Antonia's question, how do I feel about her? I feel lots of love, lots of security when I imagine holding her in my arms. Security for what, I asked myself? It's something about the wonder of the fact that I am her mother, she is my daughter, and no one can take her away. I don't have to worry so much about losing her to someone else. Though I do know, with any children, anything can happen. Maybe she'd die anyway. I feel an incredible sense of warmth towards her. I could hold her and look into her face for hours, admiring her tiny features, and finding it amazing that I carried her in my belly for nine months. It feels very different from before when I was phantomly pregnant, imagining what it would be like when she was born. Now I have a definite age to imagine her at. In my mind she is so real. I could see myself walking around the park, holding her against my breast in the colorful sling I made, supporting her with my hands. And then stopping to sit on a bench and feed her, or just hold her and be close to her. I was walking as I was thinking all this, almost in a trance, holding my baby and feeling her so real, and for a moment I came out of it and into reality, and saw how sad it was that I was walking there with my arms empty, and no child. But then I went back into it. A phantom baby is easier than a phantom pregnancy. Throughout the pregnancy I felt so scared, but once the baby is born, everything I was scared of is realized and faced, and there's nothing scary ahead after that—I just feel more wholehearted about her, rather than nervous about how it's going to change and get really difficult.

My house feels better for a baby now too. It is tidy and sweet and clean. It feels like a good place for a baby now.

# KAREN

*I wanted to go home and die*

At the age of 21 I left my then-partner of seven years and commenced living with a childhood sweetheart who turned out to be quite the undesirable. Nine months into the relationship, I found myself pregnant. I told my partner, who immediately said: "Get rid of it. I don't want any more kids." I had a four-year-old child from the previous relationship and he too had a child he never saw. I felt that it was better for me to have a termination.

I knew that our relationship would never last and as I was already working two jobs full-time, saving to buy my first home and being a full-time mum, it was the right thing to do as I would not be able to support both children on my own. I knew that my family would have a field day with the knowledge of my pregnancy, and when they found out my sister took great pride in telling me what an idiot I was to become pregnant. My mother was also not very receptive to the idea and told me I should consider getting rid of it immediately.

Although I had already made up my mind to terminate, I still thought of what the baby was (I believed in my heart that it was a boy). I went to Dr. X's clinic at ---. I spoke to a counselor who really wasn't very receptive to me. I told her what she wanted to hear just so I could get it over and done with. I then went to another part of the office and had a scan*—a fatal mistake. I could see the baby. I believe that I should never have been allowed to see the pictures on that screen because it's something that you just don't forget. I went ahead anyway and had the termination.

In the surgery** were many women waiting like lambs in a slaughteryard; waiting to be taken in to be culled one by one. No men were allowed in the waiting room, they could only come and pick you up after. There were no emotions showed by anyone; it was a really cold sort of place. A nurse took you into a room and got you prepared. There you stayed until the doctor was ready to receive you. It was so scary lying on that bed hearing the nurse talk to the other patients just outside the curtained door. When I went into the operating theater*** I remember the anesthetist telling me

*ultrasound    **clinic    ***operating room

113

I would feel a small prick in my hand and to start counting back from 100.

I remember waking up after surgery and hearing other women around me. Some were in pain and crying, some were just lying around on beds. God, it was really awful. It was like a human slaughterhouse, all these women who had just had abortions. It really was quite sickening. I felt quite empty inside. I felt a lot of cramping and abdominal pain as well. The nurse came to check on me. I said I was fine because I just wanted to get the hell out of there.

I spoke to a Filipino woman who told me her husband made her have a termination because he did not want any children. Because he was very violent to her, she agreed to the termination.

When my partner finally arrived, I walked out of the surgery across a main road and got into the car. I realized the back of my dress was covered in blood. It was so humiliating; surely someone would have seen it and yet no one said a thing. If it wasn't bad enough that I'd just had a termination, I was further degraded by the blood on my dress as I walked outside.

I was tired when I got home and wanted to sleep. Instead, I had to answer phone call after phone call. First my sister rang asking what was it like, as if I had just been on a bloody holiday, then telling me in the same breath to take the Pill. I was too tired to argue; I was just filled with resentment and felt totally alone and useless. Then my mother rang to see if I was okay. I told her I was tired and fine. She proceeded to tell me my father was not impressed and that he would call. He did. His exact words were: "What the ---- hell do you think you are doing? You had no right to get rid of that baby. Why wasn't I told?" He said he would have helped in some way and that this sort of thing must never happen again or there would be serious trouble.

About two weeks after the operation I developed pelvic inflammatory disease. My doctor told me it was very common after a termination and may never go away.

I vowed that day I would never ever terminate again no matter what. I was affected by it in a way that is indescribable. I dealt with the termination on my own. My relationship fell apart and I became a stronger person within myself. I bought my home, my daughter became a rebel and went to live with her father, and I had a new career.

In Aug. 1994 I met and fell in love with a married man. I had been seeing him for two years when I fell pregnant. I was 12 weeks into the pregnancy when I found out and told him. He was very calm at the time and said that he would support me in whatever my decision was but he felt it better for all concerned if I had a termination. He said that otherwise he would have to marry me and he did not want to do that. Those words stung. I really did not want to lose the man I loved so dearly. I wanted his love and support—instead I was being told that it would not be fair to bring a baby into the world without both parents. The next day he came to see what I had decided. He also made arrangements for me to go to a clinic in Brisbane and have a termination—he had already taken the liberty of speaking to Family Planning who gave him the clinic's phone number.

He also checked to make sure that I would get the best of care and spoke to doctors about the psychological effects. He was told there should not be any at all. I wanted to keep this baby but I just didn't know how to tell him. He knew how much I loved him but he also had other people in his life and I had to consider them as well. He never planned on having children and now I was pregnant by him. I knew he was not impressed.

I agreed to a termination.

On the way to the clinic the next day I broke down and asked my partner if we could keep the baby or adopt it out. But he said he would always worry about it. I told him about my first termination and how I felt like I was going to a slaughterhouse, about the humiliation I felt and being degraded in such a terrible way. It didn't make any difference—we still went to the clinic. He held my hand all the way as we went in. I was so scared.

We spoke to a nurse who briefly explained the procedure and took my medical details and the money for the procedure. She also explained that because of the late stage of my pregnancy, I might have to go to another clinic. My partner then waited outside for me while I went to see the doctor. I told him we already had children and did not want any more. He was satisfied with that explanation and told me that because I was in the 13th week of pregnancy, I would have to have the operation at his other clinic. He said the operation must be performed ASAP, as a baby doubles its growth every day at this stage of the pregnancy.

The next day my partner came to pick me up at 5:30 am. Before he arrived all I could think about was running away from him, not letting him come near me, thinking to myself, "Please don't do this to me; please let me keep this baby." Then I would think, "No, it is for the best. I must do this for my man—his life cannot be ruined by my selfish wants and needs." One moment I was praying, "Help me get through it," then I was thinking, "Quick, run away now; he won't find you.' But I was scared. I did not want to have a baby by myself. I wanted and needed him more than anything else in the whole world. He was and is my world.

We arrived at the clinic at 8 a.m. It was a nice sunny day. The nurse took my details and told me I would be there for at least five hours because the doctor would have to put a special medication in my cervix to soften it in order to perform the operation. My partner left me at the clinic and waited on the beach while the operation was performed.

The medication was inserted—that was stage one. Now I had to wait three hours for my cervix to soften. It was not nice at all. I saw girls come and go in that three hours, all for the same thing. Some were only 14 and 15, so young and pretty, all having abortions. The doctors and nurses were very caring towards them all, not like [the other clinic] where you were just hauled in and out of the room like a culling house.

When it was finally time for me to go in I was still uncertain. I wanted to run and hide. I cried, but I knew it was too late. Silently I talked to myself, saying, "I will be fine," but I wasn't fine. I could feel the pain in my heart. I was fighting with myself to let go of my baby. I remember looking out a window in the theater, hoping I would not remember any of this day.

When I woke, I was in extreme pain. The doctor gave me an extra shot of pethidine.* After half an hour I said I was fine, even though I wasn't. I just wanted my partner to hold me and get me away from the place. I wanted to go home and die. Never before have I felt such a sadness. I felt so alone. My partner took me home and put me to bed. He stayed with me until I went to sleep and then left.

The next morning he called to see how I was. I knew he would do more if he could; he had other worries and work as well. Later that day I really had the blues. I felt so much regret for what I had done—I felt like I had murdered someone. I kept thinking about what the baby would have been like had I kept it. I tried to get the thoughts out of my mind but it was hard and it just got worse. When I slept I dreamed of the baby and what I had done. Did it feel what happened to it? Did it cry in pain? This thought sent me insane with worry.

*a painkiller

I felt that the only thing for me was to end my life the way I ended my baby's life. I would wake up and see the baby staring at me, as though it was asking, "Why did you do it?" I felt like pulling my hair out; I felt like I was going mad. The more I stayed awake, the worse I got. The more I slept, the more dreams I had. I started looking for drugs to take. I wanted it to end.

My partner rang me and I told him I felt as though I wanted to end my life. I begged him to help me. He rang every hour from 4 p.m. to 11:30 p.m. He told me to get some sleep but I didn't. Instead, I stayed up all night and wrote to my partner and told him of my regrets. I just could not sleep so I went to work at 4:30 a.m. I cried all the way. I rang my partner to talk to him and discovered that over the weekend he had moved [to another] house. That hurt me even more.

The next day I discovered that my breasts were filling with milk. No one told me this would happen. How was I to cope with this by myself? I really began to resent my partner now, but I stayed with him. One week had gone by and all I could think of doing was ending my life. The depression got so bad I went to see my doctor and broke down in his office. He was very understanding and told me I was grieving and needed time to recover.

After a few months a friend told me her daughter was pregnant. The news shattered me. All my feelings came back and I thought of the baby again.

About a year later, despite being on the Pill, I was pregnant again. I did not tell anyone—I did not want anyone to take my baby away from me. I became her protector even before she was born. When I was five months pregnant I read an article in the Sunday paper. It told of fetuses being aborted as late as five months and gave a full description of how the doctor pushed a hole into the head of the baby and pulled it out of the mother. I was even more determined not to tell of my pregnancy. I did not want the lectures or sneers of my peers. When I eventually told my partner of the impending baby we split up for a while but now have a beautiful baby girl. We are back together but he is still married and living with her.

After the baby was born I became fiercely protective. I did not want anyone near her. I kept thinking that someone would try to hurt her. She was seven weeks early and there was no way in the world I wanted anyone near her. My partner came to visit every day for three-and-a-half weeks while she was in hospital. A nurse said I had post-baby blues. I knew it wasn't. I firmly believe I would have killed for her at the time. The only place I felt safe with the baby was in hospital—it became my haven where no one could hurt us. I felt like a wild animal in a cage, just waiting to strike at anyone who said or did something wrong to us.

I knew I had to get my act together for the sake of the baby and I did. But it was hard. I felt the guilt of what I had done even more. But my partner and I have a good relationship and we make a happy family, although we never speak of that day in 1996. I'm glad we don't talk of it although I do think of what my baby would be like now. I do have regrets but I have my little girl. I am lucky.

To this day I have never been the same. Not a day goes by when I don't think of my baby and what I did. It's been two years now since that terrible day and I have only just been able to throw away my sonogram pictures. It was like letting go; I felt it was time to say goodbye.

# MARIA

*So immobilized*

In 1994, I was 18, single and carefree. Every weekend I went out to my favorite nightclub with friends. That was my life. One night I met James, also 18. We had a short-lived relationship that left me abandoned and pregnant. He went out of his way to woo me with flowers and promises of good intentions for my 19th birthday. I had a feeling that he wasn't all that sincere and our two-month relationship soured when I told him I had missed my period and that I may be pregnant. He seemed distant and uncaring.

When I found out I was pregnant through a blood test I knew I was not ready to have a baby, even though I had strong feelings for James. I wasn't going to sacrifice my life for the chance of him coming back to me by having his child. As much as it hurt, I knew I couldn't have this baby, as I was a baby myself. I knew it was a phenomenal responsibility. We had not used contraception. So we both were to blame (just last year he got another girl pregnant and abandoned her when the child was born). I remember approaching him and telling him that I was pregnant and that I had strong feelings for him. He replied, "See, I didn't want it to get that deep."

I confided in a family friend and she ended up telling her mother, who in turn told my mother against my wishes. This did not help my relationship with my mother; it made it worse. My mother and this lady were bombarding me with, "Do not breathe a word to anyone," putting this shame on to me that I can't seem to shake. They wanted me to pretend that it never happened, like it was a dream, but it wasn't. My mother didn't even come with me to the clinic when I had the abortion. She sent the lady who had told my mother about the pregnancy to go with me so my father wouldn't get suspicious. When other girls went with the support of their partners or family, I had to go with the biggest gossiper in the Greek community.

The counselor at the clinic didn't help me much. I don't think she respected my feelings. She just expected me to have no feelings. She had no idea. That day I detached myself from what was going on.

But my feelings came to the surface after, when I had trouble after trouble. I moved out of the house for a while, having to take out a restraining order against my father. I had to leave my job when everyone found out about the pregnancy. I found out my friends were not true friends when they outed me. I threw my morals out the window and had several one-night stands. My mum was always down on me, calling me a "slut" and saying I had shamed the family. I dabbled a bit with drugs, smoking marijuana, taking a little bit of coke and speed.

The abortion changed my life. I haven't been or felt the same since. I now suffer anxiety and bad panic attacks. I'm a bit of a hypochondriac and suffer depression. I can't sleep. It's a struggle facing each day. I have been out of work for over a year-and-a-half; I don't have a driver's license, and I feel apathetic about life. People make me feel anxious. They make me feel I'm the black sheep of the family. I feel so immobilized. (I wrote this in 1997 but it took me a year to send it in.) My psychiatrist wants to stick me onto anti-depressants when I just want someone to talk to.

I have no feelings towards James now, whatsoever. I have since met someone wonderful and we are still together, planning on getting married in the not-too-distant future. He knows about the abortion and has suffered from my baggage.

I resent not being told that having an abortion had aftereffects.

Late last year I went back to the abortion clinic for counseling. The lady I spoke to made me feel like an idiot when I cried and said I wanted to die. I asked her about [the group] Women Hurt by Abortion. She said not to contact them. She was not impressed that I rang for counseling so long after my abortion. It was like, "What do you want?" They don't want to see us again, once we have an abortion.

# MARION

*Sarah, Lily, Edward, and Mary*

I come from a Liberal-voting family, and grew up on Sydney's North Shore. As a teenager I was more interested in my security than in rebellion and by the time I left school I fitted the mould of middle-of-the-road conservatism. I had never been exposed to left-wing thinking and it came as a surprise to realize there were deep issues to be understood in our society. During my university years I began to awake to this and realized I'd been brought up to think that principles didn't matter, especially if they led to conflict.

My response to the revelation that it was possible to think globally and act locally was to embrace feminist ideology. It was stimulating, challenging—an interesting and exciting new way to look at the world. The transition took me through my four years at university and into my working life. Within six years, the transformation was complete. I was as feminist as I could be—and still have a husband and children.

By the time I'd finished my social work degree, I knew I wanted to be working with strong women who fought for social justice and the rights of women to take equal and powerful positions in the country. I was delighted to witness the creation of positions for women's advisers to premiers and the Prime Minister through the late 1970s and early 1980s. Great was our rejoicing when federal funding allocations for long-daycare began their meteoric rise— the struggle had been worth it. Finally we were to see the funding of programs which gave women greater freedom and wider choices in their homes and workplaces.

Friends introduced me to a prominent feminist figure who employed me to showcase one of the first work-based childcare initiatives in Sydney: I was to take my 13-week-old baby to work.

But I had to learn quickly how to make my personal rhetoric conform to my feminist beliefs. A reporter asked me why I'd decided to take my baby to work instead of leaving him with a caregiver. I said I thought a child was better off with his mother before the age of two. The response at work was swift: What did I mean? Why had I said it? I didn't believe it, did I? "No," I said, I didn't believe it ... "Yes," I said, I'd been misquoted.

I was impressed by the sure basis for living these women seemed to possess. I felt challenged, educated, guided by these people who spoke such sense. I loved being a woman with these women. They were fun, they had purpose, they were principled. I remember being grateful that I had a firm and useful basis for my future.

A new position as project officer at Community Child Care was a challenging job. We began to plan the lobby to raise federal government funding for long-day-care centers as a political issue. Subsequently, the budget allocation increased from $30 million to over $100 million annually in a few short years.

Women's housing, employment, legal rights, health, children's services—I believed these things were worth speaking out for. I was personally challenged to come to a firm position on other issues as well, such as legal abortion services.

The only conflict came when I announced I was pregnant with my second child. Immediately I was lectured about this. The point was emphatic: I'd crossed back over the line from feminist-woman and aligned myself with the barefoot and pregnant woman of mainstream Australia. I'd moved from savior to one who needed saving. Despite my joy about the pregnancy, I felt like a sell-out—until another woman in the office also announced she was pregnant. Apart from this one episode, I was able to live out my new beliefs for a few years. Feminism made such sense.

And then, my world fell apart. One night my husband didn't come home from a work party. Suddenly I was facing the deepest crisis of my life—the despair of a broken marriage. And I was pregnant with our third child.

As the nausea of pregnancy intensified and the ten-year marriage crumbled before me, I turned to the only source of security I now knew—my feminist friends. They walked me through the most harrowing period of my life. But I was about to live out the most disempowering decision I had ever made.

The decision to abort my baby was born of fear and the belief that to decide to abort was a show of your strength. I was a feminist who believed a crisis pregnancy was easily solved with an abortion. Certainly, no one had ever suggested that abortion carried any consequences.

During the next few weeks, I lived in a blurry whirlwind. My family relationships were disintegrating. Everything I'd ever taken for granted was dying.

My husband said he didn't think it would be a good idea to have another baby "under the circumstances." My friends all agreed it was best—a difficult but sensible decision. We had a session where we said goodbye to the baby who might have been the daughter I'd always wanted. None of us acknowledged this contradiction—how does someone say goodbye to what we all claimed publicly was nothing?

I was so afraid of having a baby by myself. It became a question of me or the baby—my sanity or a situation I couldn't handle. The essence of myself was at stake. I was empty like a blown-out egg. And anyway, plenty of women had abortions, didn't they?

So I rang the clinic. Inside I was dying and nobody could hear. I had nobody to give me balance. I confided in no one who was not of my thinking. I isolated myself from anyone who could offer something else. I'd been such a strong woman and everything had gone so terribly wrong. I was unable to eat, to work, to look after my children. I had to have control over some area of my life.

The clinic in Sydney was quite like my great-aunt's house. What a feeling of homeyness there was as I sat in the waiting room. And for the first time in weeks, my husband had agreed to see eye to eye on an important issue. He sat in the waiting room with me. And, like the experienced childbirth couple that we were, we'd demanded that he be allowed to come all the way through the abortion with me as my support person! The clinic would just have to accommodate our needs.

I saw the "counselor" alone so I could discuss, without pressure from my husband, whether I wanted to go through with the abortion. We discussed the "procedure"—something about dilation of the cervix with long rods. I was told I could expect to feel a pulling sensation in my abdomen, and that it would take about 10-15 minutes. Afterwards, I'd be taken to a recovery room for a few hours, issued with a contraceptive script,* and given an emergency phone number in case I had excessive bleeding.

On the outside I was my chatty old self, but inside I was shutting down—especially when I met the doctor who was scheduled to do the abortion. He had to clear the request for my husband to come into the operating room—and of course he had little choice since he knew us from our home-birthing classes the previous year. We even had a chance to catch up on the news about our 12-month-old babies.

With my legs up in stirrups, the procedure was strangely like my first childbirth experience. White coats and sheets, metal instruments and bowls, chatty staff, comforting nurses. I can't remember

*prescription

how long it took, but I couldn't hold back the sobs that made my whole body shake. Is this what my life had come to? Why couldn't I have decided to have this baby? If she'd been conceived a few months earlier, before my husband's affair, I wouldn't be here, would I? I was politely asked to keep my legs from shaking. The counselor stroked my face, and my husband said he'd take care of me from now on. I was desolate.

The room became quiet as the machine was turned off. All I could do was lie still. I asked if I could have a look at what they'd removed. Maybe I'd be allowed to take it home and bury it? I was shown what looked to be bits of tissue paper floating in water in a specimen jar. And no, I couldn't take it home. Looking back, I believe they kept from me what was really removed.

I went home. In my mind I was relieved that one of the problems I'd been facing was now gone. Emotionally, I decided the abortion would not penetrate me—it had been a good, strong decision. My heart closed down, and I lived with the feeling of being "dead inside" for the next 13 years.

Despite this deadness, I felt I had to show my gratitude to the clinic by becoming an abortion advocate. I considered applying for a job as a clinic counselor when one became available. At the next International Women's Day march, it was me who held the "Free and Legal Abortion" banner. When a close relative discovered she was pregnant and came to Sydney for an abortion, I was encouraging about how easy and safe it was.

I was outspoken about a woman's right to have an abortion—yet I kept my own a secret from everyone except a few friends. I faced total confusion—this great decision I'd made was exactly aligned with feminist ideology, yet my heart was broken and I was emotionally destitute. I had destroyed a life—a life which I knew would have looked just like my two living sons. I could hardly breathe for the anger and disgust which rose; I was not worth the air I breathed.

My head said one thing; my heart said another. My head would have to win if I was to keep my sanity. I became very "strong" on the outside—no one would know what was underneath. I took a job heading up an affirmative action unit. Feminist trailblazer by day, emotional cripple by night, I often cried myself to sleep curled up in the corner of my lounge* room.

I hated myself. I had a sharp anger inside which I couldn't show.

*living room

I was smoldering away with a depression I couldn't get rid of. I often imagined what it would be like to go to sleep with pills and not wake up.

I tried relationships with women—not for me, really, but I didn't care. As time went on, I didn't care who I slept with—as long as they were reasonable looking. There was often someone different every month—or every week.

I found I could get through the best part of a wine cask if I "needed" to, and gin was often on the shopping list—it stopped my heart from hurting too much for a while. My once-a-week social smoking turned into 20 a day.

Within a year I was pregnant again. I spoke with the father of the baby just once before the abortion. He wasn't interested and suddenly became too busy to return phone calls. I didn't even have to think about what I'd do. I just phoned the clinic. Friends took me to the appointment while my ex-husband looked after the children.

Although I went on to have two more abortions after this second one, I now realize how I "trashed" this second baby. It was the only one conceived in an unloving relationship and I wanted more than anything to throw it away. The anger I had inside turned to cold rage and it took all my energy to keep it from exploding. So I turned it towards the pregnancy and the rottenness of the person I now was. I hadn't cared to use contraceptives, and I didn't care how much the abortion hurt me. I knew I was killing my child this time—but she was dirty to me and I didn't want her.

Sometime later I met the man I'm now married to; later again I changed jobs and moved into industrial relations in the film and television industry. Again I was pregnant, but I was too busy in an interesting job to have a baby, although we'd talked about having children from the first week we'd met. The clinic was the obvious solution—I almost didn't think about it.

This time the clinic told me I had a pelvic infection; they refused to do the abortion and sent me home with double strength antibiotics and a warning that I must come back. I started the course of antibiotics. At work on the third day I had the strangest sensation, as if the baby was moving and turning inside me. The memory is so imprinted on my mind that I know exactly where I was standing and what I was doing. I was struck with the cold fear that I was feeling the baby dying inside me; he was strong and healthy and fighting for his life. He was so strong. Yet, I was only ten weeks pregnant and wouldn't normally have been aware of fetal movement. I put my hands on my stomach and whispered goodbye, too scared not to go back to the clinic.

After we moved to Queensland, I found I was pregnant again. What a wonderful occasion—just one of the dreams we'd had which had led us to leave Sydney. We told a few people with rejoicing. But as the morning sickness overwhelmed me, and the isolation of being alone in a new place settled over me, I announced to my husband that I was getting an abortion. I was so sick that he caved in to my demands. I boarded a bus and went back to Sydney. By now, even the clinic was asking me why I kept mucking up my contraception. I didn't know—I just wanted it over with.

When I recently sat down to look at the dates of the abortions I had over this four-and-a-half-year period, I found each abortion was obtained when the previous baby was due to be born (either the same year or one or two years later). My next child was conceived when the fourth aborted baby would have been born. I now know that I was about to repeat this pattern—except that I became a Christian in the meantime. I believe this is the only reason my next child lived.

Four-and-a-half years of destruction. The next eight years were lonely and sorrowful as I worked through what I'd done to my children and the sort of person I'd become. A slow dawning took place: I realized I could no longer live this brand of feminism.

I learned that the founding foremothers of feminism were actually opposed to abortion, that they recognized it as disempowering and exploitative and a result of social injustices against women.

I was stripped naked by abortion; it made me so weak. I became a slave to an abortion cycle I didn't even know I was in. Abortion worsened each difficult life decision I had to face. It never liberated me, but merely exchanged one problem for another. I began to recognize myself as part of a group of walking wounded as I met other women who felt lessened through an act they were told would be a positive solution.

I began to grieve the gullible and uninformed person I'd been. I grieved that I'd not asked questions, but just accepted what was served up to me. And as I grieved I started to become more my own person.

And something was also happening in my heart. I began to miss my children. It was as simple as that; I missed holding the children I'd never see. When I kissed my new baby's head, I was reminded of the possibility of the other four. There were times when I sobbed until I was overwhelmed with the despair of not being able to hold my children, or dress them, or do their hair.

It was a time of swinging highs and lows, fear and self-condemnation, frustration and boundless sorrow. There were times of great peace and rest—at last I was dealing with the greatest darkness in my life. Although in mourning, I began to feel hope for the first time. I felt that eventually, I'd be free of my dead heart.

As I grieved and my broken heart was healed from deep within, I came to forgive myself.

As time passed, I let my children into my heart, grieved them and then let them go. Today I know them as Sarah, Lily, Edward, and Mary. My children.

# IRIS

*Silent long enough*

The abortion was in 1960.

It was illegal. Sam and I had been going together for a while. I had met him through friends I was nursing with at a hospital.

When I found out I was pregnant I told Sam and Mum and Dad in a letter, as I was living away from home at the time. Mum and Dad sent my birth certificate and consent for me to marry. I was 19. Sam said I would have to get an abortion to save the family name (he is Italian). He saw a friend and borrowed money to have it done and got in touch with a doctor in Sydney. That morning I went to have the procedure. I was a bit far along.

I was taken to a house to stay overnight. There were six of us. We slept in a big room. There was a can with a toilet seat on it for us to use during the night. Later in the night I got bad pains and got up and used this can and for some reason I wanted to know what my baby looked like and reached into that can and pulled him out. Yes, it was a perfectly formed little baby boy. I just put him back in the can and went to sleep (you see, from a small child my way of dealing with hurt in my life has been to suppress my feelings).

The next morning we were taken back to Sydney. I had no money for fares home so had to go and see Sam where he worked and borrow from him (he never had money and always had to borrow from mates*). I went home to the converted garage. I was very sick and my friends were worried about me. I had no medical follow-up or counseling. In those days you could be put in jail for having an abortion.

About two years later Sam and I were married. I did it mainly because all my friends were. I was very immature. At 21, I still had to have my parents' permission.

I was having lessons on becoming a Catholic from the local priest and Sam and I were going to Sydney to have marriage counseling (this was a requirement before you could marry a Catholic). The priest led me through my first confession and I told him I had an abortion and it was Sam's baby. "Try to forget it, Iris, and get on

*friends

with your life. Say six 'Hail Marys' and two 'Our Fathers' and your sins will be absolved."

I just started crying. Was this all my baby's life was worth? My two future sisters-in-law could not work out why I was crying. Confession wasn't that hard! "What's wrong?" they asked. I said nothing. "I'm just upset." (I had never told them; however, his mother guessed and told me to forget it and get on with my life.)

The marriage lasted only 18 months. I had a daughter by him, who was reared by my parents as their own. I lived in my parents' home for about three years or so. They constantly told me I was an unfit mother and to get off my ---- and get a job. I worked at a local hotel to support my daughter. Sam would come and visit our daughter and stay in the hotel. He invited me to his room. I asked him, "What sort of fool do you take me for?"

I finally found a male friend and had a relationship with him. I found out I was pregnant and as I did not want another abortion, a doctor arranged for me to live and work at St Margaret's Women's Hospital in Darlinghurst. Unmarried pregnant women were housed in a former nurses' home. We lived in cubicles on the first floor and did domestic work until our babies were born, for no wages. There were government payments six weeks before and six weeks after the birth of our babies. The pregnant women were not allowed out of the hospital grounds without permission.

Society in that period treated women that were unmarried and pregnant as wicked women that should be hidden away. Nice girls didn't get pregnant. We were treated like lepers.

The doctors thought I was putting on too much weight so I was given a glass of water with Epsom salts, which was meant to take off the excess weight. All it did was make me thirsty and of course, I retained the fluid. Close to the birth, I told the nurse that I was on the verge of toxemia with my previous baby. I was given a glass of orange juice with castor oil in it. This was meant to "clean me out" prior to delivery. Later that night my second daughter was born and taken straight from me. All I heard was her cry. I asked if it was all over. "Yes, thank God," was the reply. I was taken down to the ward with other mothers but with no baby. We were all kept in bed for three days, no shower, only dish wash*, tummies and breasts bound and given pills to dry up the milk.

One of the old nuns came to me on the fourth day to take me to the doctors' dayroom where I worked making sandwiches and

---

*sponge baths

bread-rolls for the canteen and serving the doctors' meals, morning and afternoon tea. She wanted to show me the improvements they had made in the dayroom. I felt faint and had to sit down.

My baby was never spoken of by them or me.

I got the gardener to take me into Sydney to get the train home. He told me I would be back next year to have another kid to adopt. "Don't worry; they all come back eventually," he said. "I won't be; no one is ever going to do that to me again," I replied.

A couple of weeks after the birth, a solicitor came for me to sign the papers for her adoption. He explained but I didn't hear. I had blocked myself off.

For the first few years I would look into the faces of children to see any resemblance. I frightened a little girl at a beach by staring. She was about three, with beautiful hair.

I started searching for my daughter in the mid 1970s. I knew eventually I would find her and I did. We are slowly getting to know each other. But my son I will never see and I only have myself to blame. The abortion of my son was a pain I live with every day. Thinking to myself, "What would he have been like? Would we have been friends?"

In these last two years I have finally forgiven myself for having aborted a beautiful baby son. Because all I wanted was a son and I had gone along with what others had wanted me to do.

Today I look back at my life and see a woman who bowed to others' wishes. I have no family because I made wrong choices in the man that was to be my husband and having an abortion; blocking off my feelings, having no one at the time to talk to about it and eventually marrying that man; having a daughter who my parents reared; in seeking love having another daughter to another man, a daughter who I knew could only have a decent life when I gave her to be adopted. It hurts when I look at other women who are grandmothers with their children around them.

I have failed to take control of my life. I started in 1991 to search for answers to my own life and am now finally saying what I want to do with the rest of it, and that is to finish my schooling and go to university to learn to teach English and math, to write, and tell my stories. I have tried not to speak to people about these aspects of my life because of the judgment I face and faced in the past. I have been silent long enough.

---

*lawyer

# MARY

*So much of me died*

Iremember the events surrounding my abortions clearly. There are some things that are so utterly terrible, so devastating, they never fade from the mind or heart. I idolized my boyfriend, whom I met when I was 17. I was 23 when I first became pregnant by him. We had been living together on and off for several years. Despite his treatment of me, which at times could be very cruel, and his vicious temper, I truly loved him. My parents' marriage had always been spectacularly happy and I guess deep down I believed that our relationship would be the same. I just had to try harder, or be better, or take more care to avoid upsetting him. I dreaded his temper and would put up with just about anything to avoid a scene.

I think that he became aware of this gradually, because over the years his dominion over me increased to a point where he became a tyrant. I had to wear what he said, do my hair the way he wanted, never have friends of my own over unless he was out of town. I really never stopped to analyze any of this. I guess I was too young and besotted with him to realize that ours was not a normal relationship. I believed that if only I could please him more, everything would be all right.

When I found out I was pregnant, I was thrilled. It had not been planned, but I was truly happy. I spent most of the day working out the baby's due date, who it would look like, and thoughts of that nature, but when my boyfriend arrived home and I broke the news, he flew into a terrifying rage. I wept, begged and cajoled, but to no avail. He was adamant that I have an abortion.

A week later I was in the abortion clinic with him, supposedly to receive "counseling" from a clinic staff member. She was aged around 40, and wore glasses and a white coat. She seemed so motherly and sympathetic at first; she even told us that she had four children of her own. I was crying my eyes out, saying over and over that I did not want the abortion. I was desperate; I knew it was impossible for me to stand up to my boyfriend on my own, but I thought that this "counselor" could support me and perhaps help him see reason.

Instead, she sided with him. I now had two people haranguing me. I was saying over and over that I wanted to have the baby, but the two of them just bulldozed over me completely. I felt cornered. I was sitting down, and they were both standing over me. I had once received training in how to close a sale, and I felt that this "counselor" must have been to the same sales training seminars.

There was a momentary lull in the bulldozing, when I almost blurted out, "What sort of commission do you get?" but of course I didn't. I just sat there and wept. I was never asked how I felt, or what I wanted. Nor was I offered any advice as to what resources were available to single mothers. The option of adoption was also never mentioned. I was simply told, over and over, that I could not possibly survive on my own with a baby, that sooner or later I would fall in a heap, that my boyfriend would never see me again, that my parents would never forgive me, and so it went on.

One memory which stands out very strongly from this episode is the false information given to me by both the "counselor" and the doctor who was to perform the abortion. This was, that at that stage of my pregnancy the baby was not in any way human; it was merely "a collection of cells, no bigger than a match-head." I have since learned, of course, that by eight weeks my baby's heart had already been beating for more than a month, and that many other organs had begun forming. The baby had already grown far bigger than I was led to believe.

While I was still crying my eyes out, an appointment was made for my abortion to be carried out the following week.

I will never forget that abortion, or the week leading up to it. I have tried very hard to bury the memories and go on as if life were normal, but how can it ever be normal again when I have to live with the knowledge that my baby was killed and dismembered inside my own body? It is a fact too horrible and repulsive to cope with. My only hope was that the enormous sacrifice I had made for my boyfriend would make him happy.

After the abortion, his treatment of me grew worse. He seemed to enjoy being cruel to me, and would either laugh or storm out in a rage when I cried, which I did often. He had always had affairs before, but now he didn't seem to care if I knew about them. I put up with it all. It must seem incredibly stupid, but I suppose my reasoning was that after what I had done for him, there was no way I could let our relationship fail now—otherwise my baby's murder would have been for nothing. I had done it to keep him; I couldn't give up on him after that.

And so it went on, he becoming more and more sadistic and me taking more and more without complaining. By the time I became pregnant a second time, there was no question as to what would be done. By now I was so conditioned to being under his control that I booked myself into the clinic and had the abortion, after seeing the same "counselor" and being perfunctorily reassured that, of course, I was doing the right thing. As with the previous abortion, I felt that I had nowhere and no one to turn to, so it was easier to go along with everyone. Besides, so much of me had died with my first baby, there just wasn't any fight left.

Unbelievably, I became pregnant a third time. This time I knew I could not go through with another abortion. I would have a nervous breakdown or commit suicide. My work took me out of town for two months at this time, so I waited until I was safely in another city before I rang him and told him of the pregnancy. His reaction was, as before, absolute fury. He must have called me nearly every night I was away—but never to say he loved me or missed me, just to yell into the phone that the first thing I'd be doing when I got home would be to have an abortion.

I had a lot of free time while I was away, and I spent most of it resting and daydreaming about the baby. I felt certain it was a boy, and I talked to him, saying how precious and loved he was. I felt strong enough, when I returned home three months pregnant, to break away from the relationship and raise my child alone. Two days later, however, this treasured baby was aborted too, at the same clinic, amid tears and indescribable anguish. My boyfriend and the counselor shared a coffee nearby.

A few weeks later he had to literally drag me by the wrists to visit his sister and her newborn baby boy. It was the hardest thing I ever had to do. My heart and my spirit were utterly broken. I was so grief-stricken that I thought I could never go on living.

Eventually I did manage to stand up to him. I had a family—his children—and despite not being married to him when our first child was born, my parents were loving and supportive. My children are wonderful and I am truly happy. We divorced when our third child was born, as he had again tried very hard to persuade me to have her aborted and I refused.

I love my children more than I ever thought possible. The children who were taken from me, however, will always live in my heart. There is no way of conveying the enormity of my grief or guilt, or of saying how desperately I still yearn for them. What keeps me sane are my children; what keeps me going is the certainty that we will all be reunited in Heaven one day.

# JILL

*All I wanted was my baby*

My boyfriend and I had been going steady for over 12 months, sure we were going to wait until we got married. I was 16 and a virgin, but we saw each other every day and one time the petting went to the point of no return. I had just had an appendix operation and I thought that was why my period was late. Think again: sure enough, I was pregnant.

By three months my pregnancy was starting to show. My boyfriend and I were really happy about it. I bought my first maternity dress and baby bundle.

One Sunday night, instead of going to church, we decided to tell my parents. Their reaction took me totally by surprise. They told my boyfriend, whom they never liked anyway, to get out. Their only words to me were, "You are having an abortion!"

ABORTION! That was something that had not even entered my head. Abortion was murder. I loved this baby growing in me; I didn't want to kill it. But I wasn't asked what I wanted.

The next step was an appointment with the family doctor. Yes, no worries—hadn't he arranged the same thing for his daughter when she got into trouble? Anything to help a friend.

Dad told me how one of his girlfriends had become pregnant and had an abortion and years later had thanked him that she had. I didn't want to know; all I knew was they were trying to kill my baby.

My boyfriend and I were going to run away to Melbourne. I saw him waiting outside in the car that night but Mum and Dad just wouldn't go to sleep so I could sneak out and in the end I fell asleep.

A couple of days later Dad and I flew to Sydney. We went to see another doctor and I was taken to a hospital with chandeliers. I can still picture them as if it was yesterday. The nurse came in to give me my pre-med needle. I begged her to let me see the doctor. "You will see him in the theater,*" she told me. A group of about 15 women were sitting in the waiting room. There were two open doorways and one closed door that led to the theater. A nurse

*operating room

continually walked past one doorway with a stainless steel bucket with a lid on it. I had nightmares about that bucket for years. Even though it has been almost 23 years, everything is so clear in my memory.

When my turn came, I walked into the theater and promptly told the doctor that I wanted my baby and didn't want it killed. "Fine," he said. A nurse was called in and I was taken to a room on my own. When Dad rang later to see if I was all right he was told that I hadn't gone through with the abortion and he suffered a heart turn in the phone booth.

When I returned home I got hell from Mum, Dad, and Grandma. I was told how stupid I had been and what were they going to do with me now. They argued the baby was sure to be deformed after the appendix operation. By now my nerves were fragile and I was a constant wreck. Under continual pressure, I agreed to return to Sydney.

This time we drove down. Mum bought me a new outfit because you could see my bulging tummy in the one I was wearing. Dad had to do a lot of talking to the doctor to get him to agree after I had said no the first time. That week, however, there was no room in the hospital and we would have to come back yet again.

The next week Dad and I flew down to Sydney once again. We stayed at the ritzy Double Bay. Dad took me to the movies and restaurants and bought me new clothes trying to make up for what he was about to do. All I wanted was my baby.

The next day back to that hospital with chandeliers, back in that waiting room with a different group of women, into that theater with my legs up in stirrups. I woke up with intravenous drips in both arms, an empty womb and a terrible pain in my heart. I was 16 weeks pregnant; the baby they threw in that horrible bucket that day was a fully formed baby with even its own fingerprints, a small beating heart and a body that had been moving around feeling protected inside his mother. I felt it was a little boy. We flew back home that night.

For the next few days I didn't eat, or bathe or even brush my hair. All I did was cry. The nightmare had only just begun. How does a person live with the fact they killed their own child? My baby was killed on Sept. 20, 1973, my sister's 21st birthday. There was a party for her and I was expected to act normally, but my mind and body would not let me forget. I had milk in my breasts. I told my sisters what had happened and they were also surprised at Mum and Dad, but now it was over and nobody was to mention it again. In those days there was no counseling, no discussing it. I had bought shame on the family; the sooner it was hushed up the better.

I was forbidden to see my boyfriend but with the help of a friend, I secretly met him. One day I got caught out. What did it matter? Life wasn't worth living anyway. The doctor had put me on nerve tablets—I came home and took the lot. I can't remember the next three days. For the next few years I would hear babies crying, think something was chasing me, and have nervous blackouts. I was terribly depressed. In 1975, I married the same man; we moved into a rented double-story house. He came home one day to find me trying to hang myself under the house.

In 1976, I had another child, a boy, but I couldn't love him. If I loved him like I did the other one, someone would take him away too. Even though I was married this time I remember how angry my grandfather was at me being pregnant. Years later my grandmother said she had never seen anyone turn their back on a baby the way I did.

My marriage broke up. When I wasn't working I was partying. After all, didn't Mum call me a harlot when I got pregnant the first time even though I'd only ever been with one man? I'd leave my baby with Grandma all the time and I was drinking heavily. I became very bitter, never said anything nice to anybody. The daughter of the doctor who helped Dad organize the abortion was murdered. I couldn't have been more pleased. How I laughed when I heard the news: he had taken my child and now someone had taken his. I even fantasized that it was me who killed her.

It all came to a head about 18 years later. I had remarried by then and had another son, but instead of enjoying the children I had, I continually lived in the past. My eldest son even asked me one day, "Mum, why are you always cranky?"

I went into a catatonic state twice. I really liked it in there where nothing could reach me or hurt me. I ended up in a psychiatric ward.

I had turned away from God over the years. I had blamed him as well as a lot of other people for everything that had happened to me. I came back to him after the breakdowns. Now most of the bitterness is gone. The barriers between myself and my sons have been broken down. For the first time, I could tell them I loved them. I have learned to forgive my parents. I learned that Mum had had an abortion too. Recently my nephew's girlfriend also had one. That means my parents' first child, grandchild and great-grandchild have all been victims of abortion.

Recently my son's girlfriend discovered she was pregnant just after they broke up. My son wanted her to have an abortion. Despite a lot of pressure and opposition, she is having the baby. I feel a curse has been broken. My grandchild will be born and his grandmother will love him dearly.

# CARISSA

*My last goodbye to the little baby I never met*

I can feel the pain as real as if it were yesterday, and it was five years ago.

I had always believed we would be together, marry, have kids. So it wasn't so much the shock of being pregnant at 19—it was just a few years too early. I knew I was pregnant before I had the test and I knew the nurse at the hospital was only delaying telling me because she thought I would be shocked. I could almost read her thoughts as she asked me when my last period was.

Telling Mum was one of the hardest things I have ever had to do. Telling her something she never wanted to hear. I felt so sick, and imagined all the different ways of telling her—but all with the same ending: disappointment. I knew she would be deeply disappointed in me and that hurt, because I loved my mother so much that hurting her would hurt me ten times more.

So I just said, "Mum, I'm pregnant." I think she almost thought I was joking for a second. I could see the pain in her face and neither of us could talk. So I went to bed, and she sat up. The following morning, Mum dragged me out of bed to tell me she wanted to talk.

So there we were, at opposite ends of the kitchen table, her standing, seeming so big and wild, with her face twisted, and me sitting, hugging my knees, head buried and hot tears streaming down my reddened cheeks.

According to my mother, there was only one answer—this was not a multiple-choice question. We had a meeting with my boyfriend and his mother. I was so embarrassed with Mum chairing the meeting and telling it the way it was as if nobody else was in the room. I may as well have been in another country, as I was not spoken to, or even asked how I was.

After my mother forced me to make all the necessary arrangements, I met David's mother in the city one afternoon for a chat. She told me I had a choice, and she would help me. Unfortunately, I was scared of being rejected by my family. After the reaction from Mum, I begged her not to tell Dad because I knew he would literally hunt my baby's father down and kill him after beating me within an inch of my life. So the decision was made for me.

My mother told me that if I had the baby I would be destitute, the father would leave me and I would have nowhere to live because she would not allow me to live at home as a single mum.

Unfortunately for me, David was not reliable; in fact he was downright unreliable most of the time. I can see that now—I couldn't five years ago. I had two counseling sessions booked with a social worker at the hospital; it was a prerequisite to the surgeon performing the procedure, so I went alone.

As soon as I arrived, I wanted to leave. How do I explain my partner wants our baby but he can't be bothered coming to the counseling session with me? The social worker asked me how I felt about my decision. I lied and replied coldly, "The sooner this is over the better, so I can get on with my life." Then I asked if I could leave after the physical aspects of what would happen to me were explained. I was completely unaware of any emotional distress I would feel afterwards.

So the dreaded day arrived. I had arranged for David to drive me to and from the hospital and his mother was going to meet us there. My mum didn't offer to come with me, not that she would have been any support anyway. I had to get up at 6 a.m., to leave by 7 a.m., to be at the hospital by 8 a.m. Seven o'clock came; 7:15 a.m. came and went. I rang David's house—no answer; I assumed he was on his way. I was feeling very nervous. I was running out of time. I wished the earth would open up and swallow me. I realized I would have to drive myself and had to borrow $10 from Mum for petrol.* It was then Mum said, "Perhaps I should come with you, but I'll have to tell your father everything." I replied, "Don't bother," and walked out the gate. I drove to David's house and found him drunk in bed—he had a late night. I didn't know there was anything to celebrate. All I could do was throw the alarm clock at his head and walk out crying.

I sat in the partitioned hospital room in an armchair for over three hours, dressed only in a gown. I tried to cry as quietly as I could, so the other women in the room wouldn't hear me. There were about 20 of us altogether: some young, most with their partners.

We were taken to the top floor in alphabetical order. Just before I was due to go up, I saw two sets of shoes from under the curtain. It was him, with his mother. I told him to get out. The rage was choking me. His mother told me not to get angry; what's done is done and he's here now. It felt like little consolation to me.

*gas

We entered the elevator. No one spoke; it was a long ride and my heart was beating so fast I felt I would faint. David's mother told him to put his arm around me—even that was clinical. I didn't want him to touch me. As we entered the area where I was to wait until called, I looked through the huge glass windows and saw a doctor with his hands up to his elbows in blood and the patient with her legs in stirrups. There was a woman on a gurney next to him who had already had the procedure performed, but was still under, and another on the opposite side prepared for her turn. I kept thinking about the pain I would feel after, but my emotional self felt numb by then.

My turn came and I lay on the gurney, alone and frightened, quivering. I held the nurse's hand so tight as she administered the anesthetic; I didn't want to let go. She told me everything would be fine.

When I awoke, I said to myself, "Thank God that's over." The girl next to me was crying. Little did I realize, the fetus may have been gone, but I was going to carry this experience with me for the rest of my life.

David wanted to go out drinking that night. He reasoned that because he had to take the night off work, he didn't want to waste it. I just wanted to go home and lie in his arms, and for him to tell me everything would be fine and that he loved me. Instead, I ended up being the designated driver. I wasn't supposed to drive at all for 24 hours. So I drove him home drunk, and I went home and lay in bed in the darkness, alone. I felt so empty and betrayed and wondered what I had done to deserve this treatment. Was it my fault? Should I have spoken up and said I wanted my feelings considered? Or should I do as Mum said, "Just get on with your life, and put it all behind you."

I was starting a new job the following day. Mum said if I took any time off I would have to tell my employer the reason, so I'd be better off going to work. Once I got there and started moving around, my blood loss increased. I had to keep going off to the toilet to clean myself up. At one stage I had blood dripping down the backs of my legs. I lost so much blood I fainted after work.

Within six months our relationship was finished (after almost four years), and I had developed the first stages of anorexia nervosa. I would go out all night and drink, and I couldn't sleep, so I was a constant mass of nerves. My hair started falling out and I had panic attacks. Every time I tried to talk about it with Mum, she would change the subject. Sometimes I felt like screaming at the top of my voice, "Please, listen."

For 12 months or more after my loss, I suffered vivid dreams about my baby. One I particularly remember was hearing my baby crying and not being able to get to him. The dream made me wonder, will I ever meet my baby in another life, and is he really okay?

It was almost a year before I told anyone about the abortion. I was told never to speak about it. One night I found myself talking to a friend, and she brought up the fact that she'd had an abortion. Well, then everything came out. We exchanged stories, tears and hugs, and I almost felt as though I was let off the hook for a moment. It certainly made me feel less isolated, and that what I was feeling was natural.

Four years later I was married to a wonderful person who helped me work through a lot of old emotions. We had a son. Ironically, my water broke on the day my first baby was due—even though he was born 19 days later.

I had mistakenly believed my nightmare would disappear. But after our son was born I suffered post-natal depression for six months and the anorexia returned, only this time much worse. I wonder whether the birth had subconsciously dragged up the past. I wonder if by punishing myself I thought I would make things better, or perhaps the pain of harming myself on a daily basis was a twisted reminder of what I had done.

Now I have recovered, as much as any anorexia sufferer can. Writing these things is my last goodbye to my pain and heartbreak, and the little baby I never met.

# LEE

*I have terminated myself*

I was 37 when I discovered I was pregnant. My children were 15 and ten and I had decided that I didn't want any more. I had a vague sense that I was slowly moving back into my own life. I didn't have great plans, just a sense of a new vista—having reached a kind of pinnacle and viewing the plains beyond.

I had strong views on abortion and, without reservation, placed myself in the pro-abortion "camp." I believed abortion was a fundamental right, critical to women's autonomy, power, control and independence; that if men got pregnant, there would be no question about abortion; that if ever I had an unplanned pregnancy, that was also unwanted (as I assumed it would be), I had a right to safe abortion. I believed an abortion for me would always be simple and straightforward, accompanied by passing sadness, and regret that the pregnancy had happened, but predominantly by an all-consuming relief.

Discovering I was pregnant, I found, much to my consternation, my personal convictions wavering. I couldn't decide, but wasn't sure about a baby, so I went ahead with the abortion at seven weeks. What followed was the worst experience of my life.

I cried for six weeks.

I only got out of bed to go to work (at night).

I had no strength.

I had no life.

My legs constantly gave way with the depth of my grief.

I cried and screamed and raged and hit and smashed and talked.

I filled four journals with writing and drawing.

I saw, or spoke to, ten counselors and spent $700.

I expected some sadness and thought if I cried enough the grief would be worked through, then would ease and I'd recover. But nearly seven months later, my heart was still broken. I never felt relief, only the deepest regret and remorse. What made it worse was that I had trouble finding anything to read that described what I was going through. I could not believe no one had ever felt like this before, and that no one had written about it. I wanted to hear other people's stories.

There are two standard camps on this issue. I write from the largely uncharted territory in between.

\* \* \*

After every birthday for the last few years, I told my partner that I didn't want more children and wanted him to have a vasectomy. He was very reluctant but coming around to the idea, as I pointed out again and again that I had done all the contracepting, all the pap smears, all the pregnancies, all the birthing, all the feeding, taken all the responsibility so far and it was his turn.

The first year it was, "You want all the control and what if you leave and I want more babies with someone else?" The next year it was, "You and your feminist friends want to emasculate all men." The next year he agreed.

I had been using a cervical cap together with "safe" days for eight years. The Pill gave me thrush and IUDs made me bleed. I think he got as far as going to the local doctor to get the number for Family Planning. We had that conversation [about vasectomy] in July. At the beginning of November, after having routine blood sugar and hormone levels checked to investigate another case of thrush, my progesterone level was very high and a pregnancy test came back positive.

I was so shocked I couldn't speak for two days. I was so angry with my partner I wanted to kill him.

I rang the local abortion clinic and made an appointment for three weeks time. I had it in my head that I could live with an abortion as long as the embryo was still very small and didn't have a heartbeat. That gave me a deadline of seven weeks.

My house is filled with photos, trinkets, ornaments, gifts. It is full of my life ... When I found out I was pregnant I no longer felt my life held anything good. I wasn't cared for, loved or respected. It was all a sham. It felt bare and empty. I took everything down off the walls and packed it away. My house then felt just like I did. My daughter asked me if I was in mourning.

\* \* \*

I remember at the clinic being asked to consider the two possible scenarios: having a baby and having an abortion. I said I didn't want a baby and hated my partner. I also said I was scared of feeling a great sense of loss after the abortion, that I was very ambivalent about the situation and while I didn't think it sensible to have a baby, I was really shocked that part of me wanted to keep it and couldn't bear to lose it. The counselor told me that ambivalence was normal. She said she had seen women who were 80/20, 70/30, 60/40, even 51/49 about whether to have an abortion, and they were okay afterwards. *Ambivalence was normal.*

She described the procedure and told me I may feel upset afterwards, so to give myself time and space to grieve if I needed to. As the session drew to a close and she asked me how I was feeling, I wanted to drop to the floor and sob, "But you don't understand, I want this baby." But I didn't. Such ambivalence was "normal" and no one should have a baby just because they couldn't face an abortion.

I knew it was possible to be sure about an abortion because I had one 13 years earlier, when my daughter was two. I knew I could not look after her and a baby. I knew my limits. I knew she would suffer and I knew my first responsibility was to her. My only regret was that I got pregnant.

I rang a few places like Family Planning, but I was told they didn't offer pregnancy counseling. I was left to sweat it out alone.

### Three weeks to go

After my anger had cooled a little and I could speak to him again, my partner and I made all sorts of lists. We talked late into every night about how we could fit this baby into our lives.

I swung wildly from one extreme to the other. My journal illustrates this:

> How long will this bliss last? How can I lose it. I don't want to lose it. It feels special and secret and connected like it never has before. Is this my last chance to do it and love my partner at the same time? Why did you come to me?

> I just can't do it. I can't have another baby. It's all bull[---]. It is just hard work and stress. And all those stupid people who have "accidents" just don't have the courage to make the hard decisions. I can't go on caring for other people for an extra ten years.

> I can't take on more responsibility.
> I've had it.
> I've done my time.
> Fifteen years down, five to go.
> Not 15 years down, 20 to go.
> Another 20 years of this.
> White socks, cut lunches, 24-hour duty.
> Who am I kidding.
> I'll be doing it. No one else.
> When my head is clear I see it for what it is.
> The time for babies is done.

I cannot bear the thought of being at the abortion clinic. Making small talk, sitting in recovery with people who might not even care about their abortions and certainly don't care about mine. How can I let such impersonal people do something to me that is so personal and has meant, and will mean, so much to me, to us?

We don't need such a test.
There's too many babies in the world.
I need a rest.
It's foolish and idealistic and I can't take such a path.

My whole body feels alive and buzzing. My nipples ache. My dreams are getting so big now.

Can I whisk it out and put an end to it all?
Can I put an end to another chance?
All these dreams of babies, love, wonder, joy, sharing.
Can I end the dream of letting it grow, loving it,
have other people love it too?
How can I let it be sucked out when I can't think of a good reason—can't feel a strong reason, can't hear a loud definite voice?
All I hear is, "Another chance. Another chance." Is this a reward?
Am I looking for meaning where there is none?

Would I panic if we went ahead? Would a morose disbelief, shock and resentment settle in and never leave me? Could I embrace this experience despite my doubts? Could I accept myself because I couldn't go through with the abortion—because in the face of all this potential, all this conjecturing, I couldn't have it sucked out as though it meant nothing more than it is—a scrap of tissue?

Have an abortion. Have a vasectomy. And on we go.
With that little whirlpool of dreams behind us
Like an eddy.
Gone through and past
Having touched and changed us forever
Can I let it go?
I just don't know
I don't know if I can let it go.

Babies don't know when a good time is. They just take every opportunity and it's up to us to decide.

"What do you want?"
His reply: "What do you want?"
Do we just savor this time? Wallow in it? Float and drift in it? Indulge in it? Entertain all the fantasies of it? Talk and think and dream about it? Let passion course from it? Fill our heads and hearts with the laying to rest of tired old wounds and the prospect

of a lucky last chance to feel love and joy and sharing and closeness at least once? Is this our next project together? If we're going to be together then why not this?

Leave him in the waiting room
Go and lie down
Jump up and run out
Back to his arms
"I can't let them
I can't let them take our thing we've made."

Our dreams
Our second chance
The fifth member of our family
To hell with it
Too bad about rationality and logic
Let go for once
And believe it will turn out well.
Jump into that white water raft
Take the dare
Take the danger
Take the adventure
Take the exhilaration.

I don't want to brush anyone else's teeth ever again
No more doctors, dentists
No more schools, homework, tables or books
No more crises, no more dramas
No more bedtimes
No more resentment
No more unshared parenting
No more unbalanced responsibility
No more mothering
No more caring.
No more domestic struggles
No disruption to a system that is working well and where everyone's needs are being pretty well met.
P&C meetings with a pram*.
What will they think?
That I succumbed?
That I love it after all?
That I love all the servitude and slaving and back-breaking drudgery and monotony?
That I love the forgoing of my own life?
That I'm too scared to make myself the subject of my life after all this time?

*stroller

He says he can work from home so he can be involved in the care of the baby. Three days later he says he can't; it's impossible.

## Nine days to go

My head is spinning. I am in a constant state of fright. I have to hold my head together to stop it blowing off.

I want to pray but don't know who to. One morning I get up on the roof to watch the sunrise. My journal entry:

I feel the warm breeze on my face and watch the leaves on the gum trees set against the pale sky. I want to see the sunrise, meditate on it, be touched by lightness, find wisdom in the enormity of the forces that rise the sun and tint the clouds. I want clarity, peace from my stillness. I want to be touched by Grace as I sit in this holy time of the day.

Something comes to me—to mark the "event" with a ritual. Make a speech, hold something in my hand from my friends, light a candle, listen to Maddy Prior and Mozart. Send this little spirit back from whence it came.

A few days later I am at the pool. Something comes to me as I am swimming:

To everything turn, turn, turn
There is a season turn, turn, turn
And a time for every purpose under heaven.

My time for babies has gone.
This baby's time is not now.
I cry so hard I have to stop and hold onto the lane ropes. I cry and wail into the water. Be strong, be wise. I cry and my tears become the pool.

I wake one morning and think, "Great, we've found a way to keep it." The next it's, "Nah, what was I thinking. I don't want another baby. An abortion is no big deal. It's so small."

## Seven days to go

A friend gives me "the abortion spiel": She tells me she had an abortion a few years ago. "If there's one thing women have a right to control, it's when and whether they have children. Abortion is stage two of failed stage one birth control." I couldn't agree more. I feel decided. Until the next day.

Another friend tells me, "When I thought I was pregnant the thought of another baby made me feel very anxious. The thought of an abortion made me cry and cry. So once I'd decided where it would sleep I started to get used to the idea."

**Four days to go**

I love being pregnant.

I love what's happening inside me.

I love the special secret of it.

Nobody knows.

I want to give birth to and meet this baby.

Once I was into it, it would be different and we'd just have to do it. I'd love it too.

Another one to know and watch.

Another brown-eyed creature.

### One day to go

If I think, "This is my baby. Just like my other two babies," I can almost keep it. Only thing is, I don't want another baby. With all my heart I don't.

But when was I ever ready?

I don't want another baby. I don't want an abortion.

I clean the house and put all my things back up to come home to.

I feel like I'm in a vortex. Inexorably and inevitably sliding down the sides to the center.

I say to my partner, "It's some comfort to me that you're going to have a vasectomy. Because I want you to go through something painful and traumatic. I hope you're scared to death and it hurts like hell."

I got to the clinic—stony, wooden, paralyzed, an automaton. Shaking, trembling.

The nurse takes me upstairs to check my temperature and blood pressure. She asks me if I'm sure about this. I can't speak. She asks again. "It's hard," I snap at her. Finally they call me.

I go through the motions.

I get changed.

I get on the table.

It's finally happening.

I'm really here.

I start to cry and shake.

Here where I never wanted to be ever, ever again.

"You've got music. You're all organized," someone says to me.

"I've been planning this for weeks," I say.

Then the dam breaks. I start to sob.

It hits me. I am finally here. At the gates of hell. Here on the termination table with the chair for the doctor to get at my cervix. To suck out my insides, to open and pull and drag away the thing growing in me.

My legs close, my cervix clamps, I can feel the embryo in me. I want to protect it. "I never wanted to be here ever again. That bastard." I can't do it. How can I let them take it out?

The doctor says, "You've got plenty of time, a few more weeks. You can come back later."

"I don't want any more babies," I say to her, "But I don't want to do this either." I cry and cry.

"Sounds like you know what you want but this is hard," the doctor says. "Would you like some sedation? The anesthetist is here. It will make it less traumatic. Or some entanox?"

"No," I sob. "Tell me how big it is again?"

She goes and gets a six-and-a-half week embryo in a plastic container.

It is white and fluffy, about half-an-inch across.

"Yours will be a bit bigger. About a 10-cent piece. It is not a baby. But it will be if I leave it there."

"Okay," I say. "Take it out."

I lie down. I ask the nurse to put her hand on my arm.

The doctor examines me. Feels my uterus.

"Just seven weeks, I'd say," she says. "I'm going to explain what I'm doing. You can start your music any time now."

I turn on Maddy Prior.

"I'm putting in the local—it will sting. Your heart will race." It does.

God, how can I let them? How can't I let them?

"I'm going to dilate your cervix. You may feel some cramping." I do.

"I'm going to start the suction now—sorry about the noise."

I tremble and cry. Will I say, "No, no, stop, stop. Leave it there?"

I close my eyes, listen to Maddy Prior and cry silently. My jaw trembles, the tears escape, under my lids, down into my ears. How will I ever live with this?

"It's over," she says. "It's gone."

She vacuums and scrapes through Mozart. Sucking and scraping, sucking and scraping. Tugging, pulling and drawing. All the anxiety and nausea sucked away.

"That's it," she says. "I've finished."

She puts it in a jar full of clear liquid and shows me. It is like a small sea creature—frilly and white. I know it's the sac with the waving fronds of a developing placenta around the edge. It's about two centimeters across. She pulls it out of the fluid and it's just a blob of mucus—it collapses to nothing in the air. All this agony for that. It is nothing. Not a baby. Nothing. My pregnancy but very, very early. "That's not like the books," I say.

I wait in recovery for a few hours. I feel very relieved.

It's comfortable and peaceful and cool. My experience is validated. I'll stay a while.

I thought this was the end.

My journal entry:

> We go home. He sits on the lounge.* I lie under the fan. It's 42
> degrees outside. I tell him what it was like. How I couldn't let them
> take it, I couldn't surrender it.
> "I thought maybe one day we could have another baby," he says.
> "Who with?" I ask. "I told you I didn't want any more babies."
> "There's no point in laying blame. What about my dream of having
> a son? That's over," he says.
> "Don't bull[---] me," I say. "That's dreams. I lived through a termi-
> nation today. That's reality."
> "Now I know we don't want any more," he says.
> "I had to go through this for you to know that? Thanks."

That night when the weather has cooled a bit, we have a "serv-ice" for the baby that never was to mark its very brief existence. I burn colored pieces of paper in the fire and send the little baby spirit up with the smoke, back to Mozart—from whence all things come and to where all things go.

* * *

The next week, and many to follow, were spent in shock, disbelief, denial. Raging, blaming, crying, sleeping, clutching the rose quartz I had with me during the abortion, writing, drawing, reading, talking to the baby and mostly acting as if I hadn't decided yet and the decision about the pregnancy was yet to be made.

Journal:

> I spend my days sobbing and sleeping. I light candles, burn incense,
> reread the Bible passage, wear a single black earring, play the tape. I
> cry and cry because I let them take it out. Because I had to choose.
> Because it was so awful. Because he did this to me. Because my
> pregnancy is gone and I miss it. Because it was hideous.

> I feel so heavy I want to fall, so spend most of my time lying down.

*sofa

I want this loss to stop so much I think, "Let's have one we want. Let's do it and keep it."

I feel so full of self-pity. I see a photo of myself the day I found out I was pregnant. My heart breaks for me.

When I surrendered and closed my eyes and let them take it, something broke and cracked deep inside me. In my brain. In my psyche. I had to go against all my instincts and let them into my body. I wanted to keep my pregnancy. Tighten in and close up and clamp shut to hold it in and keep them out. Keep it safe and embedded and floating and growing and awesome, but I opened up and let them suck it out and put it in a jar. I could never have another abortion. If I'd have had just a tiny glimpse of how it feels now, I would have kept it.

A friend comes and brings a letter she's found that she wrote to her ex-husband when she had an abortion about eight years ago. When I was pregnant, she told me she would not keep a baby under any circumstances. After she found this letter, however, she said she'd forgotten what it had been like and she knew she couldn't do it again. She said: "I would just have to keep it and face the tragic consequences."

Would I have acted differently if she had told me that before the abortion?

I read *Ended Beginnings* (Claudia Panuthos) and *Loss of a Baby* (Margaret Nicol). Thank God they included abortion in their books:

> When a woman's life feels too unsafe to nurture a child, she may think little of her possible feelings of loss until the abortion is done. (*Ended Beginnings*)

I don't shower for days. I just sit or lie. I go back to work.

My elder daughter asks if someone has died. I tell her, "No. Daddy and I have been trying to decide something really difficult and I've found it incredibly traumatic and stressful. I can't tell you just yet, but one day I will. No one's sick or dying or leaving."

Replaying the abortion but telling them to stop: "No! No! Wait! Please don't take it out. I don't know what will happen but please don't take it out. I can't do it. I can't let you take it. We're having a baby."

Catch 22: Had to go through an abortion to understand why I would keep it. Couldn't keep it without going through the abortion.

Please, please make this nightmare end.

### One week later

Journal:

> Woke up this morning—felt relieved—for an instant. Then started to cry and cry. That dead weight hit me and I couldn't get up.

I let them take it.

In a jar. Real and floating. Planted, growing, burrowed in.

I could not have another baby ... I think ... but if I could ... Oh, my God ... what a terrible, unspeakable thing I've done.

My body was ripening and changing. Something else lived. Something deep in me. Vibrant and electric, coursing through me. How can I make sense of losing it?

I wish someone had said, "There would be losses having a baby, but don't underestimate the loss of having an abortion."

I hate you because you didn't listen to me. You have put me in a pit and I can't see how I'll ever get out. I hate you because you play golf and I can't get out of bed.

I draw myself stabbed in the heart with a spear thrown by him.

I draw myself in a deep pit with sandy sides.

I draw myself with every part shattered and cracked like glass.

I need penance, healing—to respect, to grieve.

### Two weeks later

I am still reeling from the shock, the decision, the hysteria, the disbelief, the loss, the terrible vacuum, the emptiness that followed the charge, the heightened senses, the fantasies, the longing, the yearning.

Did I just discard and dismiss it so easily?

I feel like something was snatched from my grasp.

I hardly had a chance to see it, to think about it, to really decide—and poof!—it was gone.

I didn't want our baby days to end this way. Not with a little white thing floating in a jar.

No baby is as bad as this sadness. Should I have another baby to end this sorrow?

I wish the counselor had picked up more on my stated ambivalence and absence of a "good" reason and that I said I was worried about how I'd feel afterwards given those things. Even in my crazed state, I wish I'd spoken to an anti-abortion person who might have said, "You might think it very easy and no big deal to have an abortion, but be very careful, you might feel VERY bad afterwards if you're not clear in your mind. Think about it

VERY carefully."

I draw myself reaching up as far as I can to try to catch something that's flying up and out of my reach.

I draw myself on the abortion table, the jar with the embryo floating in it being held up for me to see.

I draw me walking through my life with a massive explosion just behind me.

## Three weeks later

I buy myself a black and white kitten.

I go back to the clinic to use their post-abortion counseling.

I see [a different counselor]. She tells me that I made a choice that day based on reality, not on dreams.

"You know you would be the primary caregiver and you know what a baby would be like."

"Reality ... reality ... reality ... ," I chant.

She tells me there'll be more babies—grandchildren. I don't want grandchildren! It doesn't touch my grief. I say I need to see someone; I'm falling to bits. She refers me to a "body worker."

I draw a hideous picture that I can't look at even a year later. It's me at the gates of hell. The devil is a huge grinning evil face that fills the whole gateway. I am kneeling before it in supplication with a little floating embryo over my head. I have written underneath, "The Gates of Hell. Where I have been and can't seem to get back."

## Four weeks later

It's Xmas. I am withdrawn, thin and preoccupied. People notice and ask what's wrong. My brother thinks I have cancer.

Someone says I have to put it behind me. I can't let it ruin my life. Oh, so easy. She says she thinks I did the right thing: Life's full of chances. These things happen.

Ambivalence: 70/30, 60/40, 50/50—but how the hell do they cope with the loss afterwards?

I dream I'm in labor. The midwife is busy so I don't disturb her and just push the baby out. It doesn't breathe at first so I rub it. It flinches and squirms. I call the midwife. It's a little girl. I wake up so happy.

## Five weeks later

A new year.

I take my black earring out. Sorry, baby, sorry you couldn't come.

I still feel as bad as I did five weeks ago.

How do I get out of this pit?

I wish I'd considered it more—just a joke between me and my friends—pregnant—how scary, how awful, always a chance. Then, how funny, it was me at lunch, at the folk festival, at my friend's, at the court, at the fete, at *Jesus Christ Superstar*. Me with the embryo sneakily embedded deep inside me; me with the choice; me caught between a rock and a hard place, between the devil and the deep blue sea; me both wanting and not wanting it; me trying to make the same rational, hard-headed decision while pregnant; me thinking an abortion was easy, being the cool feminist at the local abortion clinic, exercising my rights.

Why did that idiot woman not listen to me when I said I was ambivalent—telling me it was no reason not to do it?

The only thing that lifts my heart and draws me out of this sodden misery is the thought of having another baby ... I keep grabbing at that thought because if I don't grab at that I grab at nothing. I want to make the other choice. Go back.

If there is no baby, then I have to live with this. Take it away. I don't want this cup.

My daughter asks me if I'm dying.

I have spent the last five weeks in bed. Crying, sleeping, staring. One day I couldn't even take my younger daughter to school. I don't want to do anything. Now or ever. Everything is too hard—from thinking to eating. My head is full of clouds. My body made of lead. My heart overflowing.

I draw myself still in the sea. I have one hand on a life raft. It is keeping me afloat. In the life raft is a tiny, tiny baby.

I draw myself looking out into a completely arid desert—my life. There is nothing. Nothing to do. Nothing to hope for. Nothing to look forward to. Nothing to get up for.

He shows me the pumpkins growing in the garden. He tells me they're not setting and tears open a flower to pollinate it. I see a tiny pumpkin "set" under one flower. It's too much. Pollinating flowers with his fingers. Setting fruit.

Suddenly everything is too hard again. Too empty. Too heavy. Too bleak. Too blank.

### Five and three-quarter weeks later

I am plagued by thoughts of "getting the baby back." To choose again. To end this anguish.

My dialogues with my baby cover pages and pages:

Hey, baby, it's me again. I feel so much better when I talk to you. I feel some of that joy and brightness in my heart that I felt when you were inside me. It's a great comfort. I'm so sorry you couldn't come. I hope it didn't hurt you.

I dream I am bathing a little boy, about three or four. I dress him in his 'jammies but then I have to go out. Halfway through the night I remember I didn't empty the shower—it's a deep one. When I come home I can't see him. No one's seen him for a while. I'm too scared to look. I ask my daughter to look for him. She finds him. He has gone to sleep in the shower, lying in the warm water. Suddenly there are two naked babies under the water. We quickly get them out and I check for their pulses. We push and pump and the babies begin to cough and breathe. I am so glad they're alive and we've saved them. I wake up with a powerful sense of relief.

## Six weeks later

I keep thinking: "One day I will know whether or not to have another baby." If I think it's lost and gone forever I just lose my grip and slide back into this distress, denial, disappointment and devastation—this sick kind of slide, a gray slippery cliff of screaming horror.

We have sex for the first time since the abortion. It feels very weird and I am not in it. This is what caused all this. One orgasm and that was it. I cry and cry afterwards. I don't want this. Too bad. Too sad.

I ask my partner if he weighed Relief and Regret, which is greater.

"I have no relief," he says. "Except the money. I'm relieved we can give lots of things to the girls. Another baby might mean less money. Other than that, I have only regret."

I tell my elder daughter. While I cry and cry, she just listens and tells me she guessed. She seems to take it in her stride and tells me she wouldn't have minded another baby but she's not disappointed that she won't get to experience it.

"You might be later," I say.

I am relieved both by her reaction and that I've told her.

I go to the "body worker," the only referral I got from the clinic. She asks me to "be my uterus" and ask it what it needs. She takes me through a visualization of pregnancy, birth and a baby in my arms. She tells me to then give it away and say goodbye. I feel like she doesn't appreciate how difficult and serious this is for me.

I know I am in a terrible and precarious state and don't know how to help myself. $85.

Without rhyme or reason, I begin to make plans—how to make another bedroom, how to rearrange the house. I make an appointment with the gynecologist to ask her about treating thrush in pregnancy. I organize to have my rubella immunity checked. I contact "Foresight" to get information on pre-conception care and making healthy babies. If I don't have these "have a baby" plans, I have to face something I cannot bear to face.

### Seven-and-a-half weeks later

Since the abortion there has only been one voice—the voice that wanted it—shocked and outraged: "HOW DARE YOU? You have devastated and crushed me. How could you?"

> Take this cup away from me, for I don't want to taste its poison.
> (*Jesus Christ Superstar*)

I see a grief counselor. She gives me a single white rosebud for my baby. We talk about what the grief is about. $50. I have one more session with her and then she says she thinks relationship counseling would be more appropriate. She doesn't see how deep my agony is.

I have been dismissed.

Finally his patience wears thin and evaporates. He turns on me in a fury and tells me I have destroyed his chances of having a son and that he had no say in the decision.

Not have a say???!!!

If I ever hated and despised and loathed this man, it is now.

"You had a say, you ----. You said what I said: 'Yes. No. Too hard.'

"If you ever say I destroyed your chances of having a son again, then this relationship is finished. If you had said you'd truly wanted it and would commit to making changes in your life, I would have done it. But every plan was ultimately 'too hard.'

"Now you tell me you would never have babies with me because you hate me so much."

I decide I need time away. I will stay away every night and on the weekends. Whenever he's here, I won't be. Separate sleeping. No talking.

I need space—driving to the world out there—cool evenings, rivers, trees, the sea, the bush, the stars. I talk to my little lost baby and tell him again how sorry I am. How I couldn't bring him into this. I sense him near me—as he always will be—a spirit, an energy, something that touched me and spoke to me.

### Nine-and-a-half weeks later

I make a list of "Life post-dependent children" to try to remember what I had in mind before the pregnancy: study, work changes, music, learn to type—but I don't have any enthusiasm or energy for it anymore. And then I think, "A baby wouldn't stop me."

I have a rubella shot to boost my inadequate immunity. Just in case. Gives me three months enforced waiting. I decide that I will wait six months and see then how it all goes. My Chinese Birth Chart says a boy month is June—so June is when I'll decide. I have to give myself this possibility—it seems the only way to bear this.

### Ten weeks later

I write to the abortion clinic:

Dear Counselor,

It's been just over two months since my abortion. I hope you will share this with all the counselors at the clinic. I found it an extremely difficult decision to make and was very ambivalent right up to the time of the abortion. I believed it would be an easy thing to do and I would primarily feel relieved. I certainly didn't expect to feel completely devastated, cry for weeks on end and find myself swamped by full-blown grief. To try and make sense of such sadness and pain I [eventually found] a few books on pregnancy-related losses only to find grief following abortion covered in quite a lot of detail and certainly describing how I felt. Obviously I was not the only person to ever have reacted this way to an abortion ... Now I don't know if you deliberately don't mention the possibility of such a depth of grief because it hardly ever happens OR you are not aware of it happening. If the former, then I think women have a right to know ... If the latter, then I hope this letter ... will change that ... I realize a pro-abortion stand serves you and most women well and it is a stand with which I wholeheartedly agree, but the deep and strong feelings that go with an abortion, especially when the woman is ambivalent or unsure, must never be trivialized, denied or ignored.

\* \* \*

No-one understands that I miss that baby. He was so much a part of me. (*Ended Beginnings*)

That terrible surrender against my very soul to let them suck it out.

You assumed such proportions in my life baby. Try as I might, I can't shake you.

## Eleven weeks later

We thought about how it would be to have the baby.

We didn't think about how it would be to not have the baby.

I yearn and wonder and want it back.

How do I live with a wrong decision of such magnitude? Irredeemable.

I draw myself on a path blocked by an enormous boulder. There is no way over, under, around, through or back.

I make financial plans—to "afford" to have a baby. I make plans A-F and rank them in order of preference, 1-6. "C" is my No. 1 choice.

If he said, "I don't want to do this again, this was the right decision for us and I am not disappointed to not do it again," would I even consider these plans? I give the plans to him to consider and get back to me. He comes back with plan "C."

## Twelve weeks later

The counselor at the clinic responds by phone to my letter.

She says, "But you were sure about not wanting another baby."

I say: "Yes, I was sure about not wanting another baby, but I didn't know how it would feel to lose it."

I have thought since to say:

"Yes, I was sure about not wanting another baby, but I had one. To make the decision about another baby when you're not pregnant is one thing. To make the decision about another baby when you are pregnant can be a completely different thing."

"Yes, I was sure about not wanting another baby, but I was not sure about terminating the one I had."

"Yes, I was sure about not wanting another baby, but I thought having an abortion would be simple."

"Yes, but 'don't want a baby' doesn't necessarily mean 'want an abortion.'"

"Yes, but I didn't not want a baby enough to live with an abortion."

What if she had taken her cue?

But she didn't.

She gave me no indication that an abortion could be this hard. She gave me no warning that I would cry for weeks, sitting beside the toilet, unable to sleep or stop crying or get up. She told me ambivalence was common and that it would be okay and if I was sure about not wanting another baby, then abortion was the next step. Never did she point out, and never did I anticipate, that you also have to be clear about wanting an abortion, to live with one.

I put myself in their hands. The hands that say, "Don't want a baby? Here, simple, have an abortion." I thought I knew what they knew: "Abortion is simple. Don't bother about those tears and doubts, ignore those reservations. I hope you can live with an abortion because too bad if you can't—that's the only choice, if you don't want a baby."

I write another letter to the clinic [and make the points above].

My daughter says, "Having a baby would be better than having an abortion you weren't sure about and grieving so deeply. You might be sorry for the rest of your life about the abortion, but you wouldn't be sorry about having another baby. You won't have to end your childbearing years with an abortion. A baby might be the only way to feel happy again."

She likes the idea of a baby and is annoyed I didn't tell her before I had the abortion.

I worry all this grief will weaken me and I will get seriously ill. I see a Chinese herbalist. Her herbs might help but her advice and hardness doesn't. She tells me not to have a baby because my family is "stable." My family used to be stable. Now it has a wreck of a mother and no stability.

## Thirteen weeks later

A social worker says she will help me to end that pregnancy. That hits me like a blow. I don't want to end it. I want there still to be a chance.

I go to an anti-abortion group after I see an ad in the local paper talking about post-abortion grief. I don't realize at first that they are anti-abortion, and I don't really care. If this is someone that understands this, they'll do. She tells me such grief is common and can last for months or years. She says it's a shame I didn't get counseling to consider the impact of an abortion. She suggests rituals: name the baby, plant a tree, etc. She tells me some women do get pregnant again to try and deal with the feelings of loss, emptiness and grief.

That sounds like good news: "Lots of women feel like this," "Another pregnancy helps some women," "There is a way through this, not necessarily with a baby." She wants to show me how big a seven-week embryo is. That's when I remember why I hate anti-abortion groups.

Almost everyone I tell about the abortion speaks like I would have spoken: "A baby! Oh, my God! How could you? All that stress. How could you go back? I think you did the right thing. I don't know what I would do. You'll get over it."

They don't consider an abortion might be too hard to live with, despite the consequences that such a choice may take you where you never imagined.

Perhaps I should give myself a baby to get through this.

I tell the gynecologist I had an abortion and promptly burst into tears. She's always big into statistics and facts. She says: "About 10 percent of women feel very bad after an abortion. The ones that it's hardest for are women in stable relationships who don't want any more children but find themselves pregnant. Do you think about having a baby?"

"All the time," I say.

"Well, think about it. If you're this upset still, then it's not good."

"Do you know women who have done that?" I ask.

"Yes," she says.

"And how are they?"

"Good. It helps them. You may regret not doing it more than doing it."

I feel hugely comforted by this visit: for her facts, her simplicity, her directness, her treating me as a known statistic. I tell her I need some more counseling and ask can she refer me to anyone. She says "no" and gives me the impression there is only one way out. I also wonder where the "10 percent" statistic comes from—who has studied this? Nobody knows about me—I am not on any kind of register or record.

I dream someone I know is four months pregnant. I race into the clinic and say, "Wait! Do you know how big it is? How will you feel? An abortion can be a big deal." Her face changes from tears to relief and smiles.

I wake up crying and crying.

### Fifteen weeks later

I'm in a state of limbo. Of deadness, non-feeling, non-thinking. Of haziness, fuzziness, inertia. Two impossibilities—a baby or living with an abortion.

I sleep like I'm awake. I wake at four and lie awake—my mind feverish, tortured, agitated and without rest.

I think about the last and unexpected baby we made. Feels like it was wrenched away and I am still doubled over with the blow—winded and gasping.

I buy a totem tennis to whack. My litany of curses and abuse quickly dissolves into tears and grief for my lost baby. I fall to my knees and put my head on the ground. Please something, come from the earth and heal me.

I stand on the verandah and throw beer bottles into a plastic tub. There are not enough bottles in the world for me.

I want a chance to leave it there. I want more time to get my head around the idea of a baby. More time for my head to release my heart to its growing joy, happiness, passion and desire. I want to say, "Well, I just had to," and indulge myself. I want a chance to know deliciously and wildly every day that I don't have to decide. I want to take a leap of faith and give my heart free rein.

I receive two parcels today that capture my mood. One is from the abortion clinic: cold, dismissive, justifying, hard, emotionless, taking that same old line—we did, and continue to do, what we consider is the "right" thing. The other, from the social worker: a newspaper article by Drusilla Modjeska about the ambivalence and conundrum of abortion—"Don't kid ourselves that the fetus is less charged than it is." "Consider what it means that it is a fetus and not a tonsil that is coming out." I am reduced once more to sobbing collapse, whimpering through this overwhelming and penetrating sadness over what I lost, how my heart broke when I surrendered my embryo to their machine.

## Four months later

> From the beginning, the future child had been too powerful a presence for Herta, both consciously and unconsciously. In a certain sense, the image of the child refused to allow itself to be cancelled out. It had already established a place for itself in Herta's psychic life. I had the feeling that Herta had found it psychologically impossible to follow the course on which she seemed to have decided consciously. (*Abortion—Loss and Renewal in the Search for Identity*, Eva Pattis Zoja)

I thought I could remove this little aberration, this little hiccup in our comfortable existence and go back to normality. But I was destroying something that had already come into existence—that was already planted and rooted in our psyches.

## Four-and-a-half months later

I am more depressed than I have been so far. My days stretch endlessly and bleakly. There's nothing I want to do.

Please, God. Please help me.

I surf the net searching under "Post+Abortion." I find an article: "Women at Risk of Post-Abortion Trauma" by David C. Reardon. It identifies those women at high-risk of "Post-Abortion Trauma":

> Feel pressured into having the abortion, or feel uncertainty or ambivalence about their choice—the existence in the patient of any reluctance to have the abortion, or from a conflicting desire to keep the baby.

The article continues: "Feelings of Self-Betrayal":

> Women seeking abortion may feel maternal desires to protect their pregnancies ... Abortion is not a glorious right by which they are able to reclaim control of their lives ... She is internally divided by an emotional war within and against herself. On one side are her ... maternal desires. On the other side is her abortion experience which represents a choice to act against those feelings. These two sides are irreconcilable. The unresolved feelings which arise from this internal warfare can manifest themselves as a wide variety of psychological illnesses ... [Some] women develop an intense longing to become pregnant again in order to "make up" for the lost pregnancy.

Thus it is in anti-abortion literature that I find myself described and have my feelings validated.

## Five months later

Much as I thought I would be moving towards resolution and acceptance of the abortion, I seem to be inexorably and uncomprehendingly moving towards preparing my body and my mind for a baby: on this inevitable other course. I've done enough crying, farewelling, writing, talking, screaming, raging, smashing to begin to live with my choice, but to no avail.

He says, "I think we should have a baby."

And I feel so happy and all my fears are at bay.

If I don't have a baby, my life will change. There will be no more us. He, too, will become a casualty.

I don't want anything. Except death. Except my children. I want relief from this agony.

I write again to the clinic:

> ... I now know that for me to have an abortion without a "good" reason and without being sure, was a disaster for me. I had no "answer" afterwards to the part of me that wanted it ... Your biased, one-eyed approach did not serve me well. And now I must live with it, not you ...

## Six months later

I draw myself wedged between two solid rock walls that narrow in the center. I can't move forward or back. I tell a friend about how bad it might be to be pregnant. She says: "Could it be worse than this? At least you wouldn't be stuck."

In a dream I look in the fridge and am trying to remember something. Suddenly I do and I can't believe it. I've had the baby. It's here in the fridge and it's finally okay.

He says: "I wish you could forgive me. If you are going to hate me forever, then where does that leave me. I'd rather have a chance to make it up to you. Make something good of it."

What is there otherwise? Just ashes and ruins.

I feel dead. Like a stone. I trudge and drag. I have no spirit. I have lost heart for this life. I move like lead. I am lead. Nothing lifts my mood for long, except for the disillusioned dream of a baby.

I have terminated myself. I have surrendered and have not been the same since. I am dead.

The relationship counselor says: "Babies widen cracks and gaps, not fix them." I feel annihilated and broken and crawl like a slug.

When anyone says, "No," to a baby, I go into a state of great agitation and stress. When anyone says, "Yes," I feel okay.

I draw myself with a heavy cage around my heart, chained to a metal ring outside me. How long can you feel like a corpse before you become one?

And what of the territory of our relationship—a barren, empty, hateful, bitter, blaming, disappointed domain.

It's two weeks until June ovulation. Two weeks until I reach my own deadline—to accept that I've given it my best shot and it's time to decide.

All will be revealed.

I will do what I must do.

I will accept my task with courage and faith.

I must let this baby back. For myself. For my heart. For this emptiness. For this pain. For the loss. For my dead spirit. For letting them take it. For the space that was made. For the Wanting. For being haunted.

I feel open and yielding. I have no more resistance.

## Seven months later

I am ovulating. My temperature has spiked. A glorious rainbow arches across the sky. As I get home from work, I look to the night sky and invite the little spirit back.

When it comes time to have sex, I am swamped by a stony deadness. Time seems to be suspended. In a matter of minutes my life could be completely altered. I become frozen. Immobilized by the worst thoughts and fears—that huge bony head tearing out of my body, my age, school, prolonging something I sometimes can't wait to end. I lie comatose for over an hour.

I know I don't want to wake up to the same life in the morning. I want a new life. I want an end to this bleakness.

All night I think about sperm swimming into the deep recesses of my body.

The next day, I wake up and I remember. I know at once that my life has changed. I walk the dog and feel deeply contented, relieved, and happy. My inner self has been transformed. In the next week I finally send off my uni* application. I inquire about a computer course; I want to be able to type this in the Xmas holidays. There's a counseling course that sounds good.

It's like a spell has been broken. At once I feel released, unlocked, liberated.

How can it be that the seeds of my liberation come from being entrapped? The whole world opening again as I set out to tie myself irrevocably and totally.

Will it make us or break us? Now we are only broken.

Now it feels like enough to care for my children, to provide for them. To feather their nest until they leave me and I can fully embrace my own life and freedom.

With my first baby, I wanted to give birth without drugs.

With my second baby, I wanted a baby to love.

This time I want a pregnancy to keep. Something to end that awful despair and deadness, that devastatingly awful feeling of being winded and left vacant.

And if I don't conceive? Have I been healed enough to weather that pain now? To not be pregnant could plunge me back into emptiness, despair and bleakness.

I wake at night in a delirium of the blackest horrors—a baby choking and only I notice and get up to save it.

For the first time in over seven months I know there is something else, other than a lost pregnancy. I have been catapulted back to myself.

Two weeks after I ovulate, I start bleeding. ----! Did we leave it too late? Why didn't it work?

*university

**Eight months later**

I am ovulating again. This time we won't leave it so late.

It's Day 30 of my cycle. My breasts are sore and I can't wait to know. The test is positive. I feel quietly, delightedly, irrationally happy.

**Nine months later**

I have an ultrasound at seven weeks and see the tiny embryo. It is 6.5 millimeters long and has a heartbeat. Its heart, that will beat all its life, has already started. I cry for my little embryo, and for myself.

At eight-and-a-half weeks, I have some bleeding. "Aren't you staying with me, little baby?" I want an ultrasound to see if it's still alive, but the doctor says, "No, go home to bed."

**Ten months later**

The doctor says, "Have you had a pregnancy test? Have you had a scan?*"

My heart sinks. There is no baby. Only a seven-week sac and a blood clot. It must have died when I started bleeding.

It takes a while to sink in. The Fetal Welfare Lab don't know about miscarriages and shuffle me off down to Emergency to book a D&C. I am stunned.

No, no, no—not a dead baby. Now I have to wake up and not be pregnant tomorrow. I feel too old. Is there another chance or has time run out? I feel anxious and my confidence is badly shaken. I feel old and empty and barren and foolish.

The next day I hope it will come out, but it doesn't. I don't want a general [anesthetic]. I ring an abortion clinic and ask them if they'll do a D&C. No problem.

I have bloodstains on the inside of my legs that stay there for days—all that's left of my baby.

I am advised to wait one cycle before trying to conceive again. I have a sneaking suspicion, going on my past post-abortion bleeding, that it will take my body at least three cycles to recover.

I am consumed by a sudden desire to knit booties. Knitting a "baby space."

**Eleven months later**

It is spring—and the feeling of light and warmth and new life is hard to resist. I look forward to trying to conceive again. I want to

*ultrasound

be filled with spring. I want to be filled with life and warmth and spirit and magic and sparkle and glitter and fizz.

I meet a woman at the pool who is 40+ and has a six-week-old baby.

"I had to have this baby," she says, "because of the unresolved grief of my miscarriage. I didn't want to look back in ten years and wish I had."

This waiting is agony. Waiting to see if I'm pregnant. Waiting to see if it stays there. Waiting to see if it's born alive ...

I'm not sure how to weather this waiting or if I can. Looking forever for traces of blood. My temperature starts to drop. Bleeding starts on Day 32. Perhaps I should have waited those three cycles.

I want to conceive and fear I won't.

* * *

*Lee gave birth to a son in Oct. 1999. In a letter written shortly after his birth, she said: "I feel the most incredible and profound sense of relief. We both spent the first two weeks crying at how we nearly didn't have the baby and how we'd finally made the right decision ... it seems absolutely like the only thing I could have done—to heal, to soften, to make a new start, to begin to forgive ... From great grief, pain, rage, regret has come new life, new hope, a second chance, and a beautiful baby."*

# AFTERWORD

*[S]logans may become substitutes for analysis*
Rebecca Albury[47]

Giving Sorrow Words is replete with the stories of women who have been dismissed with a slogan: women whose abortion experience has not been analyzed because of the silencing power of the abortion-rights mantra.

But beyond the slogan are the women who were desperate, pressured, harangued, bullied, pushed, pulled, shoved, cornered, abandoned, cheated, and left damaged and desolate. Beyond what Naomi Wolf has called the "free market rhetoric about abortion,"[48] are significant numbers of wounded women.

While the primary aim of this book is to tell the grief story, there are common themes that emerge across the accounts in these pages which warrant comment. What follows is by no means an exhaustive list of the issues they raise.

## Disclosure

Concealing information relevant to a woman's decision-making and future health should be recognized as an act of coercion. Deceptive information presented as fact, for example, that post-abortion trauma is a "myth," also acts coercively on a client. If a woman chooses abortion without having been apprised of the facts about potential harm and suffering, she has not chosen freely: the decision-making process has been rendered defective. The normal requirements for informed consent prior to undergoing a medical procedure should not be suspended when that procedure is a termination of pregnancy.

Informed consent means that, prior to the decision to have an abortion, the patient must be fully advised of all physical and psychological risks associated with abortion, even if the doctor considers those risks minimal.

In 1992, the High Court of Australia in *Rogers v. Whitaker*[49] stated expressly that every patient must be provided with complete information, including the most remote risk, flowing from or which may flow from the proposed medical procedure. In that case, a specialist was held to be negligent for not advising a woman

of a one in 14,000 risk of incurring blindness from an eye operation. She was the one in 14,000.

The ruling effectively means that a decision to undergo a medical procedure is void unless it is made on the basis of relevant
information.

But in the field of abortion provision, there seems to be an attitude that women need to be "protected" from such information,
that they might be confused by material other than that which
presents abortion as quick, easy and virtually risk-free.

The U.K. Commission of Inquiry into The Physical and Psycho-
Social Effects of Abortion on Women, referred to previously,
heard from a Dr. Alan Rogers, Consultant Gynecologist at Marie
Stopes Park View Clinic, who said that he was confident he could
"tell" when a woman was ready for an abortion. The Commission's
report stated: "We were unable to establish how much information
is actually given to women at Dr. Rogers' clinic prior to abortion."[50]

A doctor who said he could just "tell" when a woman was
"ready" for any other medical procedure, without having first provided her with information about that procedure and its possible
risks, would be reminded that the days of "doctor-knows-best" are
over.

Other medical practitioners, in Australia and overseas, have noted with concern the dearth of information about risks provided to
women considering abortion. Some have called for mandatory
reporting of abortion complications.[51]

It is not enough to tell a woman she might "feel sad for a few
days" and that such feelings are "hormonal and will pass," which was
the reductionist message on abortion after-effects given to most of
this book's contributors.[52] She needs to know she might experience
what the women in this book experienced—a long-lasting mental
and emotional backlash, and, in some cases, significant physical
ramifications—even if the clinic staff don't think these possibili-
ties worth mentioning.

Women who leave their beds at night to breastfeed a "crying"
(aborted) baby, or who buy teddy bears they pretend are their
babies, or who cut themselves with razors, or whose bodies cannot
sustain future pregnancies, are suffering what may be described as
a form of socially and medically sanctioned repression. The
repression began in the clinic or hospital when they were denied
information about possible outcomes of abortion, and continued
when they were denied a forum through which to address the toll
abortion has taken on their lives.

The filtering of information to suit a particular agenda must stop. As Lee wrote to the clinic where her abortion was carried out: "Your biased, one-eyed approach did not serve me well. And now I must live with it, not you."

An informed woman should not be seen as a threat. Women should be made aware of their legal rights to pursue damages for physical/psychological harm suffered of which they were not forewarned. A number of Australian women are taking legal action for the trauma they suffered and were not warned of.[53] "Ellen" received an out-of-court settlement in 1998 in the County Court of Victoria in an action for damages for psychological trauma suffered following an abortion at Melbourne's Royal Women's Hospital,[54] as did a woman known as "Cynthia" in 1999 following an action in the District Court of New South Wales against a Sydney clinic.[55] (Malpractice actions against abortion providers are listed in the endnotes).

In an article arguing the need for informed choice, including information about "fetuses, complications, even long-term grief," pro-choice Canadian writer Lindalee Tracey, who has had an abortion, states: "We shouldn't flinch from what it is we don't want to know. No matter how politically inconvenient."[56]

"Politically inconvenient" information would certainly also include that on the link between abortion and suicide and, even more controversially, what appears to be a link between abortion and breast cancer. In a study reported in the *British Medical Journal* researchers in Finland found: "The suicide rate after an abortion was three times the general rate and six times that associated with birth ... Suicides are more common after a miscarriage and especially after an induced abortion than in the general population."[57]

Cancer studies have demonstrated an abortion/breast cancer link. Of the 31 studies published worldwide, 25 link abortion to an increased risk of breast cancer.[58]

The "Information Paper on Termination of Pregnancy in Australia," cited "A recent editorial in the *JAMA* [*Journal of the American Medical Association*]" which, the authors of the information paper claimed, "concludes that, at the present time, there is not sufficient evidence to require the practitioner to warn the woman of a possible increase in risk of breast cancer if she terminates her pregnancy unless the woman herself raises the issue."[59]

This is strange wording indeed—and not only because it isn't actually what the *JAMA* article said. Leaving that aside for now, do the paragraph's authors mean to infer that there is "sufficient evidence" if the woman does raise the issue? And if there is a risk, even a small one, shouldn't a woman have a right to be informed of it? And why should the onus be on her to ask for it in the first place? Is this what the report's authors—most of whom are involved in abortion provision or advocacy—really think: don't tell her unless she asks?

Dr. Janet Daling, a pro-choice epidemiologist whose landmark study linking abortion with breast cancer found that women under 18 who had an abortion after more than eight weeks gestation had eight times the risk of developing breast cancer by age 45,[60] has commented on the influence of politics on breast cancer research:

> If politics get involved in science, it will really hold back the progress that we make. I have three sisters with breast cancer, and I resent people messing with the scientific data to further their own agenda, be they pro-choice or pro-life. I would have loved to have found no association between breast cancer and abortion, but our research is rock solid, and our data is accurate. It's not a matter of believing. It's a matter of what is.[61]

## Unwanted Abortion

We hear a lot about "unwanted pregnancy," but nothing about "unwanted abortion;" much about the "right to choose," but not the right to refuse: the right to resist, to step back, to say "no"— and for that decision to be respected, even if verbalized only moments before the operation.

"No" means "no" when a woman is the subject of an unwelcome sexual advance. But, according to Laurel Guymer, the former abortion clinic nurse quoted in the introduction, "no" was not always given the same respect in the abortion clinic setting:

> What if they said "no" when entering the operating room? In this instance I felt compelled to reassure them they didn't have to go through with it and walked them back to the change room. This was not welcomed by my colleagues at the clinic. I was reminded that this is a business and any slowing in the production line costs money. Constant threats were made that the anesthetist had another list at another hospital and any more discussion with the uncertain woman was wasting precious time. Their patronizing remarks that some women will never be 100 percent sure, and that I should encourage them to go on and get the abortion over quickly, were not comforting. I could no longer participate.

For many women, the abortion was not wanted but undergone

due to coercion applied by others and by circumstances. There seems to be no real screening process to protect women from unwanted abortion. If the woman is aborting at the direction of another person and the abortion provider ignores evidence of this (the force being applied by Mary's boyfriend, for example, should have been obvious to the counselor), then they are clearly complicit in forced abortion. Advocates of women harmed by abortion in the U.S. speak of unwanted abortion in the context of "wrongful death" and are examining litigation options on this basis.

## Recognition of Social/Cultural Influences

Women often felt pressured by their financial circumstances to terminate a pregnancy they would have preferred to have continued. As Elizabeth Moore Sobo has pointed out, "Poverty itself negates the right to make free choices."[62]

A New South Wales study of 2,000 women found two in three gave a reason for aborting as, "Can't afford a baby." (Sixty percent named financial reasons, 38 percent said having a baby would change their life in undesirable ways and 29 percent said they did not want to be single mothers. Participants were invited to give more than one reason for having an abortion.)[63]

The workplace has been shown to be unfriendly to pregnant women. Overt or implied pressures have been placed on women whose pregnancy is seen as inconvenient by an employer. Differential bargaining power, the casualization of the female workforce,* the large numbers of women engaged in insecure employment, inflexible working hours and the fact that women continue to be paid less than men[64] combine to erode a woman's ability to be equitably treated in the workplace.

A *Sunday Age* editorial recently observed: "Despite the great influx of women in the workforce and the growing number of educated women, the bottom of the work pyramid is disproportionately female."[65]

Feminist historian Marilyn Lake has written recently of the masculine nature of the workforce:

> Women have taken on the world, but the world is still, by and large, structured on men's terms. Women have won equal opportunity and the formal right of equal pay, but the organization of the workplace is still geared to the masculine experience of autonomy,

---

*lack of full-time employment

mobility and freedom from domestic responsibilities.[66]

Sex Discrimination Commissioner Susan Halliday told a parliamentary committee of cases of women aborting to keep their jobs:

> Sadly, we see the practical, day to day evidence where an employer goes in and collects the information from the Employment Advocate, bins it* on the way out, never talks to the employees about their rights and responsibilities. When you have women in that situation who do not speak the language, who are not unionized, who cannot access a working women's center, what happens? Where do they go? What do they do? In some of the sadder cases, to keep their job, they terminate their pregnancy.[67]

The Human Rights and Equal Opportunity Commission's *Pregnant and Productive: Report of the National Pregnancy and Work Inquiry*, authored by Halliday, found discrimination, along with inadequate maternity leave, was forcing women to limit their children to one, if any. The report found the careers of pregnant women were being sidelined or terminated, and women with the potential to become pregnant were denied work and training.[68]

The New South Wales Anti-Discrimination Board report, *Why don't you ever see a pregnant waitress? Summary Report of the Findings of the Inquiry into Pregnancy Related Discrimination*, found that: "... some employers still refuse to employ women of childbearing age and include questions on plans for children and contraceptives in application forms and interviews."[69]

Women are less able than men to negotiate work times, with only 19 percent able to make daily variations compared to 24 percent of men.[70]

Actor Hunter Tylo was fired from "Melrose Place" because she was pregnant. Her pregnancy discrimination lawsuit alleged that one of the producers of the Fox TV show had said: "Why doesn't she just go out and get an abortion? Then she can work."[71]

Migrant groups say the imposition in Feb. 1997 of a two-year waiting period for migrants before they are entitled to receive social security benefits has caused severe hardship to many women and their families, who find themselves in severe financial hardship after arrival.[72] It is not difficult to see the sorts of pressures denial of these benefits could place on a pregnant migrant woman.

Women pregnant with babies believed to be abnormal are making decisions in a climate where abortion after pre-natal diagnosis

---

*throws it away

is regarded as a positive option—not only for themselves but for society at large.[73] A paper on Down Syndrome detection, presented at a conference at Westmead Hospital in New South Wales in 1998, included a "Cost Benefit Analysis" table which calculated the cost of caring for Trisomy 21 children, as against the cost of screening: "$47 million spent saves $1136 million [bold and underlined]" was the conclusion.[74]

The recently exposed widespread sterilization of women with disabilities also reflects an underlying view that to allow such women to have children would be breeding further disability, that they must be prevented from bringing "another one like them" into the world.[75]

In recent times, women have spoken of the pressure applied to them to undergo "fetal reduction" procedures in multiple pregnancies which were a result of fertility treatments.[76]

HIV-infected women are another vulnerable group pressured to abort their pregnancies. Ms. Vivienne Munro, an HIV-positive representative, says pregnant HIV-positive women face discrimination: "There is pressure to terminate and to have sterilizations."[77] A study conducted by the National Center for HIV Epidemiology and Clinical Research in Sydney found almost 50 percent of HIV-positive women who became pregnant had terminated the pregnancy.[78]

In the New South Wales study of 2,000 women cited earlier, 29 percent of respondents said they did not want to be single mothers.[63] Though perhaps not quite as despised as in the past, the term "single mother" continues to be used as a sneer. Single mothers, or those potentially so, are another group particularly vulnerable to cost-benefit type assessments of the "best thing" in "their case."

Single mothers continue to struggle. They are now the largest social group living in poverty.[79] A high proportion of those who are custodial parents do not receive maintenance* income for their children.[80]

Further hardships to custodial parents—mainly women—were highlighted during debate over changes to the Child Support Scheme.[81] Sole parent** groups also claim 755,000 children will be seriously disadvantaged by a decision to exempt child support payments from GST-related indexation.[82] They are also concerned by potential cuts to benefits foreshadowed in a discussion paper released by Family and Community Services Minister Jocelyn

*child support      **single parents

Newman in Sept. 1999[83] and by a federal government proposal to withdraw pensions* for sole parents once their youngest child reaches the age of 12.[84]

In 1990, single women or women with dependents comprised 47 percent of households in public rental housing.[85] The Australian Institute of Health and Welfare concluded in 1994 that "the demand for low cost housing considerably exceeds supply."[86] There were 154,800 households which indicated they were registered on a waiting list for rental housing from a State or Territory housing authority. The majority on waiting lists were sole parent families (29 percent) and couples with children (27 percent).[87]

Those who try to break out of the poverty trap find childcare fees are too high to make their low-paid jobs worthwhile. *The Age* recently reported on the case of a 28-year-old single mother with two children. "When she found work as a casual** clerk, the cost of child care for the week was almost equal to her wage. And there was another catch. She needed to repay social security for exceeding her $100-per-week income limit." That left her with $37 after working for six days.[88]

Observes Marilyn Lake: "The situation of single mothers could become dire in the years ahead ... Unable to pay childcare fees, they will become trapped in what is left of the welfare state."[89] Cutbacks to public spending on health and social welfare services also have a disproportionate effect on single mothers.

Young single mothers who continue with pregnancies others believe they should not have continued bear the brunt of the welfare backlash. Contrary to popular belief, less than 10 percent of single-parent families fit the stereotype of the young unmarried mother. About half are the result of the breakdown of marriages and de facto relationships.[90] Deserted women are a significant proportion of recipients, though this fact seems often forgotten in the welfare debate which focuses on stereotypes such as "paying schoolgirls to have babies."[91]

Researcher Barbara Riley Smith comments:

> The myths about sole-parent pensioners are staggering; that most are young girls who get pregnant to get the pension; that abuse of the system is widespread. Yet only four percent of sole-parent pensioners are teenagers ... The vast majority ... are more than 25 and have been married. Typically, they need the pension for two or three years to get on their feet after divorce.[92]

*government assistance    **part-time

Even some pro-life people, particularly in the U.S., support proposals to remove welfare payments to single mothers, even though doing so could, theoretically, increase the number of abortions. They decry that single mothers frequently live in poverty, yet want to remove the little public sustenance they receive.[93]

Women have been abandoned to their autonomy in the abortion decision: "It's your choice," "You're on your own." The same attitude carries over to the woman who chooses to continue a pregnancy. She finds she's on her own in that as well.

Women should not be pitted against their pregnancies because of structural and other biases.

There should be a greater focus on measures to ensure an end to discrimination against women in benefits, housing, work, or education. Ramona Koval wrote in the *Weekend Australian*: "Why should you [a 17-year-old] be denied the chance of completing your education at the whim of anti-abortion zealots?"[94] Name-calling aside, why should you [a 17-year-old] be denied the chance of completing your education because you don't "choose" abortion?

But there are other, more subtle, social and cultural influences operating on a woman contemplating what to do with her unplanned pregnancy. The associated costs of having children are high and rising.[95] Body image—the *Beauty Myth* exposed by Naomi Wolf—plagues many. Young women in particular, fearing significant alteration in body shape as a result of pregnancy, can feel pressured to access abortion to avoid this unnecessary weight gain. Three women who aborted and later regretted it told me one of the factors in their decision was a fear of "getting fat."

In *Disenfranchised Grief: A study of the long-term emotional effects of abortion*, Jo Hutton succinctly captures some of these more subtle influences on a woman contemplating an unplanned pregnancy:

> [Abortion is] practiced in a cultural milieu which privileges rationality, individuality and control ... the modern technology of abortion functions to maintain modern women's self-identity as a person in control of her reproductive function and her life ... The pregnant body can be experienced as out of control and dangerous by women who may fear loss of attractiveness and sexuality, weight gain and changes in shape. Pregnancy brings fears of loss of self, of life being never the same again. Anxieties, common in pregnancy, are multiplied in the post-modern era ... In a society which values control and rationality, an unplanned pregnancy may be seen by some women as a moral and personal failure.[96]

In *Sex and Destiny*, Germaine Greer also observes the way idealized conceptions of the female body can affect the way a pregnant woman can feel about herself:

> Perhaps more difficult to bear than the physical discomforts of pregnancy is the psychic discomfort of feeling unattractive. The feeling [has more to do with] the accepted aesthetic of female appearance ... The preferred shape of Western women, narrow-hipped and small-breasted, is desirable partly because of its denial of fecundity.[97]

These direct and indirect influences which act on many women in their resort to abortion must be ameliorated. Options must be provided for the pregnant woman who feels constrained by a lack of them. The ready availability of abortion should not be used as an excuse to tell women: "Don't bother me with your problems."

As one woman who asked not to be named wrote:

> Anxiously you enter the medical system in a state emotionally unable to make a clear decision. Guidance is needed, not some medical magic—you come in pregnant and go home unpregnant. Women are not machines you can clear of a mechanical fault: we have emotions and needs which have to be addressed by the medical profession.

### End the Isolation of Motherhood

Pregnancy and the rearing of children has become privatized as a sense of community has been eroded by many factors. Where once the burdens of raising children and the demands of domestic life were shared by extended families and tight-knit communities, many mothers face these challenges alone, feeling cut-off and detached from the broader community.

Wrote feminist legal theorist Catharine MacKinnon:

> Women who bear children are constrained by a society that does not allocate resources to assist combining family needs with work outside the home. In the case of men, the two are traditionally tailored to a complementary fit, provided that a woman is available to perform the traditional role that makes that fit possible ... When women begin to "show," they are often treated as walking obscenities unfit for public presentation. Inside the home, battering of women may increase during pregnancy. Pornography makes pregnancy into a sexual fetish, conditioning male sexual arousal to it, meaning targeting sexualized hatred against it.[98]

Jessie Bernard, in *The Future of Parenthood*, expounded on the hazards to mother and child of the institutionalized role of motherhood:

> The way we institutionalize motherhood in our society—assigning sole responsibility for child care to the mother, cutting her off from the easy help of others in an isolated household, requiring round-the-clock tender loving care, and making such care her exclusive activity—is not only new and unique, but not even a good way for either women or ... for children. It may, in fact, be the worst. It is as though we had selected the worst features of all the ways motherhood is structured around the world and combined them to produce our current design.[99]

In *Sex and Destiny*, Germaine Greer has also commented on the disconnected, insulated nature of modern mothering:

> The woman who becomes a mother suffers a crushing loss of status; as a "patient" she was at the bottom end of the health professionals' social hierarchy. At home she is a solitary menial. Fewer and fewer women can expect the support of another family member during their maternal isolation, and fewer still could expect or would welcome the help and support of neighbors. Modern dwellings are arranged in such a way that housewives carry out identical tasks in isolation from one another, in suburbs which are deserted by day except for their lonely selves and their babies.[100]

Greer observes earlier in the same work:

> If ours was a society which welcomed and enjoyed children, and if each parturient woman was surrounded by people who wanted her child even more than she did, she could ease her feelings of responsibility and inadequacy.[101]

It is time society recognized the necessity of better support structures for the primary caregiver (female or male) and that more was done to engender communitarian obligations of care and justice to ensure shared responsibilities for the raising of children.

The task of mothering needs positive reinforcement. Otherwise, as Greer observes, "women will cease to do it ..."[102]

### Reexamination of Sex-based Inequalities

In light of Rebecca Albury's astute observation at the beginning of this afterword that slogans can become a substitute for analysis, it is difficult then to understand her labeling of those who criticize abortion practice and point out sex-based inequalities underlying it as "anti-feminist." She writes:

Anti-feminists have argued that women are exploited by abortion itself. They say that open access to abortion makes it hard for women to continue accidental pregnancies; a man, they argue, can avoid the responsibility for his sexual activity by insisting that the woman terminate the pregnancy as a condition of continuing the relationship.[103]

Much of this statement rings with solid feminist—not anti-feminist—analysis. Catharine MacKinnon, for example, has drawn attention to the unequal conditions under which women become pregnant.[104] Abortion, she argues, was legalized to serve a man's requirements for sexual access to women and to enable him to be free of the inconvenient results of that access; that is, children. "[W]hen convenient to do away with the consequences of sexual intercourse (meaning children), women get abortion rights. Women can have abortions so men can have sex," MacKinnon writes.[105] She continues:

> Women often do not control the conditions under which they become pregnant; systematically denied meaningful control over the reproductive uses of their bodies through sex, it is exceptional when they do. Women are socially disadvantaged in controlling sexual access to their bodies through socialization to customs that define a woman's body as for sexual use by men. Sexual access is regularly forced or pressured or routinized by denial ... Poverty and enforced economic dependence undermine women's physical integrity and sexual self-determination.[106]

In MacKinnon's view, abortion actually demonstrates the reality and scope of women's oppression. She employs Adrienne Rich's depiction in *Of Woman Born* (1976) of abortion as violence against women.[107]

Because abortion is born of a woman's inequality, MacKinnon urges action to reverse that inequality. "Those who think that fetuses should not have to pay with their lives for their mothers' inequality might direct themselves to changing the conditions of sex inequality that make abortions necessary," she states.[108]

The stories contained in this book raise large and difficult questions about the way males continue to be raised. There are many examples here, and in other places, of male domination over a woman and over her desire for the baby she wants to bring to birth.[109]

## More Research on Post-abortion Grief

The public health significance of the psychological effects of abortion must be examined.

Steinberg, writing in the *American Journal of Law and Medicine* in 1989, stated: "We must examine the impact on these women because their numbers are so great and because the political and social volatility of this issue locks so many of them into silence."[110] More than a decade later and these women remained "locked into silence."

Abortion has for too long been a loss negated by society. Speckhard and Rue have observed that: "Post traumatic stress is more damaging and more difficult to treat if those around the affected person tend to deny the existence and/or significance of the stressor."[111]

A presumption exists that those who did not return to the abortion clinic or hospital afterwards must have experienced no after-effects, an assumption that women who don't complain about their experience must have benefited from abortion.

It is also irresponsible to assume that abortion will solve problems without causing additional ones. Jane, the young Melbourne woman quoted in the introduction about how she wished she'd done what she wanted, not what others wanted, wrote:

> Looking back now, if I had have known then what emotional
> torment I would go through as a result of having the abortion,
> I would never have gone through with it. I told her that I still
> didn't know whether I could go ahead with the abortion, but she
> just fobbed it off by convincing me that this was the best thing
> for everyone.

But those who raise questions about the effect of abortion on a woman's well-being are labeled as heretics, traitors to the cause of abortion rights. Tracey, quoted earlier, makes the observation:

> In the rush to be right and dominate public opinion, we lose the
> chance for greater insight and an opportunity to improve pre- and
> post-operative care for women wanting abortions. Women who may
> question the blob theory, who may experience grief after an abortion,
> are silenced by the fear of losing their membership in the club.[112]

Unfortunately, there has been significant resistance to further research into post-abortion trauma from supporters of abortion choice.

## Abortion as Disposal

In their fascinating and compelling history of the treatment of single mothers in Australia, Shurlee Swain and Renate Howe document the removal of women with distended abdomens and without wedding rings to faraway places where the mark of their moral failure could be hidden:

> Where other pregnant women were given specialized care to ensure the safe delivery of a healthy child, single mothers were isolated from society and subjected to a period of often punitive reformation in order to cleanse them of their sins.[113]

Teichman, cited in Swain, observed that, at least until the 1960s, "the shame of being a single mother was the worst possible shame a woman could suffer. The disgrace spread to all her immediate kin who were expected to purge their shame by expelling the guilty woman from the family or by hiding her away somewhere. Secrecy about illegitimate birth was absolutely mandatory."[114]

Perhaps today, rather than being dispatched to a maternity home to conceal her secret, a woman is dispatched to a different building (the abortion factory, Laurel Guymer and her colleagues called it): a place where she won't have to stay long but which will achieve the same purpose—concealment. Willingly or unwillingly, but most likely poorly informed, she goes to have removed the outward manifestation of the disgrace of a pregnancy that was not perfectly planned and timed, that didn't fit with the proper order of things. The swelling uterus need never meet public view: the woman is invisible as a pregnant woman or as a woman who once was pregnant. No one else need be embarrassed, inconvenienced, put out.

### Allowing Women to Explore the Meaning of "The Baby"

The stories related in this book demonstrate that a woman must also be permitted expression of her desire to reflect on the meaning of "the baby." Many women told me they had tried to do this during pre-termination counseling but received curt, dismissive answers: "a scrap of paper," "a 10-cent piece," "just cells," "nothing there."

"The doctor said: 'Don't worry, it's not formed till after 12 weeks.' Then I saw the *Human Body* program [on the ABC]. I would not have gone ahead if I'd been told the truth about the formation of the baby," said Sue, from New South Wales.

Naomi Wolf has written about the trivialization of the fetus— which she labels the *fetus-is-nothing paradigm*.[115] A New Zealand woman involved in post-abortion counseling and who has had an abortion says the fetus is the "F-word" of the abortion establishment.[116]

Laurel Guymer was disturbed by the deception of women who asked for information about their fetuses[117] after the abortion. She told me:

> When the women woke up in recovery they often whispered to me, "Was it a girl or a boy?" I was instructed to tell them it was too small to know for sure. But occasionally a woman would ask, "Can I see the fetus?" The standard line in an abortion setting was "a pregnancy is a bunch of cells, too early to differentiate" (unlike in IVF, where the women having miscarriages at earlier stages are told they have lost the "baby"). But some women insisted on seeing the fetus, so we would check how many weeks they were and select the appropriate pot off the shelf.
>
> None of the containers had a fetus in them, nothing recognizable to the naked eye at least. The contents resembled pavlova mixture: egg whites stiffly beaten, floating in a clear solution. They never saw their own fetus. It had been dismantled by the abortion procedure, suctioned into a glass container, then strained like peas in the slush room, the foot measured to estimate gestation, then finally discarded in the biohazardous waste.[118]

For many contributors, abortion had a personal moral dimension not necessarily linked to a religious background. They sought answers for their moral and spiritual pondering, but the abortion assessment process did little to facilitate these deeper questions— and they were not allowed the time.

Genevieve had cancelled two appointments at the abortion clinic in Canberra. Before the next appointment, she spent four hours walking around the clinic, her mind battered by conflicting thoughts, incapable of making a decision. In a submission she forwarded to me, written for the government-commissioned report "Services for Termination of Pregnancy," she described trying to express her deep inner conflict:

> I collapsed in sheer exhaustion. I told her that I had been outside for hours. I cried hysterically, curled over with my head in my hands on my knees. I said that "I feel like I'm depriving my child of life." Our conversation was cut short by the doctor. The pressure was on. I stopped crying in disbelief when the counselor told me that if I was going to abort then I would have to do it right now. The counselor said, "Look, I'll give you five minutes to think about it and when I come back, I want your answer." I couldn't believe it. Now I was going into a state of panic and shock. I could now

barely speak ... The counselor glared at me, sighed a deep sigh and
impatiently said, "Look, they're all waiting for you, you know ..."
They seemed angry at me. They were sick of me and in the end I
weakly obeyed their commands.[119]

Genevieve's expression of deep psychic pain—she felt she was
"depriving my child of life"—was dismissed. There was no time
for philosophical ruminations, nothing would be allowed to hold
up the process.

Lee also, in retrospect, wished others had facilitated her need to
reflect more on what the loss of the baby might mean to her, as
she wrote in the story you've just read: "I wish someone had said,
'There would be losses having a baby, but don't underestimate the
loss of having an abortion.'"

Writer Esther Harding, an associate of Carl Jung, believes interfering with pregnancy touches a woman at the deepest level of her
being:

> Inasmuch as there were no external results, it might be supposed
> that nothing of importance could be happening within. Yet even
> where the external situation has been passed over merely as a dis-
> agreeable necessity, much like an illness, its inner effects do not so
> pass. Any other minor operation is an experience which can be
> accepted at its face value, and after the pain, anxiety and convales-
> cence are over it falls into the background, leaving no long train of
> inner consequences. But an interference with pregnancy does not
> act this way, for pregnancy involves more than physical changes.
> The bearing of children is a biological task. The roots of the
> maternal instinct reach back into the deepest layers of a woman's
> nature, touching forces of which she may be profoundly uncon-
> scious. When a woman becomes pregnant these ancient powers stir
> within her, whether she knows it or not, and she disregards them
> only at her peril.[120]

## The Need for Resolution

If a woman has not been allowed reflection on the meaning of the
baby in the pre-termination process, she may well need to reflect
afterwards. Contributors to this book described many ways of trying to understand what happened to them, searching for a place of
"healing" or "resolution" or "peace."

Some, such as Anne, Jill, Marion, Liz, Sue (the pregnant homeless teenager), and Anita found it through a religious experience. In
the words of Sue: "... my Father in heaven who gave me my life

back, forgave me and helped me forgive myself." Anita wrote that she received "forgiveness from Him whom I offended and so my wounds have healed." Liz found healing after the experience of holding another woman's dying newborn baby and kissing her goodbye. "I felt elated, not because the baby had died but because I was there at her passing. This was a closing in God's hands," she wrote. She also had a commemoration service for her own baby. Another woman, Lyn, found her "conscience started getting more and more overwhelmed" and she thought she was "going mad" until she "finally found something that dealt with the pain in my heart." "It wasn't until I said, 'I had an abortion and it was wrong,' that's where the healing came for me," she wrote.

For others, comfort came through being part of a special ceremony for those who have lost babies. Some "named" their babies and wrote them a letter. Asphyxia created, and Justine adopted, a grave, to have a visible, meaningful place to reflect on their babies. Others, such as Barbara, became involved in support services for pregnant women. Marion became a counselor with a post-abortion counseling service. Then there were those who, like Catherine, found resolution through long and intense therapy. For Lee, resolution came in the birth of another baby.

All contributors had in common a need to find a way through crushing grief and to give expression to their mourning and sense of bereavement. A few were able to find a pathway to resolution; others still look for it.

But many more have not been permitted expression of their pain, nor been allowed to seek a way through it. They remain locked in, shut up, shut out of the discussion. Surely the time is long due that they too be encouraged to speak, to give their sorrow words and so help resolve their grief.

# WHERE TO FIND HELP

## ORGANIZATIONS

The following organizations have experience in the area of post-abortion recovery.

**Rachel's Vineyard Ministries**
1-877-HOPE-4-ME (1-877-467-3463)
www.rachelsvineyard.org

**Hope Alive** (Canada)
(250) 642-1848
www.messengers2.com
Email: iiplcarr@islandnet.com

**Hope Alive** (USA)
www.HopeAliveUSA.org
Email: HopeAliveUSA@aol.com

**National Office of Post Abortion Reconciliation & Healing**
1-800-5WE-CARE (national referral number)
www.noparh.org

**P.A.C.E. (Post Abortion Counseling and Education)**
1-800-395-HELP
www.optionline.org

**Ramah International**
(941) 473-2188
www.ramahinternational.org

**Victims of Choice**
1-888-267-3998
www.victimsofchoice.org

## WEB SITES

**After Abortion**
www.afterabortion.info
www.unchoice.info

**American Victims of Abortion**
www.nrlc.org/outreach/victims.html

## BOOKS

James Burtchaell, *Rachel Weeping* (San Francisco: Harper & Rowe, 1984)

Jack Hayford, *I'll Hold You in Heaven: Healing and Hope for the Parent Who Has Lost a Child Through Miscarriage, Stillbirth, Abortion or Early Infant Death* (Ventura, CA: Regal Books, 2003)

Nancy Michels, *Helping Women Recover from Abortion* (Minneapolis: Bethany House Publishers, 1988)

Sue Nathanson, *Soul Crisis: One Woman's Journey Through Abortion to Renewal* (New York: New American Library/Penguin Books, 1989)

D. Reardon, *Aborted Women, Silent No More* (Springfield, IL: Acorn Books, 2000)

Teri Reisser and Paul Reisser, *Help for the Post-Abortion Woman* (Niagra Falls, NY: Life Cycle Books Ltd, 1994)

T. Selby, *The Mourning After: Help for Post-Abortion Syndrome* (Grand Rapids, MI: Baker Books, 1990)

S. Stanford-Rue, *Will I Cry Tomorrow? Healing Post-Abortion Trauma* (Fleming, NJ: Revell, 1986)

M. Symonds, *And Still They Weep—Personal Stories of Abortion* (London: SPUC Educational Research Trust, 1996)

K. Winkler, *When the Crying Stops: Abortion, the Pain and the Healing* (Milwaukee, WI: Northwestern, 1992)

*Victims and Victors: Speaking Out About Their Pregnancies, Abortions, and Children Resulting from Sexual Assault* (Springfield, IL: Acorn Books, 2000)

T. Burke with D. Reardon, *Forbidden Grief: The Unspoken Pain of Abortion* (Springfield, IL: Acorn Books, 2002)

# ENDNOTES

## Foreword

1. V.M. Rue, et. al., "Induced abortion and traumatic stress: A preliminary comparison of American and Russian women," *Medical Science Monitor* 10(10): SR5-16 (2004).

2. Studies carried out in the U.S. found that homicide is the leading cause of death among pregnant women, and in many cases, it was known that the murder was carried out after the woman refused to undergo an abortion. I.L. Horton and D. Cheng, "Enhanced Surveillance for Pregnancy-Associated Mortality-Maryland, 1993-1998," *JAMA* 285(11):1455-1459 (2001); also J. Mcfarlane et. al., "Abuse During Pregnancy and Femicide: Urgent Implications for Women's Health," *Obstetrics & Gynecology* 100:27-36 (2002). See the report, "Forced Abortion in America," at www..unfairchoice.info/resources.htm for more information.

3. D. Reardon, *Aborted Women, Silent No More* (Springfield, IL: Acorn Books, 2002) 12, 333.

4. Rue, *Medical Science Monitor,* op. cit.

5. David M. Fergusson, et. al., "Abortion in young women and subsequent mental health," Journal of Child Psychology and Psychiatry 47(1):16-24, 2006.

6. See T. Strahan, *Detrimental Effects of Abortion: An Annotated Bibliography with Commentary* (Springfield, IL: Acorn Books, 2001). More information on recently published studies linking abortion to negative outcomes can be found at www.afterabortion.info and in the "Research and Key Facts" booklet posted at www.unfairchoice.info/resources.htm.

7. Nick Grimm, "Higher risk of mental health problems after abortion: report," Australian Broadcasting Corporation, Jan. 3, 2006. Posted at www.abc.net.au/7.30/content/2006/s1541543.htm.

8. Colman McCarthy, "A Psychological View of Abortion," *Washington Post*, March 7, 1971. Fogel reiterated the same view in a second interview with McCarthy in 1989. See Coleman McCarthy, "The Real Anguish of Abortions," *Washington Post*, Feb. 5, 1989.

9. M. Gissler, et. al., "Pregnancy Associated Deaths in Finland 1987-1994—definition problems and benefits of record linkage," *Acta Obsetricia et Gynecologica Scandinavica* 76:651-657 (1997); and M. Gissler, et. al., "Suicides after pregnancy in Finland: 1987-94: register linkage study," *British Medical Journal* 313:1431-1434 (1996).

10. M. Gissler, et. al., "Injury deaths, suicides and homicides associated with pregnancy, Finland 1987-2000," *European J. Public Health* 15(5):459-63 (2005); M. Gissler, et. al., "Methods for identifying pregnancy associated deaths: population-based data from Finland 1987-2000," *Paediatr Perinat Epidemiol* 18(6):448-455 (Nov. 2004).

11. D.C. Reardon, et. al., "Deaths Associated With Pregnancy Outcome: A

Record Linkage Study of Low Income Women," *Southern Medical Journal* 95(8):834-841 (Aug. 2002).

12. Ruth Hill, "Abortion Researcher Confounded by Study," *New Zealand Herald,* Jan. 5, 2006.

13. APA Briefing Paper on The Impact of Abortion on Women, posted at http://web.archive.org/web/20050304001316/http://www.apa.org/ppo/issues /womenabortfacts.html.

14. Ruth Hill, *New Zealand Herald,* op. cit.

## Preface

1. The phrase "writing as resistance" is taken from Rachel Feldhay Brenner, *Writing as Resistance: Four Women Confronting the Holocaust* (University Park, PA: Pennsylvania State University Press, 1997), which features the writing of prominent Jewish women from World War II: Etty Hillesum, Anne Frank, Simone Weil and Edith Stein.

2. For example, Robyn Rowland, *Living Laboratories: Women and Reproductive Technologies* (Bloomington, IN: Indiana University Press, 1992); Janice Raymond, *Women as Wombs: Reproductive Technologies and the Battle Over Women's Freedom* (New York: Harper, 1993); Patricia Spallone, *Beyond Conception: The New Politics of Reproduction* (London: Macmillan Education, 1989) and Renate Klein (ed.), *Infertility. Women speak out about their experiences of reproductive medicine* (London: Pandora Press, 1989).

3. *Poetics,* 6. "A tragedy, then, is the imitation of an action that is serious and also, as having magnitude, complete in itself; ... with incidents arousing pity and fear, wherewith to accomplish its catharsis of such emotions." In Richard McKeon (ed.), *The Basic Works of Aristotle* (New York: Random House, 1941).

4. *Shorter Oxford English Dictionary on Historical Principles* (Oxford: Clarendon Press, 1973, reprint 1990).

5. (150 conveyed their experiences in writing, the remainder conveyed them verbally.) I also heard from six men wanting to share their grief after abortion, as well as a grandmother mourning an aborted grandchild.

## Introduction

6. From *"Of Grief,"* *Selected Poems of May Sarton,* ed. by Serena Sue Hilsinger and Lois Brynes (New York: W.W. Norton and Company, 1978) 77; in S. Nathanson, *Soul Crisis: One Woman's Journey Through Abortion to Renewal* (NY: New American Library/Penguin Books, 1989) 10.

7. From Hanna Arendt, *Men in Dark Times* (New York: Harcourt/Brace, 1955).

8. Lyndall Ryan, et. al., *We Women Decide: Women's Experience of Seeking Abortion in Queensland, South Australia and Tasmania 1985-1992* (Adelaide, Australia: Flinders University, 1994). The report states: "Contemporary medical literature betrays an ongoing concern with the clinical outcome of induced abortion, in particular 'psychological sequelae of abortion,' that is, the adverse symptoms (prolonged emotional conflict) believed to follow directly from abortion. Indeed the extent to which

this particular concern assumes a central place within the medical literature, is strik-ing." (p. 29-30) Use of the word "betrays" suggests current medical literature shouldn't have this concern. Why should such a concern be considered "striking?"

While playing down the possible psychological effects of abortion, *We Women Decide* cites a 1984 Adelaide phone survey of 93 women of whom 46 percent had positive feelings about their abortion, 36 percent had negative reactions and 17 percent still had mixed emotions (p. 6). Do the experiences of those in the last two categories—who, after all, comprise 53 percent of the total sample—not war-rant exploration? The likelihood that "… women who are more likely to find the abortion experience stressful may be under-represented in volunteer samples" should also be borne in mind here. See E. Adler, et al., "Psychological responses after abortion," *Science* 248:41-44 (1990).

9. *Information Paper on Termination of Pregnancy in Australia, Commonwealth Department of Health and Family Services* (Canberra, Australia: AGPS, 1996). The NHMRC had commissioned an "expert panel" to report on services for the termination of pregnancy in Australia. However, that report did not meet even the basic profes-sional standards of the NHMRC and was downgraded to the status of an infor-mation paper, and the NHMRC imprimatur removed. The paper was discovered to contain further flaws, for example, in the way illegal abortion numbers were wrongly calculated, and was withdrawn in Feb. 1998. ["Errors cancel abortion report," *The Sydney Morning Herald*, Feb. 17, 1998, p. 4; F. Devine, "Health research body's bad blunders raise disturbing questions," *The Australian*, Feb. 23, 1998, p. 11; J. Coochey, "Damned lies and statistics," *The Canberra Times*, Aug. 10, 1998, p. 9; A. Krohn, "Abortion Review: Embarrassingly Flawed," *Bioethics Research Notes*, 10(1):1-2 (1998)] A member of the Australian Medical Association's federal coun-cil pointed to another flaw when he wrote: "One of the great weaknesses of the NHMRC document, is that having been produced by a committee of abortion providers and pro-choice advocates, it tends to minimize the complications and side effects of termination of pregnancy." Dr. David Molloy, "The Abortion Dilemma," *Australian Medicine*, June 17, 1996, p. 24.

The Information Paper ignored significant documentation on post-abortion aftermath. It relied, instead, mostly on a study by Romans-Clarkson which has been criticized for a number of flaws [S.E. Romans-Clarkson, "Psychological sequelae of induced abortion," *Australian and New Zealand Journal of Psychiatry*, 23: 555 (1989)]. "Granted the inadequacy of measures and study design, biased selec-tion, poor follow-up, lack of controls and simplistic or non-existent statistics described by her, how can she claim with such conviction that there are no psy-chological sequelae?" [P. Dignam, *Australian and New Zealand Journal of Psychiatry*, 24:5 (1990). See also C.A. Canaris, *Australian and New Zealand Journal of Psychiatry*, 24:9 (1990)]

10. Leslie Cannold, *The Abortion Myth: Abortion and the Changing Future for Women* (Sydney, Australia: Allen & Unwin, 1998).

11. Rebecca M. Albury, *The Politics of Reproduction: Beyond the Slogans* (Sydney, Australia: Allen & Unwin, 1999).

12. "Abortion in Focus: A conference to celebrate our achievements and focus on the future," held at the Hyatt Regency, Coolum, Queensland, organized by the

Abortion Providers' Federation of Australasia in conjunction with The International Society of Abortion Doctors and Planned Parenthood of Australia.

13. Post-Abortion Syndrome is increasingly recognized as a specific type of post-traumatic stress disorder. Vincent Rue first identified post-abortion trauma as a variant of post-traumatic stress syndrome in 1981 (*Abortion and Family Relations,* Testimony presented before the Subcommittee on the Constitution of the US Senate Judiciary Committee, US Senate, 97th Congress, Washington, D.C., 1981). Since then, others have reported on research and clinical observation in this area. See S. Stanford-Rue, *Will I Cry Tomorrow? Healing Post-Abortion Trauma* (Fleming, NJ: Revell, 1986); A. Speckhard, *Psycho-Social Aspects of Stress Following Abortion* (Kansas City, MO: Sheed & Ward, 1987); R. Fisch and O. Tadmor, "Iatrogenic Post-Traumatic Stress Disorder," *The Lancet* 1397 (Dec. 9, 1989); T. Selby, *The Mourning After: Help for Post-Abortion Syndrome* (Grand Rapids, MI: Baker, 1990); L. DeVeber, et al., "Postabortion Grief: Psychological Sequelae of Induced Abortion," *Humane Medicine* 7:203-209 (1991); E.J. Angelo, "Psychiatric Sequelae of Abortion: The Many Faces of Post-Abortion Grief," *Linacre Quarterly,* 59(2): 69-80 (1992); K. McAll and W.P. Wilson, "Ritual mourning for unresolved grief after abortion," *Southern Medical Journal,* 80(7):817-21 (1987); P.G. Ney and A. Wickett, "Mental Health and Abortion: Review and Analysis," *Psychiatric Journal of the University of Ottawa* 14:506-16, (1989); Anne C. Speckhard and Vincent M. Rue, "Postabortion Syndrome: An Emerging Public Health Concern," *Journal of Social Issues* 48(3):95-119, (1992).

In 1987, the American Psychiatric Association acknowledged in its newly revised manual of diagnostic criteria, *The Diagnostic and Statistical Manual of Mental Disorders III-R (DSM-III-R),* that abortion is a type of "psycho-social stressor," capable of causing "post-traumatic stress disorder."

Speckhard and Rue (*Journal of Social Issues,* op. cit. 104-106), divide psychological complications after abortions into three types: Post-Abortion Distress, Post-Abortion Psychosis and Post-Abortion Syndrome. Reactions are classified as Post-Abortion Distress if they occur within three months of the abortion and persist for no more than six months. Symptoms include physical pain, emotional stress, a sense of loss, personality conflict and relationship problems with husband or partners and disorientation in the person's sense of values. Post-Abortion Psychosis is a general term for major affective or thought disorders not present before but directly attributable to the abortion. It is characterized by chronic and severe symptoms of disorganization and significant personality and reality problems such as hallucinations, delusions, paranoia and severe depression. Post-Abortion Syndrome is a type of post-traumatic stress disorder characterized by the chronic or delayed development of symptoms resulting from impacted emotional reactions to the perceived physical and emotional trauma of abortion. Symptoms include uncontrolled negative re-experiencing of the abortion, e.g. flashbacks, nightmares, grief and anniversary reactions. Unsuccessful attempts are made to avoid or deny abortion recollections.

V. Rue et al., in *The psychological aftermath of abortion: A white paper,* Testimony presented to the office of the Surgeon General (Washington, DC: U.S. Department of Health and Human Services, 1987), concluded that despite flaws in design and methodology, all psychological studies of abortion display some negative outcomes for at least a proportion of those women studied. They found also that the types of errors found in the many studies examined underestimate the negative responses to abortion. See also G. Zolese and C. Blacker, "The Psychological Complications of Therapeutic Abortion," *British Journal of Psychiatry* 160:742-749 (1992), who found that psychological or psychiatric disturbances occur in association with abortion and seem marked, severe or persistent in approximately 10 percent of cases. See also The Right Hon. Lord Rawlinson, *The Physical and Psycho-Social Effects of Abortion on Women: A Report by the Commission of Inquiry into the Operation and Consequences of The Abortion Act* ("The Rawlison Report"), House of Lords, June 1994, which found that 87 percent of women surveyed by the commission experienced long-term emotional consequences as a result of their abortions.

For an extensive on-line bibliography of journal articles on post-abortion issues, see, http://www.afterabortion.org/biblio.html.

14. Lyndall Ryan, et. al., *We Women Decide: Women's Experience of Seeking Abortion in Queensland, South Australia and Tasmania 1985-1992* (Adelaide, Australia: Flinders University, 1994), x.

15. Ryan, *We Women Decide*, op. cit., 7.

16. Beverly Harrison, *Our Right to Choose: Toward a New Ethic of Abortion* (Boston: Beacon Press, 1983) 16.

17. Maria Londono, "Abortion Counseling: Attention to the Whole Woman," *International Journal of Gynecology and Obstetrics*, Supp. l.3: 169-174, (1989), cited in Patricia Lunneborg, *Abortion: A Positive Decision* (New York: Bergin & Garvey, 1992) 83. Londono also elevates abortion to something akin to a "peak experience."

18. Lunneborg, *Abortion: A Positive Decision*, op. cit., 75. Lunneborg takes issue with books which describe women's mixed feelings on abortion, stating that abortion is "... profamily, prolife, moral, and good." (p. x) She lauds "... the positive consequences of abortion for women's mental health ...," listing "... increased psychological health, maturity, and enhanced self esteem." (p. xi) She also sees abortion as "... a good opportunity to reassess educational and vocational plans, and become a better decision maker in general." (p. xi)

19. Lunneborg, *Abortion: A Positive Decision*, op. cit., 83.

20. M. Tankard Reist, "An (un)informed choice," *The Canberra Times*, May 24, 1997, p. 16.

21. D. Proctor, "It's all about the freedom to make a choice," *The Canberra Times*, June 7, 1997, p. 13.

22. "Unacknowledged grief and guilt, anticipated condemnation by others, as well as the terror of reexperiencing the trauma all enable and maintain the parameters of secrecy and isolation ... By not acknowledging an abortion experience to one's self and/or to one's significant others, a psychological barrier is erected and an emotional toxicity is perpetuated." V. Rue, "The Psychological Realities of Induced Abortion," in Michael T. Mannion (ed.), *Post-Abortion Aftermath: A Comprehensive Consideration*, writings generated by various experts at a "Post-

Abortion Summit Conference," (Kansas City, MO: Sheed & Ward, 1994) 9.

23. "The power of the uterus," *The Herald Sun*, March 18, 1998, 19. Tsitas was writing in response to the author's article, "When Women Have No Choice," *The Herald Sun*, March 16, 1998, p. 19.

24. Margaret Nicol, *Loss of a Baby: Understanding Maternal Grief* (Sydney, Australia: Bantam Books, 1989) 87.

25. Glenys Collis, "Disturbing dreams of miscarried children," *The Age*, Dec. 18, 1985, p. 23.

26. John Lahey, "At last, the touch of the child she never saw," *The Age*, June 11, 1994, p. 3.

27. See for example, Kathleen Murdoch, "Never-ending story," *The Age* (News Extra), Jan. 8, 2000, p. 6.

28. M. Frith, "The stolen generation," *The Age*, June 15, 1996, p. A24. These children came to be known in Australia as "The Stolen Generations." From the late nineteenth-century to the late 1960s, Australian governments took children who were part-Aboriginal from their mothers, parents, families and communities. In the period before 1940, authorities, operating under the official "White Australia Policy," believed that by removing these children, they could "breed out the color." The *Bulletin* stated in 1901: "If this country is to be fit for our children and their children to live in, WE MUST KEEP THE BREED PURE. The half-caste usually inherits the vices of both races and the virtues of neither. Do you want Australia to be a community of mongrels?"

A.O. Neville, the Chief Protector of Aborigines in Western Australia, at a Native Welfare Conference in 1937, said: "We have power under the act to take any child from its mother at any stage of its life ... Are we going to have a population of one million blacks in the Commonwealth or are we going to merge them into our white community and eventually forget that there were ever any Aborigines in Australia?"(quoted in "Sorry," *Sydney Morning Herald*, May 30, 1998, p. 41)

David Hollinsworth, in his book *Race and Racism in Australia*, quotes Dr. Cecil Cook, Northern Territory Chief Protector from 1927-1939:

"Generally by the fifth and invariably by the sixth generation, all native characteristics of the Australian aborigine are eradicated. The problem of our half-castes will quickly be eliminated by the complete disappearance of the black race, and the swift submergence of their progeny in the white."

The Human Rights and Equal Opportunity Commission report, "Bringing Them Home," suggests that somewhere between one in three and one in ten Aboriginal children were separated from their mothers. In a period of about 70 years, tens of thousands of babies and children were removed from their families.

See Robert Manne, "The Stolen Generations," in *The Best Australian Essays 1998*, Peter Craven, ed. (Melbourne: Black Inc., 1998). Manne's essay is posted online at http://www.tim-richardson.net/misc/stolen_generation.html.

29. "Bringing them home: National Inquiry into the Separation of Aboriginal and Torres Strait Islander Children from Their Families," Human Rights and Equal Opportunity Commission, New South Wales, Australia, April 1997.

30. See for example, Kiera Jenifer Khan, "Why I grieve for the child I will never meet," *The Age (News Extra)*, Nov. 20, 1999, p. 7.

31. E. Joanne Angelo, "Post-Abortion Grief," *Human Life Review*, Fall 1996, p. 43.

32. Jane Cafarella, "The heartache of abortion," *The Age*, Aug. 28, 1992, p.14.

33. In a study comparing American and Russian women who had experienced abortion, 64 percent of American women reported they felt pressured to abort by others. V.M. Rue, et. al., "Induced abortion and traumatic stress: A preliminary comparison of American and Russian women," *Medical Science Monitor* 10(10): SR5-16 (2004). David C. Reardon, *Aborted Women, Silent No More* (Chicago: Loyola University Press, 1987) 10-26, reports on a study that found about 40 percent of women who experience post-abortion problems were still hoping to discover some alternative to abortion when they went to the abortion clinic for counseling; more than 80 percent said they would have carried to term under better circumstances or with the support of loved ones; between 30 and 60 percent had a positive desire to carry the pregnancy to term and keep their babies; about 70 percent had a negative moral view of abortion and were choosing against their consciences because of outside pressures; and more than 60 percent reported having felt "forced" to have the abortion by others or by circumstances. See also Mary K. Zimmerman, *Passage Through Abortion* (New York: Praeger Publishers, 1977) 62-70; and James T. Burtchaell, *Rachel Weeping* (Kansas City, MO: Andrews and McMeel Inc., 1982) 104.

34. Linda Bird Francke, *The Ambivalence of Abortion* (New York: Random House, 1978) 29, quotes a clinic director: "Indeed, there is almost a social obligation to have an abortion if the conditions for carrying the baby to term are not perfect." See also Daniel Callahan, "An Ethical Challenge to Prochoice Advocates," *Commonweal*, Nov. 23, 1990, p. 684: "That men have long coerced women into unwanted abortion when it suits their purposes is well-known but rarely mentioned. Data reported by the Alan Guttmacher Institute indicate that some 30 percent of women have an abortion because someone else, not the woman, wants it."

35. E. Grubner, "Social Study of Patients Admitted for Abortion, RWH March to May 1956," Unpublished paper, Social Work Department, RWH, 4-5 in S. Swain and R. Howe, *Single Mothers and Their Children: Disposal, Punishment and Survival in Australia* (Cambridge University Press, 1995) 38.

36. Structural issues are examined in more detail in the Afterword.

37. Germaine Greer, "The Feminine Mistake," *The Sydney Morning Herald*, May 9, 1992, p. 39.

38. Germaine Greer, *The Whole Woman* (New York: Doubleday, 1999) 86, 90.

39. Guymer's account of use of the abortion drug Misoprostol in a Melbourne clinic is told in M. Tankard Reist, "Misoprostol-Nurse Speaks Out on Dangers For Women," *FINRRAGE Journal*, 13-17 (March 1998).

40. The view that abortion is the best thing for certain classes of women is widespread. *In Abortion: The Clash of Absolutes*, Laurence Tribe lists "… those who are least able to bear the burden of motherhood—particularly the young, the uneducated, the rural, and the nonwhite." (New York: W.W. Norton & Company, 1990,

1992) 207. An American columnist has written that abortion is needed for the "at risk" population, "poor, black and Indian" whose children are "marked for failure," (Tony Bouza, "A Mother's Day wish: Make abortion available to all women," *Minneapolis Star Tribune*, May 8, 1989). Another commentator has described abortion as "a policy of social defense" to "save ourselves from being murdered in our beds and raped on the streets" by "a monster" (Nicholas von Hoffman in the *New York Observer*, quoted in Nat Hentoff, "Pro-Choice Bigots," *The New Republic*, Nov. 30, 1992, p. 25). A recent study in the U.S. titled "Legalized Abortion and Crime" (by John J. Donohue III and Steven D. Levitt, Stanford Public Law and Legal Theory Working Paper Series, Working Paper No. 1, Stanford Law School, California, June 1999) attributes a decline in crime rates to legalized abortion, drawing links between race, poverty, crime and abortion. Karen Cooper of Washington State's National Abortion and Reproductive Rights Action League (NARAL) wrote: "NARAL believes that the study ... reinforces the positive effects of legalized abortions for children, families, and society." ("Report Reinforces Positive Effects of Legal Abortions," *Seattle Times*, Letters Section, Aug. 15, 1999).

41. Kerry A. Petersen, "Abortion Counseling in Australia," *Australian Journal of Sex, Marriage & Family* 6(2): 93-103 (1985).

42. Lyndall Ryan, et. al., *We Women Decide: Women's Experience of Seeking Abortion in Queensland, South Australia and Tasmania 1985-1992* (Adelaide, Australia: Flinders University, 1994) 123.

43. The Right Hon. Lord Rawlinson, *The Physical and Psycho-Social Effects of Abortion on Women: A Report by the Commission of Inquiry into the Operation and Consequences of The Abortion Act* ("The Rawlison Report"), House of Lords, June 1994, p. 16.

44. See, for example, Anne C. Speckhard and Vincent M. Rue, "Postabortion Syndrome: An Emerging Public Health Concern," *Journal of Social Issues* 48(3):104, 112 (1992). The authors observe: "Abortion recovery may be unsuccessfully attempted by reenactment through a subsequent pregnancy experience. For some women whose grief about their unborn child is impacted, the compulsion is to attempt mastery of the trauma through resolution of guilt feelings and replacement of the lost object. For some, the resurfacing of the trauma in a subsequent pregnancy is too threatening and compels another abortion. When multiple abortions occur, the traumatization and resulting psychological impairment can be compounded for some women."

According to counselors working in the area, the onset of delayed symptoms is often precipitated by a triggering event such as the birth or loss of another child, the anniversary date of the abortion, failure to conceive, death of a loved one, miscarriage, birth of a niece/nephew or friends' child or grandchild, the onset of menopause, the deterioration of a relationship or some other event associated with children or reproduction. See *Post Abortion Syndrome* (Perth, Australia: Post Abortion Grief Counseling Services Inc., n.d.).

45. In what became known as the "baby in the fridge" case, a Maori mother of three requested the remains of her aborted fetus following a termination in a Perth clinic in 1997. She had wanted to take the remains home for a culturally

appropriate burial. However, after one of her children told his class that there was a "baby in the fridge" at home, the teacher alerted police and the abortionist was later charged with performing an illegal abortion. The incident led to a major abortion debate in Western Australia and the liberalizing of its abortion laws. See Chip Le Grand and Natalie O'Brien, "Historic Bill allows abortion on demand," *The Australian*, April 3, 1998, p. 4.

46. Bob Ellis, "Why We Met Jenny," *Sydney Morning Herald*, Nov. 22, 1997, p. 9.

## Afterword

47. Rebecca M. Albury, *The Politics of Reproduction: Beyond the Slogans* (Sydney, Australia: Allen & Unwin, 1999) 23.

48. Naomi Wolf, "Our Bodies, Our Souls," *The New Republic*, Oct. 16, 1995, p. 29.

49. *Rogers v. Whitaker* (1992) 175 CLR 479.

50. The Right Hon. Lord Rawlinson, *The Physical and Psycho-Social Effects of Abortion on Women: A Report by the Commission of Inquiry into the Operation and Consequences of The Abortion Act* ("The Rawlison Report"), House of Lords, June 1994, p. 12.

51. N.E. MacLean and M. Devarajah reported in the *New Zealand Medical Journal* on a retrospective study over a one-year period from June 1, 1997 to June 30, 1998. Twelve patients with "significant physical complications" were admitted to the Southland Hospital during this period. "That all 12 patients admitted to the gynecology ward after the termination of pregnancy required further surgical intervention indicates a high level of postoperative complications. The total number of physical complications may be significantly higher than this because some patients are reluctant to report and others are managed by their general practitioner and re-admission is avoided." The authors called for mandatory reporting of all abortion complications. "We are concerned that many patients undergoing termination of pregnancy are not provided with adequate information involving the complications." "Complications of legal termination of pregnancy," *New Zealand Medical Journal*, 59 (Feb. 26, 1999).

52. Minimalist information is also reflected in these extracts from information pamphlets. "It is not unusual to feel sad or depressed two to six days after the operation. This may be a result of the withdrawing of pregnancy hormones." Reproductive Healthcare Services (ACT) "Termination of Pregnancy Services Post Operative Instructions." Another RHS information sheet, "Possible After Effects & Complications" (March 1998), lists some possible physical outcomes, but states: "Please try to keep the risks we have listed in perspective." This could have the effect of minimizing the significance of these complications in the minds of some women. The RHS information makes no mention of psychological risks. "Information for Women Considering Abortion" provided by the Australian Women's Health Clinic (New South Wales), makes no mention of any risks (although it does state: "We care for you" and informs clients the cost of counseling is extra). New regulations in the ACT requiring provision of more detailed information on the risks of termination have been depicted as one of a series of "shuffling steps backward." S. Powell, "Beating a retreat in abortion war," *The Australian*, June 10, 1999, p. 15.

Of further note is a survey of American and Russian women who had undergone abortions, which found that 67 percent of American women reported receiving no counseling beforehand, 79 percent said they were not counseled on alternatives to abortion, and 84 percent said they did not receive adequate counseling before the abortion. V.M. Rue, et. al., "Induced abortion and traumatic stress: A preliminary comparison of American and Russian women," *Medical Science Monitor* 10(10): SR5-16 (2004).

53. See M. Tankard Reist "Abortion not as safe as women are being told," *The Canberra Times*, Nov. 15, 1998, p. 7.

54. See Tankard Reist "Abortion not as safe as women are being told," op. cit., p. 7; A. Bolt, "Mother wins 'abortion harm' case," *Herald Sun*, Sept. 29, 1998, p. 16; A. Bolt, "The price of grief," *Herald Sun*, Sept. 29, 1998, p. 19.

55. Cynthia received the settlement following a negligence claim against the doctor who referred her for an abortion, as well as the clinic, the doctor who performed the termination and a clinic counselor. She claimed that none of the doctors or counselors warned her of the potential for psychological trauma. According to her legal representatives, her life has been marred by depression, grief, erratic behavior and continuing regret. She has been diagnosed by psychiatrists as suffering a form of Post-Traumatic Stress Disorder. The defendant's solicitors had threatened to subpoena her parents (who had no knowledge of the abortion) as witnesses unless she dropped the case. "Cynthia" continued the action however, and the solicitors failed to carry out the threat. (Personal communication with author, Dec. 14, 1999.)

Another Sydney woman has an action pending for nervous shock after an abortion. (Personal communication with author.)

Another Melbourne women alleges she had the same experience as Ellen at the same hospital. She is considering her legal options. (Personal communication with author.) Ginny, who self-mutilates and has undergone shock therapy, is also pursuing legal action. (Personal communication with author.) A Queensland woman is exploring legal options against a doctor for the physical and psychological effects suffered as a result of the abortion carried out on her as a teenager and single parent—and the sterilization done at the same time without her consent. (Personal communication with author.)

While actions for psychiatric injury are relatively new, actions have previously been brought for abortion related physical injury.

In Sept. 1993, Dr. Neville John Marinko was found guilty of Professional Misconduct by the Professional Standards Committee of the New South Wales Medical Board over the abortions of Ms. B and Mrs. M.

On Dec. 20, 1989, Ms. B, then 17, underwent a midtrimester abortion. She suffered a lacerated cervix, lost a liter of blood and required resuscitation. "Ms. B denied being informed of any complications of the procedure," the committee's ruling stated. (The Medical Practitioners Act, 1938, Professional Standards Committee, Inquiry Under Section 32E held at The New South Wales Medical Board on June 10, July 26, and Aug. 2, 1993). On Feb. 21, 1991, Mrs. M was admitted to Sydney Hospital in a coma as a result of complications during an abortion. She suffered severe brain injury which left her physically and mentally incapacitated, requiring full-time physical care. Her claim for damages was settled for $3.7 million in April 1997. In June 1998, Justice Rolfe ordered damages of $455,170 for nervous shock to her husband. Mr. M told the court: "I lost my social life. I lost my friend. Put it this way, I lost my life, that's all. Also the kids, when I look at the kids, they lost their mother too …" (Nick Papadopoulos, "Suffering Husband Awarded $455,000," *Sydney Morning Herald*, June 5, 1998, p. 5).

While the Professional Standards Committee placed some conditions on his practice, Dr. Marinko was not prevented from carrying out abortions.

A young Chinese woman is in a persistent vegetative state in a Queensland nursing home as a result of an abortion in Jan. 1994. The Queensland Medical Assessment Tribunal found (the late) Brisbane abortionist Dr. Peter Bayliss failed to have oxygen administered to the woman during and after surgery, failed to have a cheap, effective medical instrument available to monitor oxygen levels and also did not provide qualified one-on-one post-operative monitoring. (Bayliss argued this was unnecessary). It was alleged an ambulance was not called until 90 minutes after the woman stopped breathing. Dr. Bayliss was found guilty of professional misconduct in 1998. Tribunal head Justice George Fryberg said Dr. Bayliss's negligence "was gross, perhaps even criminal." Bayliss received a three-month suspension. (*Medical Board of Queensland v Bayliss*, Queensland Medical Assessment Tribunal, No. 10 of 1995, Feb. 6 & 18, 1998, before J. Fryberg; "QLD: Patient in Coma 'An accident waiting to happen,'" *AAP*, May 8, 1996). Dr. Bayliss died in 1999.

In 1995, Dr. Bayliss was also investigated by the homicide squad after an Aboriginal girl from Boggabilla suffered a cardiac arrest and died. A post-mortem examination listed the official cause of death as "septic abortion." (N. Breen, "Inquiry After Abortion Patient Dies," *Courier-Mail*, Nov. 2, 1995, p. 3).

Massive damages awards have been made by the New South Wales Supreme Court in recent years in cases involving women irreparably injured after undergoing abortion procedures. A woman known as "C" in the case *C v. Pannikote and St. George Hospital* suffered complications following an induced abortion when she was four months pregnant. The induction process was prolonged and she suffered an epileptic fit. The ventilator supplying oxygen to the woman was apparently accidentally turned off, resulting in gross brain damage. She was left grossly spastic, suffering muscular spasms causing involuntary movement of her limbs and body. In Aug. 1993, Sharpe J awarded damages totaling $2,261,361.00 plus costs.

A Western Australian woman, Belinda Triplett, is suing an abortionist who perforated her uterus during an abortion in Feb. 1999. She required an emergency hysterectomy to control life-threatening hemorrhage. (Channel 7, March 15, 1999). A Sydney woman, known as "Marie," accepted an out-of-court settlement late in 1999 following a malpractice action against a prominent Sydney abortionist for his failure to properly follow up and treat complications following an abortion.

56. Lindalee Tracey, "Rethinking Abortion," *Toronto Life*, Feb. 1991, p. 41.

57. M. Gissler, et al., "Suicides After Pregnancy in Finland, 1987-94: Register Linkage Study," *British Medical Journal* 313:1431-34 (Dec. 1996). For more recent research on suicide rates after abortion, see the Foreword to this book.

58. See for example, J. Brind et al., "Induced Abortion as an Independent Risk

Factor for Breast Cancer: A Comprehensive Review and Meta-Analysis," *Journal of Epidemiology & Community Health* 50:481-496 (1996). This article was described by Dr. Janet Daling of Seattle's Fred Hutchinson Cancer Research Center as "very objective and statistically beyond reproach." Lucette Lagnado, "Study on Abortion and Cancer Spurs Fight," *Wall Street Journal*, October 11, 1996, p. B4. Since this time the list of studies linking abortion and breast cancer has been updated; for the most current information, see web site of The Coalition on Abortion/Breast Cancer's summary (citing Dr. Brind and others) at www..abortionbreastcancer.com/abc_summary.htm

59. *Information Paper on Termination of Pregnancy in Australia, Commonwealth Department of Health and Family Services* (Canberra, Australia: AGPS, 1996) 18.

60. Daling et al., "Risk of breast cancer among young women: relationship to induced abortion," *Journal of the National Cancer Institute*, 86(21):1584-1592 (1994).

61. J. Gelman, "Findings linking cancer to abortions a well-kept secret," *Los Angeles Daily News*, Sept. 28, 1997, p. 3.

"Politically inconvenient information" might also include informing a woman of the possibility of a live baby in a late-term abortion, as happened in the case of "Baby J" which came to light in Nov. 1999. The baby girl was alive after an induction at between 21 and 22 weeks performed at the Darwin Private Hospital and lived for about 80 minutes. Midwife Carrie Williams told an inquest that when she phoned Dr. Kai Man Henry Cho to inform him the baby was alive, he had said "So?" (Watt, B, "Abortion baby was alive for 80 mins," *Northern Territory News*, Nov. 3, 1999, p. 3.) More generally, see Nancy Rhoden, "The New Neonatal Dilemma: Live Births from Late Abortions" *Georgetown Law Journal* 72:1451 (1984).

62. Elizabeth Moore, "A Matter of Welfare," *Sojourners Washington D.C.,* Nov. 1980, p. 9.

63. P. Adelson et al., "A survey of women seeking termination of pregnancy in New South Wales," *The Medical Journal of Australia* 163(8): 419-422 (Oct. 16, 1995). More recently, a paper published by the Alan Guttmacher Institute in the U.S. reported that 73 percent of women listed "can't afford a baby now" as a reason for their abortion, while 74 percent reported that having a baby would change their life dramatically, such as interfering with their job or education, and 48 percent listed relationship problems or not wanting to be a single parent as a reason for the abortion (participants could check more than one reason). LB Finer, et. al., "Reasons U.S. Women Have Abortions: Qunatitative and Qualitative Perspectives, *Perspectives on Sexual and Reproductive Health* 37(3):110-118 (2005).

64. "Women earning 66c to male $1," *The Age*, Sept. 30, 1999, 10; and Tim Colebatch, "Women are still not equal. But Why?" *The Age*, Oct. 13, 1999, p. 17.

65. "Establishing a fairer deal for working women," *The Sunday Age*, Oct. 3, 1999, p. 16.

66. Marilyn Lake, "A battle still not won," *The Age*, Oct. 4, 1999, p. 17.

67. Susan Halliday, evidence to Senate Employment, Education and Training Legislation Committee hearing on the Employment, Education, Training Legislation Amendment (More Jobs, Better Pay) Bill 1999, Oct. 26, 1999, p. 378.

68. Sex Discrimination Unit, HREOC, 1999. See also Penelope Green, "Lives of pregnant workers at risk," *The Australian*, Aug. 26 1999, p. 3. A submission by the Australian Education Union to the HREOC inquiry said discrimination against teachers in Australian schools is rife. "Women who are pregnant or are thinking of becoming pregnant perceive that they will be discriminated against in terms of promotional opportunities, renewal of contracts and participation in information sharing processes." ("A Nice Job For A Girl—But!, Women Educators' Experience of Pregnancy and Work in Public Education Systems," *Australian Education Union*, March 1999, p. 12). The Union's federal branch president, Ms. Sharan Burrow, said pregnant teachers were frequently denied support, promotion and fair entitlements while pregnant students were often forced to compromise or abandon their education. ("School's tough for teen mums: union," *The Age*, April 20, 1999, p. 6.)

69. New South Wales Anti-Discrimination Board, Sydney, 1993, p. 6. At the time of writing, the federal government was being criticized for indicating support in a maternity protection survey by the International Labor Organization for employers being allowed to conduct pregnancy tests on women before hiring them. The government said it voted against the proposal at the ILO conference; however, critics continued to demand it explain its survey response. See Michelle Gunn, "Staff wanted, take your pregnancy test within," *The Australian*, Oct. 6, 1999, 1; Rebecca Rose, "Abbott Mum on Pregnancy Slip," *The West Australian*, Oct. 7, 1999, p. 2.

70. K. Andrews and M. Curtis, *Changing Australia: Social, Cultural and Economic Trends Shaping the Nation* (Sydney: Federation Press, 1998) 179.

71. Amanda Covarrubias, "$7.7m for actor fired over pregnancy," *The Age*, Dec. 24, 1997, p. A7.

72. See Isolde Kauffman, "Prophets Among Us: New residents show how social security law is creating poverty," Network for Safety-Net Payments for new Residents, SA, Oct. 1999; Senate Hansard, Dec. 8 1998, Payment Processing Legislation Amendment (Social Security and Veterans' Entitlements) Bill, 1998, 1380, 1420.

An attempt in June 1999 by the Australian Democrats to persuade the Senate to have the Special Benefit payment—a safety-net provision within the Social Security system for those in severe financial circumstances—exempted from the waiting period, failed.

73. It appears many women aborting on the grounds of fetal abnormality are not aware that they are in the "at risk" category for post-abortion depression. Speckhard and Rue include genetic abortion in a list of predisposing risk factors for post-abortion syndrome [(Anne C. Speckhard and Vincent M. Rue, "Postabortion Syndrome: An Emerging Public Health Concern," *Journal of Social Issues* 48(3):114 (1992)]. P.K.B. Dagg, "The Psychological Sequelae of Therapeutic Abortion—Denied and Completed," *American Journal of Psychiatry* 148:578-585 (1991), states: "… It has been clearly demonstrated that medical or genetic indications for abortion increase the risk of adverse psychological sequelae in the mothers." J. Lloyd and K.M. Laurence, "Sequelae and support after termination

of pregnancy for fetal malformation," *British Medical Journal* 290:907-909 (March 23, 1985), found that 77 percent of women interviewed experienced "an acute grief reaction" after the termination "... akin to that documented after stillbirth or neonatal death," and 46 percent "remained symptomatic" six months later. The authors also noted the lack of information provided to the women prior to termination and concluded: "... the consequences of termination were not acceptable because they had not been anticipated and planned for."

74. "Down's Syndrome detection—should we be screening everyone," Professor Brian Trudinger, Obstetrician & Gynecologist and Fetal Medicine Specialist, Westmead Hospital.

75. See Susan M. Brady and Dr. Sonia Grover, "The Sterilization of Girls and Young Women in Australia: A Legal, Medical and Social Context," Human Rights and Equal Opportunity Commission, Dec. 1997; Susan Brady, "Invasive & Irreversible; The sterilization of intellectually disabled children," *Alternative Law Journal*, 21:160 (Aug. 1996); Susan Brady, "The Sterilization of Children With Intellectual Disabilities—Defective Law, Unlawful Activity and the Need for a Service-oriented Approach," *Australian Journal of Social Issues,* 33(2):155 (May 1998); Helen Rhoades, "Intellectual Disability and Sterilization-An Inevitable Connection?," *Australian Journal of Family Law*, 9:234 (Dec. 1995).

See also Vicki Toovey, "Sterilization of Women With Disabilities—Case study presented to the Women's Rights Action Network First Australian Tribunal on Women's Human Rights," cited in *WWDA News—A Newsletter from Women With Disabilities Australia,* 16 (June 1999). Toovey writes: "The issue of sterilization brings into focus both the notions of consent and of discrimination. When can it be said that a woman has freely and in an informed way given her consent to a procedure if the woman's self esteem is so low that she does 'not believe that it would be right to bring another person into the world like me,' when her life is one of constant discrimination, denial of her worth and a limited view of her own potential."

For further reading, see that author's book, *Defiant Birth: Women Who Resist Medical Eugenics* (Australia: Spinefex Press, 2004).

76. Kate Nancarrow, "Why this woman said no to turning her triplets into twins, Life or death: a mother's multiple choice," *The Sunday Age,* April 7, 1996, p. 1. For further reading, see Elizabeth Ring-Cassidy and Ian Gentles, *Women's Health After Abortion: The Medical and Psychological Evidence, 2nd Edition* (Toronto, Canada: The deVeber Institute for Bioethics and Social Research, 2003) 175-187.

77. Rada Rouse, "HIV women 'coerced' to abort," *AAP,* Nov. 17, 1994.

78. Ibid.

79. Greg Callaghan, "A family by any other name," *The Australian Magazine*, Jan. 1-2, 2000, p. 19. The Social Security Minister has also observed that families with only one parent remain among the poorest in the nation. "Pauline Hanson Gets The Facts Wrong Again," Media Release, Minister for Social Security, Senator Jocelyn Newman, July 16, 1998.

80. K. Andrews and M. Curtis, *Changing Australia: Social, Cultural and Economic Trends Shaping the Nation* (Sydney: Federation Press, 1998) 38.

81. Rosemary West, "Youngsters become the casualties in a bitter battle of the Sexes," *The Australian*, June 6, 1998, p. 19; L. Lamont, "Sole Parent Support to be slashed," *Sydney Morning Herald*, May 20, 1998, p. 1; Balancing Act," *Sydney Morning Herald*, May 20, 1998, p. 12.

82. Annabel Crabb, "Sole parents miss out on GST support," *The Advertiser*, Dec. 15, 1999, p. 7.

83. Fia Cumming, "Plan to cut welfare for parents," *The Sun Herald*, Sept. 26, 1999, p. 3.

84. See Robyn Taft, "Parenting doesn't stop when a child turns 12," *The Age*, *(Opinion)*, Nov. 17, 1999, p. 18.

85. K. Andrews and M. Curtis, *Changing Australia: Social, Cultural and Economic Trends Shaping the Nation* (Sydney: Federation Press, 1998) 98.

86. Australian Institute of Health and Welfare (1994) Public Housing in Australia (Canberra: AGPS), cited in Andrews and Curtis, *Changing Australia*, op. cit., 98.

87. K. Andrews and M. Curtis, *Changing Australia*, op. cit., 98.

88. Andrea Carson, "Who cares?" *The Age*, Nov. 3, 1999, p. 13. At the time of writing, the government had also been criticized for recent policy changes which, it was argued, resulted in decreased affordability of center-based childcare and the withdrawal of support for community-sponsored childcare centers. See Julie Lee and Glenda Strachan, "Family Preferences, Child Care and Working Hours," *The Journal of Australian Political Economy*, No. 43, June 1999, p. 24-45.

89. Greg Callaghan, "A family by any other name," *The Australian Magazine*, Jan. 1-2, 2000, p. 19.

90. See K. Andrews and M. Curtis, *Changing Australia*, op. cit., 36.

91. Federal Liberal MP Peter Lindsay has run the line that single woman are having children just to make a "profit" from the welfare system. Paul Daley, "MP slams women's 'children for profit,'" *The Sunday Age*, Feb. 2, 1997, p. 3.

92. Quoted in A. Horin, "Staggering Myths About Sole Parents," *The Sunday Age*, March 7, 1993.

93. I am not saying there is no need for welfare reform or that the welfare system is perfect. I'm just not convinced of the alleged good which would result if public financial support to single mothers was suddenly withdrawn.

94. "Abortion zealots summon sad past," *Weekend Australian*, Feb. 21-22, 1998, p. 26.

95. Ross Gittins, "How much do you pay to keep your child?," *The Age*, Sept. 15, 1999, p. 19; Ross Gittins, "Why the high price of children is bad for business," *The Age*, Nov. 24, 1999, p. 21. See also Rebecca Valenzuela, "Costs of children in Australian households: New estimates from the ABS Household Expenditure Survey," *Australian Institute of Family Studies, Family Matters*, No. 53, Winter 1999, p. 71-76.

96. J. Hutton, *Disenfranchised Grief: A Study of the Long-Term Emotional Effects of Abortion* (Thesis, Geelong: Deakin University, 1995) 1, 4, 6, 36.

97. Germaine Greer, *Sex and Destiny: The Politics of Human Fertility* (London: Pan

Books Ltd/Martin Secker & Warburg., 1985) p. 7.

98. Catharine A. MacKinnon, "Reflections on Sex Equality under Law," *The Yale Law Journal*, 100(5):1312 (1991). See also Julie A. Gazmararian et al., "The Relationship Between Pregnancy Intendedness and Physical Violence in Mothers of Newborns," Obstetrics & Gynecology, 85 :1031 (1995); Hortensia Amaro et al., "Violence During Pregnancy and Substance Use," American Journal of Public Health, 80: 575 (1990); and J. McFarlane et al., "Abuse During Pregnancy and Femicide: Urgent Implications for Women's Health," Obstetrics & Gynecology, 100: 27, 27-36 (2002).

99. Bernard Jessie, *The Future of Parenthood: The New Role of Mothers* (London: Calder & Boyars, 1975) 9.

100. Greer, *Sex and Destiny*, op. cit., 13.

101. Greer, *Sex and Destiny*, op. cit., 9.

102. Greer, *Sex and Destiny*, op. cit., 14.

103. Rebecca M. Albury, *The Politics of Reproduction: Beyond the Slogans* (Sydney, Australia: Allen & Unwin, 1999) 22.

104. See Catharine A. MacKinnon, *Feminism Unmodified: Discourses on Life and Law* (Cambridge, MA: Harvard University Press) YEAR, and MacKinnon, "Reflections on Sex Equality under Law," op. cit.

105. MacKinnon, "Reflections on Sex Equality under Law," op. cit., 1300. Mackinnon has noted (*Feminism Unmodified*, op. cit., 144-145) the involvement of the Playboy Foundation in the funding of abortion rights.

106. MacKinnon, "Reflections on Sex Equality under Law," op. cit., 1312.

107. MacKinnon, "Reflections on Sex Equality under Law," op. cit., 93.

108. MacKinnon, "Reflections on Sex Equality under Law," op. cit., 1324.

109. One of the most extreme examples of this took place in the USA in 1999, where a woman was killed for refusing to get an abortion. Lorena Rivera, the 21-year-old mother of a three-year-old son, Angel, and at least 21 weeks pregnant, was delighted to be having another boy and had already named him Isaac, according to friends, family and her doctor. However, Nathaniel Dee Smith murdered Lorena "because she refused to have an abortion and he didn't want to pay child support," according to Assistant District Attorney Don Deason. ("Woman Killed for Refusing To Get Abortion, Jurors Told," *The Oklahoman*, May 21, 1999.) See "Forced Abortion in America," at www. unfairchoice.info/resources.htm for additional examples.

110. T. Steinberg, "Abortion counseling: To benefit maternal health," *American Journal of Law and Medicine*, 15:483-517 (1989).

111. Anne C. Speckhard and Vincent M. Rue, "Postabortion Syndrome: An Emerging Public Health Concern," *Journal of Social Issues* 48(3):108 (1992).

112. Lindalee Tracey, "Rethinking Abortion," *Toronto Life*, Feb. 1991, p. 42.

113. S. Swain and R. Howe, *Single Mothers and Their Children: Disposal, Punishment and Survival in Australia* (Cambridge University Press, 1995) 60.

114. Swain and Howe, *Single Mothers and Their Children*, op. cit., 61.

115. Naomi Wolf, "Our Bodies, Our Souls," *The New Republic*, Oct. 16, 1995, p. 34.

116. Philippa Peck, "Abortion: a woman's right to refuse." Unpublished, Aug. 1999.

117. *We Women Decide* provides another example of the effort to avoid the "fetus" (or "baby") word. "We have therefore referred to it [the fetus] (as do most women) as a 'pregnancy.' This choice of terminology acknowledges that from the woman's perspective an abortion ends a bodily process (a pregnancy) of which the fetus is a constitutent part, rather than eradicating a separable entity (fetus)." [Lyndall Ryan, et. al., *We Women Decide: Women's Experience of Seeking Abortion in Queensland, South Australia and Tasmania 1985-1992* (Adelaide, Australia: Flinders University, 1994) 4] But a significant number of women quoted in the report continued to use the "wrong" words. See for example, pages 94, 98, and 106 ("I couldn't sort of work out how you could bring babies into the world and then get rid of them"); pages 118, 127, 133, and 139 ("I sort of couldn't think of it [the pregnancy she had aborted] in any other terms other than 'a child of mine' which was comparable with the other two"); and page 154 ("... it's a baby. It's the beginnings of a baby and the whole concept of ending what is a life ...").

118. An American abortion clinic worker, Sally Tisdale, gave a graphically honest account of the deception she employed in an article she wrote for *Harper's* magazine, Oct. 1987, p. 68: "It is when I am holding a plastic uterus in one hand, a suction tube in the other, moving them together in imitation of the scrubbing to come, that women ask the most secret question. I am speaking in a matter-of-fact voice about 'the tissue' and 'the contents' when the woman suddenly catches my eye and asks, 'How big is the baby now?' These words suggest a quiet need for a definition of the boundaries being drawn. It isn't so odd, after all, that she feels relief when I describe the growing bud's bulbous shape, its miniature nature. Again I gauge, and sometimes lie a little, weaseling around its infantile features until its clinging power slackens. But when I look in the basin, among the curd-like blood clots, I see an elfin thorax, attenuated, its pencilline ribs all in parallel rows with tiny knobs of spine rounding upwards. A translucent arm and hand swim beside."

119. Submission to National Health and Medical Research Council, *Draft Document on Services for the Termination of Pregnancy in Australia: A Review*, p. 266 (later titled "*An Information Paper on Termination of Pregnancy in Australia*," and since withdrawn).

120. Esther Harding, *The Way of All Women* (New York: Harper Colophon Books, 1970) 155.

# ACKNOWLEDGEMENTS

From the time the idea for this book began to germinate in my mind, a small number of significant people helped bring the seedling to fruition. I want to thank them. To Peter for your thoughtful and gentle insights, Katrina for generous editing assistance, and Warwick for wise suggestions and for keeping me on track. To Irene and Mary for early encouragement, and Gerard, Lynne, Jeremy, Lara, Anna and Michael for feedback on drafts. To John for a quiet place in which to write and for significant input along the way. To Renate and Laurel for validating the importance of the project and for comments on the final draft. To Bob Ellis for your moving response to the proposal. To Jack for being in the right place at the right time, and to Christopher for your personal recommendation. To David, for taking the load on the "home front" and for forbearing when my life was being absorbed by the book. To Ariel, Jordan and Kelsey, for lots of love and restorative breaks from writing. To Lara and Tim for your special friendship and support. To my sister Suzanne. To Michael Duffy for having the courage to publish the book. To every one who spoke an affirming word in support of the project—you may not have realized how significant your words were to me at the time. And, most especially, to the brave and generous women who made it all possible. This is your book.

Melinda Tankard Reist

# About the Author

Melinda Tankard Reist is an Australian writer and researcher with a special interest in women's health, new reproductive technologies, and medical abuses of women. She trained and worked as a journalist in Victoria, Australia and was awarded a Rotary Foundation Scholarship to study journalism in the United States in 1987. Melinda's work has been published in newspapers and journals in Australia and overseas, and she has reported for a number of radio programs. She is also involved in advocacy and support services for pregnant women and is a consultant on bioethical issues.

In addition to *Giving Sorrow Words*, Melinda also recently authored the book *Defiant Birth: Women Who Resist Medical Eugenics*, which tells the story of women who resisted advice to abort based on perceived disabilities in themselves or their unborn children, and takes a critical look at medical eugenics as a form of contemporary social engineering.